Roslyn Young was born in Australia and after obtaining a BA and a Dip.Ed. from the University of Queensland, she taught English literature in Australian schools for a few years.

She moved to France in 1967 and worked at the University of Franche-Comté at the Centre de Linguistique Appliquée from 1968 until she retired, teaching English and sometimes French in intensive courses. She met Caleb Gattegno for the first time in 1971 in Geneva, where she saw him teach an hour of Chinese. She knew immediately that she wanted to be able to teach in this way.

Roslyn Young wrote her doctoral thesis on Gattegno's model and its relevance to his work in language teaching. She has published around 30 articles on teaching and the Silent Way. With Piers Messum, she published *How We Learn and How We Should be Taught: An Introduction to the Work of Caleb Gattegno* in 2011.

The author discussing the Silent Way. Scan the QR code below for the video of this discussion.

She worked for Une Education Pour Demain, the Gattegno association in France, from the beginning of the 1980's until 2014 when she joined Actualis in Versailles, providing teacher training for both. (Teacher training was anything between a two-day course on a specific subject and a five-year programme designed to produce a new generation of teacher trainers.)

She was awarded *Les palmes académiques* by the French government in 1999 'for services to national education'.

Roslyn Young is a director of Pronunciation Science Ltd which designs and publishes materials for teaching languages by the Silent Way.

She teaches English and French online, and provides leadership for the team at www.silentway.online—the web resource for information on the Silent Way.

Teaching English the Silent Way

Roslyn Young, with Piers Messum

Duo Flumina

First published in 2025 by Duo Flumina Ltd
112 Warner Road, London SE5 9HQ
www.duoflumina.com

ISBN 978-0-9568755-4-9

© 2025 Roslyn Young and Piers Messum

The right of Roslyn Young and Piers Messum to be identified as authors of this work has been asserted by them in accordance with sections 77 and 78 of the Copyright, Designs and Patent Act 1988.

All rights reserved. No part of this book may be reprinted or reproduced or utilised in any form or by any electronic, mechanical, or other means, now known or hereafter invented, including photocopying and recording, or in any information storage or retrieval system, without permission in writing from the publisher.

TABLE OF CONTENTS

Preface 1

SOME THEORY

1. About learning 9
    What beliefs do teachers hold? 9
    How do we learn? 10
    An example—learning to read English 12
    The four stages of learning 12
    Using the model in the classroom 13
    What place does imitation have in the learning process? 14
    The role of presence in the learning process 14
    Why speak about 'presence' rather than 'attention'? 15
    Taking notes 15
    Which gives learners better results—practice or repetition? .. 16
    The way the memory functions and the cost of learning 16
    Expensive learning—memorisation 17
    Inexpensive learning—natural retention 17
    Applying this in the classroom 18
    Constraints 19
    Knowledge and know-hows 19
    How do we construct know-hows? 21
    The notion of the 'ogden' 22
    The notion of yield 22
    The role of sleep in learning and teaching 23
    Learning to speak, speaking to learn 24

2. About language 25
    Some questions 25
    What am I aiming for in my courses? 26
    Accuracy is the priority 26
    How languages function 27
    Two sorts of vocabulary 28
    The spirit of the language 29
    Teaching a language 30
    Pronunciation 31
    Grammar 32
    The four skills 32
    Vocabulary 33

Don't teach related words as sets	33
A new discipline	34
Is speaking a language about communication or expression?	34
Separating communication from expression	35
The Communicative Approach	35
Expression	36
What should we be teaching?	37
About know-hows	38
Language as an expression of who we are	38
Implications for teachers	39
3. Teaching from first principles	**41**
One-way and two-way teaching	41
The subordination of teaching to learning	42
Two-way teaching as opposed to subordinated teaching	43
The powers of the mind	44
Developing criteria	44
Zooming in and out	45
The more you give, the less you get	46
Homework	47
Beware of students' beliefs …	48
Post-paration	48
How do I know if I have done a good job?	49
Making learning a language a joyful experience	49

BETWEEN THEORY AND PRACTICE

4. Keeping teacher talk brief	**53**
Provoking awarenesses	53
To intervene without interfering	53
Using silence	54
But I'm not mute	55
Something I don't say: Very good!	62
5. The principal materials	**63**
Cuisenaire rods	64
The pointer	65
The Rectangle chart	65
Working with colour-blind and blind students	67
The Fidel	67
The Word charts	69
Wall pictures	70

Rich Tasks	71
The Verb Tense System	73

6. Using a pointer — 75

Pointing on the charts	75
The act of pointing enhances retention	78
Diagnosing problems	78
Pointing with a 'laser finger'	79
'Blind' pointing	80
Working online	81

7. Correction — 83

A word about pronunciation	83
Do the minimum	84
Three key non-verbal techniques	84
Finger correction	85
Syllabification	89
The aeroplane gesture	91
The unexpected	91

PRONUNCIATION

8. Below the superficial — 97

The nature of speech	98
The sounds of English	102
The stress & reduction system	103
A double system	105
Articulatory settings	105
Sensitising students to their tongue	106
Speech breathing	107
The stress & reduction system	109
What I am aiming for	113
Homework linked to pronunciation	113
A need for change	114

9. Putting theory into practice — 117

Why not model pronunciation?	117
Listen first or produce first?	119
Starting out	119
Meaning can wait	120
Off we go	120
The Rectangle chart	121
Helping those who find English breath control difficult	131

Stuttering	132
After this…	133
The other vowels of the first line	134
The fourth line of vowels	134
The second and third lines—the diphthongs	136
Other consonants	138
Re-awakening sensitivity	139
Consonant clusters	140
More on speech breathing	141
The importance of the articulatory setting	141
The reduced forms	144
American English: the schwr	144
Other strategies for working on sounds	145
10. Numbers	**147**
The numbers up to nine	148
The numbers up to ninety-nine	148
The -teen line	150
Working on stress and reduction using numbers	152
The numbers beyond ninety-nine	153
Very big numbers	154
The years in English	155
The times tables	156
Ordinal numbers	158
Working thoroughly	158
Much language with little vocabulary	159

WORKING WITH BEGINNERS

11. Using the Word charts	**163**
The Word charts	163
The choice of words on the charts	163
Deciding on a progression	164
How a suitable progression is arrived at	165
A structuring which is wider still—three themes	166
Theme 1: the use of function words	166
Theme 2: the Verb Tense System	167
Theme 3: numbers and time	167
Which theme I'm working on	168
Placing virtual words using mental imagery	169
Pacing the class	170

Teaching a heterogeneous class	171
The trap	173
Feedback from students	174

12. Starting with Word chart 1 — 175
- How to begin — 175
- Using Theme 3 — 187
- Answering questions waits for Chart 2 — 188
- Class management, by me and then the students — 188
- Learning to write — 188
- Reading and writing — 189
- Moving on — 190

13. Moving on to Word chart 2 — 191
- Theme 2: the verb tenses — 191
- Theme 1: the function words — 194
- Mistakes to avoid — 200
- More on rods — 201
- Moving on — 202

14. Expressing time — 203
- The economy of learning — 204
- The months — 204
- The seasons — 206
- The days of the week — 207
- Telling the time — 212
- The temperature — 216
- The weather — 216

15. Exploring Word chart 3 — 217
- The fields of Word chart 3 — 217
- Theme 2—work on the verb tenses — 218
- How long the work should take — 222
- Letting students 'sleep on it' — 226
- Comparisons — 226
- Other words on Chart 3 — 229
- Don't forget — 232
- Moving on to the next chart — 232

16. Adding Word chart 4 — 233
- Spatial relations and prepositions — 234
- The modal auxiliaries — 238
- The other words on Chart 4 — 239

17. All the Word charts together	241
Each, Every, All, Most, Almost all, Some	241
Shorter and *Longer* ...	244
Both and *And, Neither* and *Nor*	244
Enough	244
Before and *After*	245
Making more comparisons	245
Once, Twice, Three times ...	245
The suffix *-ly*	246
The suffix *-en*	246
Say and *Tell*	247
Distances—*Near, Far, Close*	247
Look and *See, Listen* and *Hear,* and *Think*	249
Do you think ...? *I think* ...	250
Length	250
Although	251
Developing a feel for how the language behaves	252
Going on from here	252

TOWARDS THE CLASS CONVERSATION

18. Verb tenses—laying the foundations	259
Using triggers	260
Verbs at Step 1	261
Working at Step 2—Rod Stories	261
Mr. and Mrs. Green—the present progressive	262
The station	264
The story of the Greens—later ...	266
'Lines for Words' for longer texts	266
Much later ...	267
Using students' experience	268
Using wall pictures	268
The word live and where it can take us	269
Writing	272
19. Laying out a comprehensive view	273
The origin of the Verb Tense System	273
Who might benefit from the work on the Verb Tense System?	274
Preparations—some preliminary explanations	274
Step 1—The work begins	276
Step 2—Checking the negatives, interrogatives, etc.	282

Step 3—Using the various forms	283
Step 4—Taking some time to digest	290
Step 5—The future	291
Step 6—The modals	292
How I want students to understand the modals	292
Step 7—How I introduce the modals to the class	295
Step 8—Sequences of tenses	297
To sum up	300

THE CLASS CONVERSATION

20. Low-level students — 305
How I work — 306
The history of the English language — 306
No notes — 306
How I worked — 307
Discover all you can about one person — 309
A little later in the course — 310
Simple conversations, but genuine — 312

21. Upper intermediate and advanced levels — 315
Pronunciation — 316
The articulatory setting — 316
The reduction system — 316
Two kinds of schwa — 317
Working on consonants — 318
Using the Verb Tense System — 318
Getting the conversation started — 318
It was a question! — 319
More advanced students — 319
The performance piece — 320
A free, to-and-fro conversation between the students — 321
The content — 321

22. The Class Conversation — 321
Some rules — 322
Each sentence is corrected before we move on — 322
The Class Conversation is self-regulating — 324
Use of English alone is insufficient — 324
A special case: 'Tell me' classes — 324
Targeted 'Tell me' classes — 325

MOVING FORWARD

23. Moving into the Silent Way world	329
Silent Way principles	329
You, the beginning Silent Way teacher	331
Questions, and sometimes answers	333
24. Afterword	335
Acknowledgements	341
References	342
Further Reading	342
Guides	343

APPENDICES

Appendix 1: A brief history of the English language	347
Appendix 2: The Silent Way Word charts	351
Appendix 3: The PronSci Word charts	353

Preface

How do humans learn? How do humans learn languages? How do the answers affect what we do in the classroom? Have we really thought through these and similar questions?

This book is an attempt to go back to first principles and recast the whole job of language teaching. It is not a book about theory, although theoretical questions will be addressed. It is a practical book on how I think teachers should work in the classroom in order to create learning.

I want to propose a radical change in language teaching in both schools and adult education, and to describe how it might be put into use on a lesson by lesson basis. The approach requires two major changes to conventional thinking.

The first of these is to recognise that speaking a foreign language is a know-how. This know-how must be learned like any other know-how, through practice. For example, to learn to ski, we practise the activity many times, making progress as we do so, and end up knowing how to ski. We can go as far as we like in learning to ski. We may try to become champions or we may be happy to stop when we are satisfied with the level we have reached. The only way to learn is to practise until the discipline is mastered.

Learning a foreign language is the same; it is necessary to speak until one knows how to say whatever one wants to, easily, fluently and automatically. The capacity to speak a language does not develop from knowledge about grammatical rules. All the time of the class should be used for students to speak.

The second change involves a new way of thinking about what it means to teach, about how classes should be conducted.

We all know that students don't necessarily learn when we teach them. If this were the case, there would be no need for examinations. The teacher would give the lesson, would do whatever she decided to do, the same for all, and all the students would learn everything. But we know that this is not what happens. In reality, there is no necessary relationship between teaching and learning.

However, as we shall see, it is possible to create such a relationship. Instead of teaching in the usual sense of the word, the teacher works in such a way that what she does is an improvisation that arises directly from the students' learning as this takes place here and now in the classroom. The focus changes from teaching to accompanying the students, coaching them as they learn. The teacher's work is directly determined by how the students function on a moment by moment basis.

I propose that it is more efficient to go into the classroom without a clearly defined lesson plan, but with an agenda—a sense of what needs to be done—and with techniques which actively create specific conditions in which students learn; then to follow the students and guide them while they are doing it. The teacher chooses her pedagogical acts to guide the students' learning as she sees it happening in front of her while the lesson is taking place.

We should never simply assume that the students are learning; we must make sure that learning happens every step of the way.

To do this efficiently, we must know how students learn. Caleb Gattegno, the inventor of the Silent Way approach, developed a model of learning which, to this end, will be sketched out in the first chapter.

I am not proposing an easy way of working or a quick solution to every problem. As a practising teacher, I know that the habit of 'teaching', of trying to transmit knowledge and telling students what to say, can be deeply ingrained. Old habits die hard…

I would encourage the reader to try this approach. What happens in the classroom is beneficial for the students and they enjoy taking control of their learning. When the approach is well done, it is exhilarating for both the students and the teacher.

For reasons of simplicity in the use of pronouns, I assume a female teacher and male students throughout this book.

What is it, then, that will allow us to teach mathematics to anyone with a functioning mind and an inclination to learn? Simply, finding a way to make the learner aware of the powers of his mind—the powers he uses every day, those which allowed him to learn his native language and to use imagery and symbolism.

This means that the job of teaching is one of bringing about self-awareness in learners through whatever means are available in the environment: words, actions, perceptions of transformations, one's fingers, one's language, one's memory, one's games, one's symbolisms, one's inner and outer wealth of perceived relationships, and so on.

Caleb Gattegno (1974)

There is nothing so strongly motivating as realizing you can do something that is valued and valuable. The exercise of your own powers, independently, is a major source of pleasure for human beings, whereas dependency on others breeds discontent. Learners can become frustrated when the teacher or text usurps their role by doing things for them: roles they are on the edge of assuming or actions they are already able to do for themselves. All too often learners decide that their powers are not wanted in the mathematics classroom, and so they stop using them even where there is an opportunity. It is highly de-motivating and disempowering to find that your own powers are not called upon, not encouraged, not used; it is a source of pleasure and empowerment to find that you can use your own powers to make sense of phenomena, situations and ideas. Furthermore, the more you are called upon to use your powers, the more developed and sophisticated they are likely to become; the less they are called upon, the more likely they are to atrophy, or at least to be parked at the classroom door.

John Mason (2008)

It took me three days of exposure to the Silent Way to realize that all I had done in my previous years could not in fact be called teaching at all. More important, I had never known what learning was. I had merely instructed students in a subject without taking into consideration the richness and the complexity of their minds.

Cecilia Bartoli (1972)

SOME THEORY

'I do know, from what experience I have had [of the Silent Way], that the techniques without the theory are incomplete.'
Earl Stevick

1. About learning

Let us begin with a very basic question:

WHAT BELIEFS DO TEACHERS HOLD?

Human beings cannot function without using mental models. A model is a set of beliefs we hold which inform us about how we should act in all the usual circumstances of our lives. For most people most of the time, these models remain implicit. But they always inform our actions. In our fast moving lives, it cannot be otherwise.

Whenever a teacher is teaching, she is always using a model like this. But very few teachers ask themselves what they believe about learning. Their model of learning is implicit.

This is not optimal. If the model being used remains implicit even to the one who holds it, there is no way of checking its validity and no way of deliberately improving it. All teachers and more especially, all methods writers and teacher trainers, should make the model of learning that they are using explicit. How humans learn should be central to any reflection about teaching, should inform all that is done in the classroom, and should be used by all teachers to judge how their practice sits with the model they discover themselves to hold.

To set an example, here is the model of learning that underlies all that will be said later[1].

[1] *The pedagogical practices based on this model exist for other school subjects as well as language learning— maths, reading, history, geography ... The theoretical principles outlined here apply to these and all other subjects and disciplines.*

HOW DO WE LEARN?

I use the model proposed by Caleb Gattegno for two reasons.

Firstly it is the most comprehensive that I know of. It applies to all disciplines and to all people, regardless of their age or socio-cultural background.[2] It is applicable to all that is learnt over a lifetime—learning to walk or speak one's mother tongue as an infant, to play hopscotch, to ride a bicycle, to play bridge, or to speak a new language.

Secondly, I find it to be the most useful model on a moment-by-moment basis as I teach. It informs:

- how I plan my classes;
- how I work on my students' immediate needs on a here-and-now basis;
- why a student might have asked a particular question and how I should best respond;
- how I think about what I have done in class and how I can improve.

I use it as a guide to all I do in the classroom.

Learning is becoming aware

Gattegno proposes that all learning takes place by means of awarenesses. He uses this word 'awareness' as a countable noun. An awareness is a movement of the mind which allows me to become aware of something, as a result of which I choose what to do next. Once I have **become** aware of something, I **am** aware of it. I have had an awareness.

Everyone knows the 'aha moment', when we become aware of something which is new and important. What is created in the mind at that moment is 'an awareness'. Gattegno saw that awarenesses could be big or very small, and that they take place all the time. If we choose to attend to them, we can be aware of very many of them, but normally the fact that we learn and change through a succession of discrete awarenesses goes unnoticed: the process escapes us. Here's an example:

> I'm visiting an old aunt and decide to make a cup of tea. She doesn't have a kettle, so I fill a saucepan, turn to the stove and become aware that I don't know which knob goes with which burner. I look at the diagrams on the front panel, become aware that one in four of the circles in each diagram is filled in, check how the diagrams correspond to the arrangement of the burners, turn the knob I've chosen, press

---

[2] *More detailed information on learning can be found in Young and Messum* How We Learn and How We Should be Taught, *London: Duo Flumina, 2011.*

Almost all awarenesses are much smaller than 'aha' moments.

I take a mouthful of food I have made using a new recipe, and am aware that this is a new taste, a new consistency.

I am about to take a sip of tea and become aware that the temperature is too hot for my lips.

I wake up and become aware immediately from what I hear that it is raining outside.

I become aware of a slight discomfort, of a mild pain.

I become aware that I am hungry.

the lighter button and become aware that it was the right knob.

During these few seconds, I wouldn't usually have noticed how my mind was functioning. But in this case I observed and distinguished what information my experience furnished for me and what new awarenesses were necessary. I attended to my awarenesses as well as to the task itself.

When I am alert to my environment, each tiny movement of my mind from here, to here, to here, generates **an awareness**. When I say *I am aware of something*, I know that I have become aware of it an instant before; when I say *I know*, I have had the necessary awarenesses some time before. Awarenesses are what allow me to give myself know-hows and expand my knowledge. They are the foundation of all learning. They are always present when learning takes place. They make learning a lifelong experience.

> I am changing the sheets on my bed. I toss the fitted sheet over the mattress and pull each corner over its corner of the mattress. I become aware of creases, and pull each of the corners of the sheet a little tighter over the mattress until I can see (which means that I am aware) that it is completely flat and taut on the bed. I check that the corners of the sheet are tucked in as far under the mattress as possible. I know (which means I have become aware on past occasions) that this will save me time in the days to come.
>
> I throw the top sheet over the bed, using a flicking gesture with my wrists to make the sheet float over the bed and then settle down onto the bed slowly and gently. I become aware that the centre line of the sheet is not in the centre of the bed, so I throw it again, flicking it to make it glide down slowly, so that I can guide the centre fold to a better position. When it lands, I can see it is close to the centre and pull this corner and then that one until it is exactly centred.

Or

> I walk into a supermarket I have never been in before and immediately become aware that the newspapers and magazines are to my right, in my experience an unusual place to put them. I walk a little further and find the items

for the laundry. As I walk around, I discover the organisation of the shop.

Or

I walk into a supermarket I have never been in before and immediately become aware that the shelves are a little too close to each other and the alleys are too narrow for my taste. There is not enough light for me to feel at ease. I find what I am looking for and leave. I resolve not to go back.

Gattegno proposed that 'the awareness' is the fundamental building block of all learning. Just as chemistry could develop out of alchemy once the concept of the atom became available, education can become scientific once it has this basic conceptual unit, the awareness.

AN EXAMPLE—LEARNING TO READ ENGLISH

Learning to read the English language requires the learner to have had certain basic awarenesses, and we can list them:

> He must become aware that English is read from left to right, and from the top to the bottom of the page.
>
> He must become aware that the letters on the page induce the reader to produce sounds; these sounds, in order, reconstitute the spoken language.
>
> Each sound is represented by one or more signs.
>
> Etc.

A teacher who knows the awarenesses that are required can make sure that the learner has become aware of them all. If one is missing, she can detect which, and provoke it. So she will know what to do at every moment. The process is more secure and much faster.

THE FOUR STAGES OF LEARNING

Gattegno described human learning as a four stage process.

Stage One—a single awareness that there is something to be learned. As long as a learner does not realise that there is something to learn, no learning can begin. This is obvious, but absolutely essential.

Stage Two—the learner begins the learning process by doing something; he watches carefully as he makes the trial, becomes aware of the result

---

'The belief that mistakes must be avoided at all cost goes against the purpose of practice, which assumes the lack of mastery and therefore the possibility of errors. If we want to be realistic, we must accept mistakes as part of learning.'

—*Caleb Gattegno*

SOME THEORY

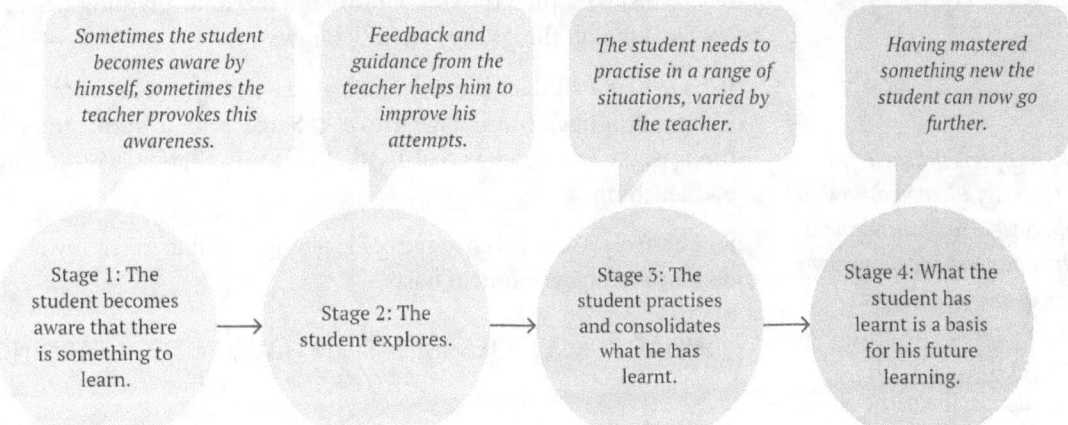

and adjusts the following trial based on the result of the previous one. He continues his trials, integrating what the feedback from the environment tells him, until he is satisfied with the result.

Stage Three—what has been learned in Stage Two gradually becomes automatised. Once the learner knows what to do, he does it again, being careful to get it right each time (which means he is present to the task).

This is a transitional stage. To start with, he must be entirely present to what he is doing. By the end, he has reached mastery and no presence is required. He is free to make himself present to something else and learn that. Our automatisms free us from the need to be present.

Stage Four—once the learner has mastered something, it is available for any future learning process. Learning is cumulative.

USING THE MODEL IN THE CLASSROOM

These four stages guide me throughout all my classes. I know when I introduce something new that the class is at Stage One. I know that they must all **see** what I put before them, and I am careful to make sure that this is the case.

When students are actively exploring in Stage Two, they cannot fail to make mistakes. I know they need feedback to make them aware of these. When I give feedback, I am keeping them in, or bringing them back to Stage Two of the process. On the other hand, if there are few

At the age of about a year, a child learned to walk; awareness after awareness, he learned which muscles allowed him to hold himself upright, to shift his centre of gravity from one leg to the other, to lift one foot off the ground, and then to take his first steps. Some years later, he learned to ride a bicycle and the balancing skills he had learned for walking were refined for bicycle riding.

Years later again, he might take up windsurfing, and the balancing skills he gave himself with the bicycle were further refined for windsurfing.

It so happens that when I was young, I learned how to walk a tightrope. Imagine a tightrope strung between the roofs of two buildings. Imagine that I say to you, the reader, Off we go! I'll go first. Just do the same as me! Would you do it? Of course not! You know that you can't imitate me in this. You haven't developed the sensitivity to your centre of gravity, the muscular power in your feet and abdomen, and all the other technical details which would allow you to do it.

or no mistakes, then the students are not learning anything new; they are working on things they already know.

If I see that a student is automatising something which is not correct, I bring him back from Stage Three to Stage Two. If I don't intervene, the mistake will become fossilised. To let this happen is quite simply bad teaching.

So I actively use the four stages of learning to guide me in my choices on a moment-by-moment basis.

WHAT PLACE DOES IMITATION HAVE IN THE LEARNING PROCESS?

Consider the example in the left margin. This is an extreme example, but a little thought shows that it is only possible to imitate someone doing something if the imitator already possesses the know-how to do it. If the learner does not already possess a movement, he cannot imitate it. He first has to construct the know-how. If simple imitation were part of the learning process, we would all be champions in any discipline we were drawn to. *Just watch me, and then do what I do.*

Imitation exists, of course, but if someone can imitate, he is not meeting something that he doesn't know, something that for him is his unknown. He is using know-hows that he already has in place.

This fact has important repercussions on our choices in class. In particular, it is inefficient to provide students with a model for the pronunciation of a new sound. If they can imitate it, they are being taught what they already know how to do. If they cannot, they have to learn to produce it.

THE ROLE OF PRESENCE IN THE LEARNING PROCESS

To learn, particularly in Stage Two, we need to be present to what we are doing, to be 'with it'. No one can learn without being focused on the task at hand.

To be present is enjoyable for all humans. The more intense the presence required, the more exhilarating the task. That's one of the reasons why people find video games so engrossing. Surfing, skiing and many other athletic activities require presence. This is why so many people like doing them.

Scan to download Non-imitative ways of teaching pronunciation *Messum & Young (2012)*

WHY SPEAK ABOUT 'PRESENCE' RATHER THAN 'ATTENTION'?

We've all heard a teacher say *Simon, pay attention!* The teacher is right: if the lesson is boring, Simon must **pay** to remain present. He pays by generating a tension to keep himself with what the teacher is saying. We can easily make ourselves aware of this tension.

> I am reading a good book, an act which only requires my presence and is therefore cost-free in terms of the energy required to remain with the task.
>
> Someone comes along and asks me to put the book aside in order to do something else which also requires my presence. As I try to settle into the new activity, I am aware that the story I was reading is still in my mind. I am with the images from my reading and have trouble getting involved in something new. I may even feel resentment towards the person who has called me away. To remain focused on the new activity, I have to spend energy in the form of an inner tension. I literally 'pay a tension'. Once I become involved in the new activity, the images from the book fade and the tension I needed to generate in order to keep myself with this activity disappears.

When learning is taking place, one of its characteristics is the presence of each learner to what he is doing. Any efficient approach to teaching a language must be deliberately conceived to enhance students' presence. It is not sufficient for the teacher to exhort, *Simon. Pay attention! Your head is in the clouds!* She needs techniques which work so well that Simon is not tempted to let his attention wander, so that he is caught up by what is happening in the class.

TAKING NOTES

I don't allow students in my classes to take notes. I want them to be as present as possible, close to 100% of the time, and taking notes divides their attention, damaging their learning.

I also want them to move away from reliance on memorisation. It's my job to make sure that students do enough practice in our lessons, because if they practise enough with presence, then what we've worked on will automatically be moved into long term memory during their subsequent

Scan to watch a video about why one teacher asks his students to put away their notebooks.

> Jacques Prévert captures the loss of presence caused by repetition in his famous poem *Page of Writing*
>
> *Two and two are four*
> *four and four are eight*
> *eight and eight are sixteen …*
> *'Repeat' calls the master*
> *…*
> *But look at the songbird*
> *passing in the sky,*
> *the child sees it*
> *the child calls to it*
> *'Save me!*
> *play with me, bird'*
> *Two and two are four*
> *four and four are eight*
> *…*
> *'Repeat' calls the master*
> *…*
> *But all the other children*
> *are listening to the music*
> *and the walls of the classroom*
> *slowly fade away*
> *And the windows return to sand*
> *the ink returns to water*
> *the desks return to trees*
> *the chalk returns to cliff*
> *the quill becomes a bird.*

periods of sleep. We will work again in subsequent lessons on anything that hasn't been retained. This is a much more efficient way of working, greatly increasing the yield for their time in class.

WHICH GIVES LEARNERS BETTER RESULTS—PRACTICE OR REPETITION?

Practice and repetition are different. Repetition can take place even while the person is mentally absent from what he is doing, thinking about something quite different. In the popular imagination, assembly line work is this kind of activity.

I will use the word *practice* to speak about activities which require the presence of the doer.

Skiing a steep slope requires that the skier be present to what he is doing, even if he has already skied down this same piste ten times today. The piste remains the same on each occasion, but the skier is different; he knows the pitfalls he has encountered already even if he cannot be confident of dealing with them successfully this time.

In spite of the seemingly repetitive nature of the afternoon's activity, his presence is required at all times, and this is the reason why it is fun to ski all afternoon (but not to tighten nuts onto bolts on an assembly line).

Unfortunately, classrooms are places where repetitive activities can often be found. Jacques Prévert's poem, on the left, is a wonderful description of children whose presence has drifted away. The schoolmaster has placed them in a situation requiring repetition, and loss of presence is the inevitable result.

THE WAY THE MEMORY FUNCTIONS AND THE COST OF LEARNING

> *'We are retaining systems and do not need to stress memorisation as much as most teachers do. We hold better in our minds what we meet with awareness.'*
>
> Gattegno (1976)

In terms of energy and time consumption, there are two types of learning: memorisation—energy-draining, time-consuming, and unreliable—and retention—natural, energy-efficient, quick and reliable. We should design our classrooms to encourage the second type of learning rather than the first.

EXPENSIVE LEARNING—MEMORISATION

Each time we have to memorise an arbitrary fact, we must spend energy to 'stick' it in our memory. The energy cost can be very high, especially if the subject does not interest us.

Much of what I learnt at school was of this type: historical dates, the vocabulary of a foreign language, the names of rivers, lakes and chains of mountains, mathematical formulae, etc. These facts are expensive whenever, from the learner's point of view, the information is completely arbitrary.

But school is not the only place where this kind of learning is necessary. The first time I meet someone, I must learn his name, and names are arbitrary for us—Frederick could have been called Henry or Michael. We remember faces much more easily than we remember the names that go with them. Telephone numbers are also arbitrary. The 'mental glue' necessary for remembering this kind of information is expensive.

Such learning is not only expensive, but also fragile and unreliable, and it requires regular revision to prevent forgetting. Most people have problems remembering these kinds of facts. Even after making a genuine effort, they still forget.

INEXPENSIVE LEARNING—NATURAL RETENTION

There is another way of learning, which Gattegno called retention. This is the name he gave to the reception and stocking of images in each of us. Whenever we look at a street, a person or a beautiful scene, photons leave what we are looking at, enter our eyes and strike our retinas, creating images which we stock. When we listen to music or a song, we make auditory images which enable us to recognise or even recall what we have heard. We make tactile images too. We may recall the feel of hot sand beneath our feet or of jam on a finger. We also have taste images; for example, the taste of lavender honey or mashed potatoes. Nobody has ever attempted to memorise a sunset, and yet we can recall images of sunsets in particular places without any effort at all. We do not pay to keep such images. We let them in by being present to our surroundings, inner and outer, and they stay with us for a very long time. Everyone possesses huge quantities of images of these and other types. It would be impossible to live one's life without them.

During my holidays one year, I went to New York for the first time and spent a week there. Some years later, I went back and was able to travel around the city easily and to go back to places I had been to the first time. I recognised many places because I could compare the images from the first visit with those I had before my eyes during the second. The experience gained from the first visit was still with me.

When I go back to a place for the second time, I never doubt whether I have been there before. I know I have, because of the images I have retained.

An example:

> I know my way around several supermarkets in my area (and quite a lot of others in places where I have been on holiday). I can write my shopping list sitting in my kitchen, mentally walking through the particular supermarket I intend to go to, mentally checking my stock at home against what can be bought in each of the aisles.
>
> I didn't try to memorise all these shops. I am not even aware of having noticed how they are set out, although I can picture each shop in my mind's eye after one or two visits. I have picked up their layout by walking around in them and noticing where they place the goods I want to buy.

This system of retention is extremely efficient. We retain huge quantities of impressions with no special effort. Although I do not retain everything, many images I have within me are decades old—the school grounds of both my primary and secondary schools, the place where I caught the bus every morning, the shops I frequented, the garden around the house I lived in when I was a child, the taste of fruit gathered off the tree and a myriad of other images. These are what allow me to keep in touch with the whole of my life, to go for a walk in my town without getting lost, to prepare a meal or to go straight to the book I want on my bookshelves. This faculty of retaining is part of our human nature.

Memorisation costs a lot and is not reliable. Retention costs nothing and lasts a lifetime.

APPLYING THIS IN THE CLASSROOM

Teachers should base what they do on our natural ability to retain, whenever possible. With a little thought, it is in fact usually possible. If we can mobilise students' presence, then retention follows. The pedagogical tools presented in this book were deliberately created to favour retention by showing what will be taught, and by calling on students to participate actively and so build faithful images.

I don't want my students to memorise words and phrases. I want them to integrate them through familiarity—'acquaintance', as Gattegno called it—using them in situations and, as you will see later, using the Word charts to remind themselves of the words until they no longer need to.

I aim for students to learn by familiarity rather than by memorisation whenever possible. For example, if a student is writing something on the whiteboard and hesitates about the spelling of a word, I encourage him to look at the charts and check it. He will stop doing this automatically when he becomes confident that he knows it.

CONSTRAINTS

Throughout my courses I constrain what the class is working on at any one time. I want the students to work thoroughly on the task of the moment. This means they can always build future learning on secure foundations.

At the start of their journey learning English there is very little that students can say. So we thoroughly explore the world of rods and colours.

But then I can relax that constraint a little and we can explore, say, the world of *giving* and *taking*, etc. A little later we can begin to talk about their everyday lives and concerns. At this stage I might begin by constraining the conversation with 'trigger' words' like *usually*, *sometimes* or *always*. A little later when their skills have advanced, we may explore the worlds of their past, and then perhaps their opinions and expectations.

Eventually, once students have a good grasp of 'the spirit of the language' they can range as widely as their desire to talk takes them.

At every stage constraining what students are working on means everything can be worked on properly and practised. This is the fastest route to speaking English well and confidently.

KNOWLEDGE AND KNOW-HOWS

How do humans generate knowledge? And know-hows?

At various moments in time, at different times in different cultures, and in different disciplines, the following story took place.

> One day, a child became an apprentice to a master craftsman—a carpenter, a cabinetmaker, a specialist in marquetry, a stonemason or any one of dozens of crafts. He began by spending his days in the workshop doing menial tasks, observing, if he was a good learner, all that took place there.
>
> Soon he was given more important tasks. His master began to show him the gestures he had to learn to perform, watched how he worked and commented—gave him feedback—so as to give him rapid access to good practice.

'Hold your plane like this. It has to be flat and level; otherwise you won't get a completely flat surface to your wood. Look, you're hollowing out a line here with the left-hand edge of the blade. Press a little less with your hand and keep the plane level ... That's better.'

Our apprentice's principal way of knowing was through his awarenesses: hundreds upon hundreds of experiences, each made up of a multitude of awarenesses gradually accumulating until he knew how to use all the tools of the shop, how to select the woods it had access to, how to accomplish the gestures required for each technique, and how to put it all together to make a piece of furniture. He had given himself experience.

He proved his skill by creating his masterpiece, the piece of work that demonstrated to his guild that he was now a master craftsman.

A few years later, he began to take apprentices himself, and the same process began again, a process repeated down through the ages.

However, one day, a strange idea came to our master craftsman. He would try and codify all he knew. He would write a book on his craft. To do this, he had to rethink the whole process. He realised he would have to state many things which in the shop were obvious. He would need to describe the tools of his particular trade. He would have to talk about the woods he used, and how to select a suitable wood for a particular job. He needed to describe how to work, the gestures necessary for each step.

The book was duly published, placed in some libraries and thus made accessible to others. The master craftsman had converted his know-how into knowledge.

Several hundred years later, I go to my local DIY shop because I want to make a wooden box. I decide to buy a book about cabinet making. I have the choice of several, all of them descendants of the first book written in this culture by a master craftsman who was inspired to create knowledge from his know-hows. When I buy the book, what it gives me is knowledge.

Creating a masterpiece

Picture: Compagnons du Tour de France – Institut Européen de Formation de Mouchard (Jura)

This tells me what kind of awarenesses I will need to give myself, but now I have to start working. If I want to become adept at woodworking I need to learn much more than I have read about my tools and how to use them; I need to try various woods until I become familiar with their qualities, to learn the gestures of the trade. In other words, I have to give myself hundreds of experiences, which will coalesce to become my experience. I know I will never write a book about cabinet making, so I will probably never generate knowledge in this field.

HOW DO WE CONSTRUCT KNOW-HOWS?

There is only one way to learn a know-how, and that is to practise until one reaches mastery. This is true of skating, of riding a bicycle, of playing the guitar or the piano, and it is also true of speaking a foreign language. This means that the language should be taught as a know-how and not as a collection of pieces of knowledge such as grammatical rules, lists of vocabulary or irregular verbs.

Suppose that you were learning to ice skate. For your first lesson the teacher says to you, *We are going to start with a lesson on the behaviour of ice indoors and the physics of turns.* Such a lesson would be utterly absurd, but it bears striking resemblance to many lessons on 'the Simple Present' or 'Comparatives and Superlatives'. If your skating teacher did say this, you would justifiably change to another teacher.

You know that what you need is a pair of skates, ice and time. If you have all three, and if you start skating, you will end up some time later knowing how to skate, better or worse depending on your aptitude and how well you spent the time.

An important advantage of know-hows is that they remain functional for many years. Even after thirty or forty years, someone who learned how to ride a bicycle can get back on and ride away a few seconds later.

There is no need to swim or to ski every day to be sure of knowing how to swim or to ski. The know-hows remain available although one's muscles or breathing may have deteriorated.

If the teacher works suitably, her students will keep their new language forever even if, after a period of non-use, it may take a few days for some of the vocabulary to come back.

MASTER CRAFTSMAN	ME THE READER	ME THE DOER
Knowledge	⟶ Knowledge	
↑		
Experience/ know-hows		Experience/ know-hows
↑		↑
Experiences	⤏	Experiences

There is no way of changing knowledge into know-hows except by going through the process which will allow one to actually build the know-hows. Knowledge does not spontaneously produce know-hows.

> *'Since knowing produces knowledge, but not the other way round, this (approach) shows how everyone can be a producer rather than a consumer of ... knowledge.'*
>
> Gattegno (1974)

So the role of the teacher should never be to transmit knowledge. Aspects of language learning that are conventionally taught through rules—making past participles agree in French or getting one's declensions and conjugations correct in German—can and should be taught as know-hows.

Practically, this means that there will be no explanation of grammar, or indeed of anything else. What has to be learnt will be made very clear, but by means of lived examples, not by means of explanations. These experiences accumulate to create experience and ultimately know-hows in the language.

THE NOTION OF THE 'OGDEN'

Good teaching is designed to avoid memorisation and to use retention everywhere possible. Teachers will systematically ask themselves whether they can find ways of increasing the proportion of retention their lessons require, and minimising the amount of memorisation.

> *One day, Gattegno told the participants in a seminar that he had been sitting in a plane and had got into conversation with his neighbour, the psychologist Ogden Lindsley, the founder of the principle of 'Precision Teaching'. He told Lindsley about the idea of the unit of energy necessary to memorise one fact. Lindsley asked him what this unit was called. On the spur of the moment, Gattegno answered, 'the ogden'.*

To help teachers to keep tabs on how much memorisation they are asking for, Gattegno invented the notion of the *ogden*. Counting ogdens helps teachers estimate the 'weight' of memorisation they impose on their students.

An ogden is a unit of 'mental glue', the quantity of energy that is necessary to 'stick' an arbitrary fact in our memory. This unit is not strictly defined: we cannot yet measure this quantity of energy in some kind of recognised energy unit or on a specific scale, but it still serves as a useful guide in the classroom.

Counting, in whatever language, is a good example, because we can easily determine the number of ogdens that must be paid in order to count up to a million. For example, to learn how to count up to 999,999,999 in English we need to spend just 21 ogdens. These elements are all that it is necessary to memorise in order to count in English. See Chapter 10 for the details.

THE NOTION OF YIELD

Strongly linked to the concept of ogdens is the notion of yield. This notion leads us to making choices based on the relative usefulness of words. Words such as *lawn* or *flower* are only useful occasionally. Others like *hello* and *goodbye* are useful for thirty seconds at the beginning and the end of each class, for social reasons. On the other hand, words like *the* and *is* will be necessary in a wide variety of sentences. So we will give priority to *the* and *is* and all the function words of this kind, at the expense of common nouns which yield much less. In the Silent Way approach, all the words presented have a high yield.

There is one exception, to be found in the material for beginners—the word *rod*. This word is to be seen as a 'joker', comparable to the *x* in algebra. It is there to be transformed into other words once the structures are in place. If my students can say *The blue rod is longer than the red one*, they can substitute *car* or *house* or hundreds of other words for the word r*od* in this sentence (and *shorter, bigger* or *faster* for the word *longer*) once they have mastered the structure.

The beginning of the learning process will be devoted to mastering the uses of the functional vocabulary, to put into place the structures of the language.

THE ROLE OF SLEEP IN LEARNING AND TEACHING

Humans integrate what they live in their waking hours when they sleep. Speaking—like all know-hows—is consolidated during sleep. This is why we must wait until Tuesday or Wednesday to know whether Monday's work has been integrated. I take the role of sleep into account when I think about my teaching of any particular class.

In a Silent Way course, the work progresses in a spiral, turning around on itself in widening circles. The deliberate choice to limit the expansion of vocabulary helps to create a dense and strong core. The class naturally comes back to each field and works on it again and again in different contexts. In the meantime, the students have slept. This leads to the use of the functional vocabulary—the grammar of the language—becoming better understood and integrated each time any aspect comes up.

'Not all learning takes place here and now; some may well be the outcome of sleeping on it.'

Gattegno (1976)

When a student is looking sleepy, I ask myself if this is because the class is going either too fast or too slow for him. If so, I need to change the way we are working, but if not, I would invite him to go to sleep for a few minutes. This gives him the chance to assimilate the work he has just done. There is no point in watching a student fight to remain awake when a few minutes' sleep will usually refresh him. The urge to sleep should be listened to. This is especially true during intensive courses where effort must be sustained over hours and days.

LEARNING TO SPEAK, SPEAKING TO LEARN

I consider the act of speaking a language to be a skill, a know-how—*I know how to speak this language.* Therefore, I believe that second languages should be taught as such.

People have known for millennia how other know-hows are learned, and therefore how they should be taught: through a process of coaching. The coach knows where to start her students off and how to move them forward. The learner tries to do what the coach suggests, receiving feedback from her on his trials when necessary so that he can adjust what he does and develop criteria for evaluating his performance. The learning happens in the successive trials, constantly adjusted, and in the ongoing development of his criteria.

It is necessary to distinguish the coaching session from the match, the music lesson from the end-of-year performance, the language class from the conversation. The first is where progress is made. The second takes place for other reasons: for the stimulus of competing, performing or conversing.

The phrase *learning to speak, speaking to learn* is meant to capture the learning process that is described in this book; in a classroom, the way a speaker learns to speak is by speaking with the active involvement of a coach.

However, by *speaking* I do not mean just saying words and phrases that are not one's own. In the next chapter, I will explain that for the purpose of second language learning it is superficial to view language as being 'for communication'. It is more insightful to see it as a means of expression, and in class it is only when students are speaking to express themselves that language is learnt as a know-how.

2. About language

SOME QUESTIONS

Let me start with some questions:

1. I talk to myself from when I wake up until when I fall asleep, and sometimes in my sleep as well. Do you?

2. I rehash what happened during recent events, and events from further back, sometimes way back. I reminisce. I recall. Do you?

3. I talk to myself about ideas and projects I'm working on at the moment. I reorganise them by talking to myself about them. I refine them. Do you?

4. I plan ahead, discussing with myself possible futures, possible outcomes. Do you?

5. I spend much more time doing these activities than talking about them with others. Talking to others takes up much less time every day than all the other things I do with language. Is this the same for you?

To imagine that 'language is for communication' is a huge oversimplification. In my case, language allows me to work out what I think, what I believe, what I know. In fact, it seems to be what allows me to be who I am, and to know who I am. I want my students to be able to reach this level in the language I teach.

WHAT AM I AIMING FOR IN MY COURSES?

As a language teacher, I believe that there are better reasons for learning a language than simply for communicating. I'm aiming for my students to be able to master this new language as well as they have their first. I won't be able to accompany them all the way on their journey towards this goal, but I can give them a firm and correct platform from which they can attain it for themselves if they decide to pursue this goal. This platform must be true to the language grammatically and the pronunciation must be very good, even if not native-like. The platform must contain foundations from which students can advance confidently, independently and successfully. To teach for less would seem to me to be an unethical limiting of their potential.

I am aiming at excellence, and I can say from experience that a very high level in a language is not as difficult to attain as most people imagine. This means that students who choose to will be able to express their thoughts and feelings accurately and correctly.

I am aiming at the spoken language first. At every step of the human trajectory, both through the ages and for individuals, the spoken language has preceded the written form, and this will be the case in my classes. How do I know if something is correct in my first language? I just know; it feels right, it sounds right. This is my aim for my students; everything has to just feel right.

In my class, students will learn the language they have paid to learn, not some degraded version of it which will get them by on their next holiday; a tourist phrasebook will do this more comprehensively than what I could teach them. It's not more difficult to learn to speak a language well than to speak one badly. However, it does requires skilful teaching.

ACCURACY IS THE PRIORITY

It is sometimes argued that 'accuracy' should be given a lower priority than 'communication' in language classes, on the grounds that a focus on accuracy somehow damages students' confidence and fluency.

This isn't my experience. Furthermore, in my teaching it is the sentences themselves that provide the 'raw material' for students' minds to construct the language. For that reason their sentences need to be made correct.

*The class has come together to learn English. I believe that this means that they should be given the opportunity to learn to speak it **well**.*

I know that if I allow mistakes to fossilise, these are likely to remain with the students for the rest of their lives.

Also, I work to develop students' internal criteria for the language. Because my students end up with good criteria that they themselves know they can rely on, they have the only solid basis for confidence in speaking.

If I make sure every sentence is corrected, they will know for themselves where they have solid criteria and where they don't. This is the true basis of self-confidence. As I will show later in this book, there are ways of getting students to correct themselves and each other that build their criteria and boost their confidence. And this is how we should teach.

HOW LANGUAGES FUNCTION

Consider these two sentences.

Plome the pleakful crotations ruggled the polanians ungleashably in the rit.[3]

Tarèque, les crotations altiènes ont ruglé les polaniens ingrésablement dans la rièse.

We know that one is in English and we may know, or can perhaps guess, that the other is in French.

Reading the English sentence, we know who *ruggled* whom; we know how they were *ruggled—ungleashably*; we know something about the *rugglers*—they were *pleakful*. We know when this happened, using two clues, the adverb *plome* and the tense chosen by the speaker for the verb—the <ed> form; and we know where this act took place—in the *rit*.

If we have a good knowledge of French, we know these same facts about the second sentence.

How do we know this? Not because we know the meaning of *crotations*, *polanians*, *rit* or the verb *ruggle*—these words were invented for the occasion—but because of the word order, the way that the nouns and verb (and in French, the adjectives) are inflected, and also because we understand the function words *the* and *in*. Despite not understanding seven of the eleven words in the sentence, a native speaker would never doubt his competence in English when reading it.

Sentences such as these illustrate that word order, inflection and function words are the heart of the language. Mastery of these words is essential if students are to speak the language well. This is why I work on these

[3] *I first met this English sentence in 1960 in a linguistics class given by Robert Cochrane. The French translation is mine.*

aspects of the language intensively before a wider vocabulary is introduced.

TWO SORTS OF VOCABULARY

For the purposes of language teaching, we can distinguish two types of vocabulary in any language: the lexical vocabulary, which ranges from everyday words to highly unusual ones; and the functional vocabulary.

The **lexical vocabulary** of the language allows the speaker to express the subject matter of his thoughts. It includes the names of objects such as *lawn* or *pike*, the labels for mental concepts such as *hope* or *fear*. The nouns *crotation*, *polanian* and *rit*, the first syllable of the adjective *pleakful*, the verb *ruggle* and the central part of the adverb *ungleashably* would belong to the lexical vocabulary of the language if they existed.

There is a subset of the lexical vocabulary that could be called 'everyday words'. There is no strict boundary between these and other content words. However, for almost everyone, the words *car* or *bus* are more likely to be needed than *chariot*. These words allow speakers to talk about what happens in their daily lives: the people they interact with, their daily schedule, the spaces they inhabit, the causal relationships that guide their choices. Words like *Thursday*, *children* or *work* cannot be considered function words, but it is certainly necessary for anyone learning the language to know them.

The **functional vocabulary** consists of the articles, pronouns, prepositions, quantifiers, auxiliary verbs and negations, of words that deal with quantity and quality, and some types of adverbs. The role of the function words is to structure the lexical vocabulary so that we know the answers to the questions above: how this happened, when, where, why, who, what, and other such questions of this nature. They allow the speaker to establish the personal, spatial, temporal and causal relationships between the content words. They structure these so as to give a precise meaning to what is being said. They are what make English English, and French French.

In my experience, the function words cannot be taught by simply explaining them. They cannot be equated with similar words in any other language because those in another language and those in English belong to different systems of thought. They don't have easy translations, even into closely related languages. The only way to learn them is to

I work from the premise that the best thing to teach students is to teach them all the things they find most difficult to learn for themselves.

use them in real but controlled contexts until one has a sense of what each allows one to express in the language.

There are a limited number of function words; around 450 in English depending on how you count them and whether you limit yourself to words in current use or not.

Consider these statistics, quoted from James Pennebaker's *The Secret Life of Pronouns* (2011, Bloomsbury Press):

> A very small number of function words account for most of the words we hear, read and say. ... Every one of the top 20 most frequently used words is a function word; together these 20 account for almost 30 percent of all the words that we use, read and hear.
>
> English has about 450 common function words in total, which account for 55 percent of all the words we use.
>
> The average English speaker has a vocabulary of perhaps 100,000 words. More than 99.5 percent of this is made up of content words. The split between content words and function words is comparable in other languages.

Of course students will need more vocabulary than just the function words, but these are the key to speaking the language well, and they therefore need to be worked on very early in the learning process, and worked on thoroughly. The content words can be added later, when students find themselves in situations where they need vocabulary and can learn the words they need in context.

THE SPIRIT OF THE LANGUAGE

The way people interact with others using their language, the way their language allows them to talk about time and the sequence of events, to describe space, to talk about causal relationships, to deal with quantities, generalisations, inclusion and exclusion—all of these and more differ fundamentally from one language to another. Gattegno summarised these aspects of languages in his term *the spirit of the language*[4]—in which he also included other factors such as the way native speakers use their energy when speaking their language.

Gattegno's proposition was that if we want to teach a language well, then we should start by spending most of our class time teaching our students the spirit of the language. If we do this, we will be teaching

[4] *For more information, see Chapter 2 of Gattegno (1963)*

them all the things they find most difficult to learn for themselves, and therefore, the things for which a teacher's involvement is most valuable.

After all, the students will almost always have the opportunity to continue working on the language after their course is over, so I don't need to try to teach them everything. My time and theirs is wasted if I spend it working on lexical vocabulary; this will fall into place, as it does in our first language, effortlessly and well, when encountered in a real context.

This is the reason why the lexical vocabulary is kept to a minimum in my courses until many of the uses of the function words have been mastered. Discovering the spirit of a language from the very first contact with it, when it is at its most foreign, arouses a pleasing and healthy astonishment and the desire to know more. This is one of the reasons why Silent Way emphasises this aspect of languages whatever the level of the students. How this can be done in the early stages of language learning is explained from Chapter 11 onwards. And from Chapter 21, we see how it can be done when working with students who have already studied the language in other learning contexts.

TEACHING A LANGUAGE

I can find out empirically what the things are that students will find most difficult to learn for themselves by looking at what people who are left to their own devices learn, and do not learn. When I talk to people who have either learnt English mainly through contact with native speakers or through studying it at school, I immediately see that they are often 'fluent bad speakers'. I usually notice some or all of the following problems:

Their **pronunciation** is based on that of their mother tongue; both vowels and consonants are assimilated to those of their mother tongue. The rhythm is wrong. They usually have no idea how to produce stress and, even more important in English, reduction.

Their **constructions** are faulty. Depending on their level, they tend to string words together one after the other in an order based on their native language.

Temporal relationships are indicated by a few adverbs such as 'today', 'tomorrow' or 'soon' rather than by using tenses or constructing complex sentences. The verb form used does not always match the adverb used

As a polyglot, Gattegno knew that languages differ from each other in fundamental ways, and that to learn a language properly means to understand how people speaking it relate to each other, to space and to time. He called these relations 'the spirit of the language'.

'Languages differ in grammar because they differ in spirit.

The earlier learners are acquainted with the choices which will define the L2, the easier it will be for them not to fall back on the choices of their own L1, thus avoiding the interferences of L1 on L2, often mentioned in the literature.'

Gattegno (1985)

in the same sentence. Lower level students sometimes use verbs in the infinitive, or in only one verb form, always the same.

Personal relationships are expressed using a limited number of pronouns which are not always correct.

Spatial relationships are expressed using a limited number of the simplest prepositions and not always the right ones.

These, then, are typical areas I know I should work on.

On the other hand, people who have picked up a language by themselves usually have an extensive **vocabulary**. So we can count on our students' capacity to acquire vocabulary when they need it.

PRONUNCIATION

Pronunciation has been called a 'gateway skill'. In job interviews, for example, if a person's pronunciation is not at the standard of his other language skills, he may not get the opportunity to display these. It is therefore important for students to develop a high level of pronunciation. I work on the oral and aural qualities of the language at the same time: both pronunciation and ear training.

Pronouncing a language is a motor skill; it involves muscles. It takes time to learn to pronounce the sounds of a language, and even more time to make their production automatic in all contexts. Pronunciation cannot be worked on in fits and starts, by introducing a new sound every lesson or so, spreading the process out over the time of the course. It will be needed for every sentence that the students say, so I will start with a few intensive hours on this skill, until the students know how to produce some of the idiosyncratic movements that English requires, although these will not yet be automatic.

At the same time, I need to train my students' ear so that they can hear the language correctly when it is spoken by native speakers. Fortunately, this comes as a corollary of production: correct pronunciation produces a trained ear, but the reverse is not true, because the students' musculature needs to be developed specifically for the new language. There will be more on why this is so in Chapters 8 and 9.

If our students leave the course knowing how to make all the sounds of English, and in different contexts; if they understand how the stress and reduction system functions; then they will have an excellent

I am aiming high for my students. I want them to attain a genuine mastery of the new language. So we work extensively on the function words.

grounding for continuing to improve, and will be able to pick out individual sounds and words in the chain of speech.

It is much more efficient to teach pronunciation in the first hours of the course, at least well into Stage Two of the learning process, and then continue to refine the production of individual sounds and the use of stress and reduction throughout the rest of the course. This can be done using micro-lessons whenever the need arises.

GRAMMAR

To master the spoken language, it is necessary to internalise the grammatical structures as functioning automatisms, not as knowledge; I therefore work on the structures as know-hows. I don't teach grammar using explanations and rules. I do not believe that applying rules will lead to the effortless grammaticality that we all have in L1. Instead, grammar emerges from real situations:

- **for beginners**, I use Cuisenaire rods to present linguistic situations which require little vocabulary but a lot of language (i.e. the grammar and use of the function words necessary to express what the students are experiencing);
- **for more advanced students**, I use their own lives as the subject matter of the class which allows them to ground their use of grammar in their personal reality. Through this process I can both rectify their misconceptions and offer them new and more precise ways to express themselves.

Inevitably, we focus extensively on the function words.

THE FOUR SKILLS

Learning a language is often presented as learning four skills: speaking, listening, writing and reading. This book focuses on teaching **speaking** because all the others are dependent upon it. They are much easier to learn once students have made progress with speaking.

Because my classes are based around speaking, **listening** is automatically worked on from the start because students listen to themselves and each other continuously.

We speak of the skills of 'reading and writing', but it would be better to reverse these words; **writing** should be taught before **reading**. When working with most of my students, I spend very little time on reading and writing. Their previous classes have been heavily focused on these

'We call "linguistic situations" those situations whose function is to make people speak.

… rods are useful because they allow meaning to be made immediately perceptible and give a chance to teachers to introduce the functional vocabulary of any language.'

Gattegno (1985)

skills and they don't need more of the same; they have come to learn to speak. However, for students who are illiterate or those who are unfamiliar with the Roman alphabet, it is necessary to work on both.

At the end of a lesson, writing helps students to fix what has been said in their minds. Obviously, it has the further advantage of leaving a trace; this can then be exploited for practice in reading. Once students have written texts, these can be passed around the class in order to give everyone practice in reading and in reading other people's handwriting.

If I ask students to write in class, it is always something they have already said. This way, I know for sure that they understand what they are writing. Also, I never stop students from copying the spelling of words from the charts. As soon as they are sure of the spelling of a word, this stops of its own accord.

VOCABULARY

The lexical vocabulary of the language will be left aside, at least to begin with. After all, we have no idea what vocabulary our students will need. Will they want to reserve a hotel room, negotiate a contract, sell sandwiches, or buy industrial products? I have no idea. Quite often, the students themselves don't know yet either. I can rely on them to learn the vocabulary on their own, just as they did in their native language.

Since lexical vocabulary is one of the things the 'fluent bad speaker' does possess; we can count on our students' capacity to acquire it when they need it. In many schools, children learn little other than vocabulary. And, unfortunately for them, what vocabulary they do learn is not operational. This is because it is learned from lists and in role plays, and is not connected to lived experience. When the learners do encounter real life situations, nothing in them triggers the vocabulary they have memorised with so much effort.[5]

DON'T TEACH RELATED WORDS AS SETS

It is usually a mistake to teach groups of words as sets—all the words for a topic, pairs of opposites or synonyms, all the words for family members, etc.—in any one lesson.

There are two dangers. The first is that the students simply muddle up these words in their minds. The second is that students remember them as an ordered set and can only reach the one they need by running

'Context is the means by which native speakers learn the meaning of words.'

—Dot Wordsworth, The Spectator, *16th November 2024*

[5] See Chapter 8, 'On Memory', in Young and Messum How We Learn and How We Should be Taught, London: Duo Flumina, 2011.

It is quite remarkable how many students who have studied English at school for several years have to go through their own language to find a simple word like 'red' or 'blue'.

When they are asked to describe an arrangement of rods—'A red rod, a blue one, a green one and a black one',—they find it surprisingly difficult.

In their hours of study, they have spoken authentically so rarely that the colour of each rod does not trigger its word in English.

through the set from the beginning. Generally, it is best to avoid these approaches and provide just the word that students need when they need it. If a student needs the word *beautiful* to say what he wants to, why also give him the opposite—*ugly*—at the same time? Give him that word when he needs it.

Occasionally there are advantages to presenting opposites and one or two intensifiers together, if that helps students comprehend the meanings of these words by their contrast.

A NEW DISCIPLINE

When someone speaks to us in everyday life, we extract the meaning from what we hear and let the words that expressed it disappear. Spoken language is ephemeral by nature. If I am asked to tell someone else what was just said, I use my own words to do so rather than repeating those of the original speaker. Indeed, if I try to use the same words as the speaker, it is often an indication that I have not understood what was said sufficiently well to have been able to extract the meaning.

If they want to learn a new language, it is necessary for students to modify this normal linguistic functioning of letting go of the words they hear. They must learn a new discipline: as well as listening for the meaning, they need to hold on to the way the message was expressed. Many students do not realise that they need to develop this new discipline. They find it difficult to listen for the 'container' as well as the 'content'. In the Silent Way, the demand for the use of correct language, means that students always work on both.

IS SPEAKING A LANGUAGE ABOUT COMMUNICATION OR EXPRESSION?

'Expression is a power of the mind; communication is an event with a certain probability attached to it, a probability that can be zero, as in disguising one's thought, and is almost never 100%.'

Gattegno (1976)

The last workshop Gattegno led before he died—ten days in the French Alps—was entitled *La communication est un miracle*: in English, *Communication is a miracle*. He pointed out that a speaker can only be responsible for what he or she emits. No speaker can take responsibility for the way the listener listens, nor for the place the listener makes within him or herself for the opinions expressed by the speaker. On the other hand, the speaker must take full responsibility for what is expressed, and how it is said. As soon as the situation is a little more complex than *Please pass the salt*, people rarely know the extent to which communication has really taken place.

This is why I aim for my students to be able to use the language as a means of expressing their thoughts, their perceptions, their opinions and their sentiments. I want them to master what they say so that they can express themselves in a clear and precise way in the new language. If they can express themselves well, then perhaps communication will take place.

SEPARATING COMMUNICATION FROM EXPRESSION

If you have been in a meeting where you had something you wanted to say, you were ready and waiting for an opportunity to say it, but an opening in the conversation didn't present itself, the conversation moved on, and in the end you didn't say it, then you have experienced the difference between expression and communication. You knew what you wanted to say—this is expression—but communication did not take place.

THE COMMUNICATIVE APPROACH

The Oxford English Dictionary gives this definition of communication:

> The transmission or exchange of information, knowledge, or ideas, by means of speech, writing, mechanical or electronic media, etc.

Note that in this definition, 'communication' is the process of transmission or exchange, not the formulation of the message that is transmitted.

As my colleague Piers Messum has pointed out, the use of the word within the scientific and engineering disciplines of telecommunications is consistent with this definition. Given the impressive achievements of these disciplines in the 1950s and 1960s, it would have been an attractive choice of name for the linguists and teachers in the 1970s who were developing alternatives to the Grammar Translation and Audio Visual approaches whose limitations had become apparent.

However, whatever the original aspirations and subsequent history of the Communicative Approach were, its current reality is realised in the textbooks that most teachers use. Generally speaking, the peg for each chapter is an issue, topic or situation from the world that is supposed to bring interest and relevance to the lesson. The language is crafted to demonstrate certain points of grammar, which are then practised in a series of exercises. Students are supposed to

---

'The experience we all have in using our own language for the expression of our thoughts, feelings, emotions, and perceptions is that words come by themselves, that we have at our disposal an extremely effective automatic system which demands almost no energy to function. Under such conditions, language is truly a vehicle; it carries our expressions to our satisfaction.

As soon as we leave our own language and concentrate on acquiring a new one, however, we find that we are engaged in struggles, that our memory becomes so important, whereas in our own language it does not seem to play a big role. In fact we can no more say that we 'remember' our language than that we remember how to stand up or walk. We know how to speak. We feel that knowing a language is a skill, not the memorization of statements, that it is ours as a functioning. So much so that, in our conversations with our relatives and friends, we never attempt to retain the words we use and hear, once the meaning has been either expressed or understood.'

Gattegno (1976)

be 'communicating' when they create and perform a semi-scripted role play, and do the exercises proposed orally in pair work or with the teacher.

As Piers notes, the net result has more in common with the grammar-translation approach than one might at first imagine. In the old days, the message to be translated into English was given to students in their native language in the form of a text. Nowadays, the message is not always given as text (it is generated in a supposedly communicative situation), but it is still formulated *sotto voce* by students in their native language before they translate it into English. Grammar-translation in the mind, however, is no more speaking English authentically than the same activity done on paper.

EXPRESSION

The Collins English Dictionary (1979) gives this definition of expression:

> The act or an instance of transforming ideas into words.

Although the transformation of an idea into words and the communication of the idea often take place at the same time, sometimes they don't, and this is where we can clearly see the difference between expression and communication. The distinction is precious and should not be allowed to disappear, particularly in language teaching.

As I watch people converse, I am aware that it is very often not a need to communicate which moves speakers, but a need to express themselves.

Can we catch ourselves in situations where we can become sensitive to the human energy that we use when we speak? I do not mean the physical energy we use to actually utter words, but the mental energy we use to create and to hold our ideas. Close observation of what happens to us in various circumstances as we live our lives gives us some opportunities to make ourselves sensitive to this energy

When I am developing new ideas, words and images appear in my mind, I stabilise them by creating sentences out of them which I can then critique, organise and rework. This process is sometimes called 'talking to oneself', but I never feel that I am divided—A speaking to B within my mind—and I certainly wouldn't call this communicating with myself. I remain one integrated person when I develop new ideas. For me, this use of language is at least as important as communicating with other people, because it allows me to know what I think.

When I watch my inner life, I see that words are present much of the time. I talk to myself constantly. My inner voice takes me back over past moments of my life as I hear myself talking about what happened or what might have happened. It talks me through possible futures and prepares me for them. I use it to work on problems, to talk them through. My inner voice helps me to lead a functional life.

When I'm talking to someone else, I sometimes have to say things like, 'That's not quite what I wanted to say'. I am aware that I constantly monitor what my inner voice says, and what I say out loud. I notice when what I have said does not correspond exactly to the idea which provoked it. I always feel the need to correct myself, and do so if I have the opportunity. How I express myself matters to me.

On the other hand, I only very occasionally check that communication has taken place. I might do this with children, to make sure that they have understood what I said. I rarely do it with friends and neither do they do it with me, even though it is sometimes clear to me, in the moment or later, that something said in either direction has not been received in quite the way it was intended. We don't seem to care as much about communication as we imagine we might, and certainly not as much as we care about our own expression.

WHAT SHOULD WE BE TEACHING?

Ferdinand de Saussure and what his work implies for teachers

In his *Course in General Linguistics*, a course given in French between 1907 and 1911 at the University of Geneva which was made into a book by some of his students who transcribed their notes, Ferdinand de Saussure (1857–1913) established the foundations of the modern discipline of linguistics. He is reported to have done this by proposing that there is a system or code called a language (*langue*) which is used by humans in order to speak (*parole*). The field of linguistics is concerned with language, the system—Saussure's *langue*—to the exclusion of speech, Saussure's *parole*.

From the second half of the twentieth century until now, many of those people who write for or train foreign language teachers have been trained in linguistics, and their teaching has been influenced by their understanding of the discipline. To make matters worse, teachers call themselves *language teachers*.

'Speakers work on their expressions and discover that there may be need for alterations to adjust to circumstances so as to obtain communication. Of course, there are many cases of non-ambiguity and these require little adjustment to shift from one's expression to one's communication. But there are also many situations which require discipline in order to reach a non-ambiguous expression.

...

Making students aware that expression is their responsibility and must be attended to carefully if communication is to have greater chances of happening will be of great help in the mastery of L2.'

Gattegno (1985)

At 17 years of age, the niece of a friend of mine had been studying French for 6 years at school before going to university. She reported to me that no one in her class used y *or* en, *two pronouns that are used frequently in French but which have no equivalent in English. Why would this be?*

I believe that when speaking and writing French, the question these students ask themselves is, How do I say this in French?, *where 'this' is the English version of what they want to say. They are translating from English words in their minds, and this is why* y *and* en *never appear.*

This has created a problem for language teachers, since our students come to us, wanting not Saussure's *langue*, but his *parole*. They come to us wanting to learn to speak the language. And all too often, teachers offer them courses in Saussure's *langue*, giving them grammar rules and vocabulary lists, underplaying the function words and their role, and providing little spontaneous use of the language. Acquiring knowledge doesn't yield know-hows; learning Saussure's *langue* doesn't yield his *parole*. *Parole* is an expression of who I am in the instant. Only practising talking about what one wants to say in the moment can yield *parole*.

ABOUT KNOW-HOWS

How does one teach a student to speak a foreign language? The English language itself gives us a clue; we say, *I know how to speak Japanese* just as we say *I know how to swim*, and this tells us that speaking a language should be seen as a know-how, like playing football or the guitar.

As we saw in Chapter 1, we learn a know-how by doing it, whatever the 'it' might be. So teaching students to speak will be about helping them to learn to play the 'language game': speaking. This does not mean simply learning words and expressions—English as a translation of your native language—which sometimes works,

Quelle heure est-il ? = What time is it?

but usually doesn't,

Je m'appelle Julie. = My name is Julie.

I need to work in such a way that the students can build up the feel for the language that is necessary for them to speak it well. To do this, we will first need to work on the spirit of the language using the spoken language to do so. Teaching students to speak requires teachers to work on students' know-hows, and these have to be developed in an appropriate way.

LANGUAGE AS AN EXPRESSION OF WHO WE ARE

In the idea that speaking a language is a know-how, I see the reason why students can have years of school English but still be tongue-tied when they find themselves in an English-speaking country with the language all around them. It doesn't spring to life in them as it does in me. Words never simply appear when needed, sometimes years after having been learned. This is because the words were never connected to a reason why one would utter them. Speaking was not taught as a means of expression.

In 2018, in *How People Learn II*, an overview of the scientific understanding of learning, the expert committee commissioned by the National Academies of Sciences (USA) wrote:

> Emotions are skills just like cognitive skills [and] without emotion, your cognition has no rudder—nothing to steer it.
>
> Quite literally, it is neurobiologically impossible to think deeply about or remember information about which one has had no emotion because the healthy brain does not waste energy processing information that does not matter to the individual.

How people learn II: Learners, Contents and Cultures *The National Academies Press (2018), page 29.*

The language needs—**needs**—to be lived to be learned. Textbooks try to be relevant and engaging, but nothing in a textbook—no role play, no exercise—will ever have the emotional charge of even the simplest sentence said by someone because this is what they want to say.

In both cases, words come out of a student's mouth, but only in the second case is language being used as we use our native one, with genuine self-involvement. This is real speech.

IMPLICATIONS FOR TEACHERS

Language teachers have to make a fundamental choice between two points of view. They can decide to consider language as being primarily about communication and adopt a communicative approach, or they can decide that it is primarily about being able to express oneself and use an approach which favours expression and works on creating appropriate know-hows. The decision a teacher makes will lead to classes which look and behave entirely differently.

'It can't be said too often: we get better at using words, whether hearing, speaking, reading, or writing, under one condition and only one—when we use those words to say something we want to say, to people we want to say it to, for purposes that are our own.'

John Holt *How children learn. London: Penguin (1967) p.124*

In a class based on communication, the guiding principle is that the message has to be transmitted. So as long as this happens, everyone should be more or less satisfied. Correction is often perfunctory, and pronunciation is to a large extent ignored. Unfortunately, this means that most students are condemned to mediocrity.

Higgs T.V. and Clifford R. The Push Toward Communication. In Curriculum, Competence, and the Foreign Language Teacher (1982) Higgs, T.V. (ed.), Lincolnwood, IL: National Textbook Co.

This problem with the Communicative Approach was raised by Higgs and Clifford as early as 1982:

> If a student has 'communicated' a message effectively he has succeeded; in principle, there is no need for a teacher to ask more of him. The result is that students soon develop ingrained bad habits. These are extremely difficult to eliminate later and these students therefore do not progress to the point where they speak the language to a high level of excellence. By the time they reach an intermediate level, many have become 'fluent bad speakers' and are destined to remain so.

On the other hand, the guiding principle of approaches based on expression is that students should be able to express themselves as well as possible. For this reason, excellence is sought after in all areas of the language and at all times. In the Silent Way, everything that is said is checked and corrected, and alternative constructions are worked on when these offer the speaker a better way of saying what he means. The students choose what they want to talk about. The route to excellent English remains open if any student decides to spend the necessary time to follow it.

'As a student of languages I wish to feel myself inching towards what natives do with themselves when they use their language spontaneously for expression in all occasions; as a teacher, I want to do the "right" things for my students. Once I understand what students have to do, I am able to invent techniques and materials.'

Gattegno (1976)

I see my role as helping the students to learn the language to the point where they can develop an intimate relationship with it, where it is as deeply embedded within them as their first. Transactional language use will never lead to this level of expertise. It can only be achieved if I help students to encounter the spirit of the language and make it theirs.

How we can build this intimate relationship with the new language is the subject of this book.

SOME THEORY

3. Teaching from first principles

Everyone recognises an excellent teacher when they are fortunate enough to encounter one, but what is it that such a teacher does which makes her so good?

There seem to be two principal factors: first, the extent to which information flows freely between the students and the teacher, and second, the extent to which the teacher has developed a personal understanding of how people learn.

ONE-WAY AND TWO-WAY TEACHING

When I was in secondary school, I had a teacher of ancient history who would come into the classroom, sit down and read to us from the history book. She would comment on what she read, expand on some details and then, when the bell rang, would stand and leave. We were not invited to ask questions so our only activity was listening. She was a kind person, but she seemed to have not enough energy to do more than this bare minimum.

This teacher was a 'one-way' teacher; information flowed from her to her students but she ignored any information flowing from them to her.

In contrast, a two-way teacher constantly adjusts what she does in the class to the students' activity as it unfolds in the here and now. She acts

'Gattegno does not challenge … education on some point of methodology; he challenges it in the way Copernicus challenged the belief that the sun revolved around the earth—that is, at the heart of its most fundamental and honored assumptions.'

—McCandlish Phillips, New York Times, 28 Sept, 1970

41

upon information flowing from them to her and this produces the second direction of two-way teaching.

Fortunately, very few teachers are as one-way as my ancient history teacher was; most teaching is two-way at least to some extent. Teachers are aware of the students they have in front of them and respond to their mistakes if these are visible, although often only to give the students the right answer. Many teachers have only a general idea of how well the students are understanding the work. After all there is a curriculum: the teachers have a lesson to teach, explanations to give, a book to work through, a pace to maintain, and this is what they do in the class, willy-nilly. They will find out what the students have learned when the next exam takes place.

In language teaching, every time the teacher 'teaches' the students what the curriculum states they should know by telling them about it and perhaps by getting them to construct a few perfunctory sentences, every time she plans her lessons in advance and teaches the planned lesson whatever happens in class, she is functioning as a one-way teacher. How can such a lesson possibly respond to the learners' immediate needs except in the most general way?

In a language class, a two-way teacher provides her students with open situations for them to explore and helps them to do so. She evaluates each of their sentences as it is produced and gives the students immediate feedback to alert them to their mistakes. This kind of teaching is 'two-way' because, first, as the students express themselves they give their teacher immediate feedback about their capacity to speak the language through what they say and do, here and now; and second, she gives the students her feedback on their production.

But even the two-way teacher is only as good as the model of learning she is using in her practice. The mere fact of being responsive to her students is not enough for her to be an excellent teacher.

THE SUBORDINATION OF TEACHING TO LEARNING

Gattegno insisted that teachers should subordinate their teaching to the students' learning. This goes further than two-way teaching. The teacher who is putting this into practice will be applying the theory of learning and the four stages of learning presented in Chapter 1.

The theory of learning tells her that learning a language means learning know-hows and that this takes place through awarenesses. As she gains experience, she develops a deep understanding of what she is teaching and finds ways in which what she knows can be presented so that her students will meet the language as a series of awarenesses. With experience, she will discover various orders in which these awarenesses can be provoked and she will find ways of provoking each one.

For any topic, she makes sure that her students progress through the four stages of learning. Once they have had the initial awareness of Stage 1, she knows that they will then mostly be working at Stage 2 and she knows that this requires that they have freedom to experiment, that they receive feedback on their trials, and that one of her jobs is to make sure nothing moves to Stage 3 until it is ready to be made automatic. Otherwise a mistake will become fossilised and will be difficult to correct at some later time.

She is aware of the need to take her students into account in her decisions about how the lesson will unfold. She deliberately creates the two-way flow of information which will enable her to work intelligently on what the students are exploring. She learns to observe them and the way each of them functions as a learner; then she can fairly accurately follow their train of thought. As the lesson unfolds, she is in a position to make an educated guess about what train of thought has caused the mistake a student is making and what awareness is required in the moment. She becomes more skillful in providing what he needs in the form of a question or some other way of provoking an awareness rather than as a piece of knowledge. She works to develop the students' criteria for correctness rather than simply to obtain 'the right answer'.

Part of her continuing education as a teacher consists in developing both her sensitivity to her students as they learn, and her capacity to work with more and more students while following them all individually. What used to be a class of 20 gradually becomes 20 one-to-one lessons taking place together. She educates her capacity to see the learning from the students' perspective to an ever-higher level.

TWO-WAY TEACHING AS OPPOSED TO SUBORDINATED TEACHING

I said that the two-way teacher is only as good as the model of learning that she is using. Let's take 'teachable moments' as an example. A teachable moment is a moment when a student has a genuine question in him and is poised to take in the answer and use it immediately. If a two-way teacher deals with a teachable moment by giving the student

'The subordination of teaching to learning requires that we meet the needs of individual students, needs unknown to everybody except their teacher if she is sensitive. The teacher must learn to find out as quickly as possible what each student is going through in the lesson, and then remain in touch with and adjust to this.'

Caleb Gattegno

The teacher's role is completely transformed. It is not to transmit her knowledge, but to get her students to work at the boundary between what they know and what they are learning.

This boundary is not difficult to establish. When a student speaks, whatever is correct belongs to what he knows, and what needs correcting lies beyond.

In A Working Model for Health *(1986), Gattegno enumerated some of the powers of the mind: awareness, concentration, presence, the need to know, discrimination, perception, will, action, intelligence, sensitivity and vulnerability, abstraction, freedom, imaging and imagination, the sense of truth, the sense of harmony, surrender, patience and wisdom, objectivation, passion, adaptation, and learning.*

He elaborated on this in The Learning and Teaching of Foreign Languages *(1985) .*

'*Teachers must be concerned with what the students are doing with themselves rather than with the language, which is the students' concern. Teachers and students work on different subjects.*'

Gattegno (1976)

the answer rather than providing what is necessary to allow him to work through the problem for himself and thus develop his criteria, she is wasting a golden opportunity for genuine learning to take place.

If the two-way teacher's implicit model of learning doesn't include the capacity to make educated guesses about what is taking place in the students' minds in the here and now, then she has no way of calibrating her response to the train of thought that produced the mistake. If she doesn't have awareness as the basis of her model, she won't know that her role is not to impart knowledge, but to change the way the students see the world. As tools, she uses awareness in general and awarenesses locally in every moment of her work.

THE POWERS OF THE MIND

Outside the classroom, my students are intelligent, witty, naturally creative people whose company I enjoy. They deal with the everyday issues they meet; they solve problems; they can apply themselves for considerable periods of time if required; they have repeatedly demonstrated that they learn well. If they don't display these qualities in my class, I know that the problem must stem from me; I'm not allowing them to be the people that they naturally are.

Gattegno described the mental qualities that underpin our learning as 'powers of the mind' or 'attributes of the self'. The Silent Way teacher who subordinates her teaching to the students' learning opens the way for her students to use the powers of their minds to the full.

On more than one occasion I heard Gattegno make this point by saying some variant of the following: '*I am not an English teacher. I am a people teacher and the people are learning the language.*'

I can say from experience that it is incomparably more interesting to be a teacher of people learning a language than to be a language teacher.

DEVELOPING CRITERIA

When students make a mistake, I don't simply show them the right answer. I silently ask questions, often using finger correction, to help them discover what they missed at some earlier point. They need to become as sure as I am that this aspect of the language is now as it should be, is right. This certainty can only be reached by working for themselves until they have criteria which allow them to be sure.

One occasionally sees a teacher using Silent Way charts and rods, and therefore believing herself to be using the Silent Way. If she is working just to get the students to say the right words in the right order, rather than having the ability to do this from criteria that they have developed, then what she is doing is a travesty of the approach. For example, she might be substituting 'visual dictation'—showing a sequence of words or sounds on the charts—for proper teaching. Too much 'help' might give the appearance of helping but the work will almost certainly have to be done again, and again …

Gattegno often told a story about a lesson he saw during a visit to a class in California. Even forty years later, when he talked about this lesson, he spoke of 'the scandal'. He watched a Grade 1 teacher during a lesson on arithmetic. The teacher said, *Two plus three?* and the pupils answered with a question in their voices, *Five?* That was the scandal!

What Gattegno saw as scandalous was the fact that the teacher had put a system into place in which, even for something so simple and obvious, the pupils felt that they had to rely on her to know whether they were right or not. The answer to the question should have been an unshakable, resounding, *Five!*, not a doubtful, *Five?* Any child in Grade 1 can learn absolutely and for a fact that two plus three makes five.

Our job is to free the students from the need for a teacher, and we can only do that by helping them to develop their own criteria for correctness.

ZOOMING IN AND OUT

In everyday life, people always have the wider context in the background while they are working on some detailed aspect of a given challenge.

- A doctor who is examining your throat is aware that it is part of a wider system, and will be considering his diagnosis in a dialogue between what he sees and his understanding of how it might fit within the larger picture.
- If you are puzzling about how to halve three eggs, it is because you have a recipe for eight people which requires three eggs, but you only have four people to cook for. Whatever compromise you come to must work with the other ingredients of the recipe to produce the dish.

We only properly understand any element of a system when we understand its relationship to the other elements and, indeed, to the system itself.

'Teachers of L2s can learn to think in terms of criteria and conceive of their jobs as being the transfer of these criteria to their students.

A good teacher is one who has found exercises which force awareness and thus generate criteria and one who makes sure that these are applied in all relevant cases—representing the practice which will make students assimilate the new criteria as belonging to 'rightness' from now on.'

Gattegno (1985)

To gain such an understanding, we freely 'zoom in' to the particular and 'zoom out' to the system.

The Silent Way makes systems visible. The materials (See Chapter 5) are designed to allow students to 'zoom out' to see where they are relative to the system they are working within and then 'zoom in' to return to the details of whatever it is that they are working on.

The charts are all syntheses of some aspect of the language. The Rectangle chart shows the sounds of the language, their articulatory relationships and the stress and reduction system, the Fidel shows the sound/spelling relationships and the Word charts show the function words and allow students to discover the spirit of the language. The Verb Tense System described in **Chapter 19** shows how temporal and modal relationships are expressed in English.

In each case, when a student works on a specific aspect of the language he does so within the context of the whole system. He situates what he is doing, and can see how much remains to be worked on. He is forced to make deliberate choices between the elements of the system and it becomes clear to him that he needs criteria for these choices.

Students are not troubled when presented with a whole system within which they have so far only worked on a small part. They simply ignore what they have not yet met. This is preferable to presenting them with simplified or partial versions of the language which have to be constantly revised and expanded so that students never know how much more there is to learn.

THE MORE YOU GIVE, THE LESS YOU GET

Charles Curran, the developer of Community Language Learning, described the phenomenon of a teacher being 'sick to teach': having a pathological need to explain something she knows. Learning to resist this is part of a Silent Way teacher's development but it becomes easier as one learns to notice students' awarenesses and becomes more adept at provoking them. Then one can take real pleasure in seeing students work out for themselves what one would have previously explained.

There is another form of interference when a teacher constrains the work so much that the students lose choice, lose the opportunity to explore. This may take the form of guidelines for what to say or write, 'help' in deciding how to express it, exercises which are so vapid that there is no challenge at all—detailed guidance of all kinds.

Experience tells me that the more 'help' I give, the less the students feel inclined to mobilise themselves to learn. The task simply becomes too boring. The lack of freedom reduces their sense of adventure, of enterprise, of pleasure in working and exploring. If they do not need to mobilise themselves, they simply settle back into passivity and, if they are free to do so, they soon drop out.

One source of motivation stems from being successful in rising to real challenges, even small ones. One of the major tasks I have, therefore, is to propose challenges which are correctly pitched to the students' level. Much of the thinking I do outside the class revolves around finding suitable challenges to propose. Much of my work inside the class is about repeatedly inventing challenges right now for situations I had not envisaged.

HOMEWORK

As a general rule, I don't give homework to students in my classes. If the work is done properly in class and I make sure they have done enough practice, then homework is not needed. The natural process of sleep will consolidate what they've learnt.

Scan to watch a video of a teacher giving students a 'manageable challenge'.

There are exceptions to this.
- Pronunciation usually requires students to do more work to train their muscles. So I ask them to spend a few minutes each day practising saying the sounds, words and phrases we have been working on.
- If writing is an important part of the course I may ask them to write me letters for homework (see previous section).
- When we start working on the Verb Tense System at intermediate level, there is a small amount of work on the irregular verbs that is better done by students individually (see Chapter 19).

Some students want to do additional work in between lessons. For these students I recommend that they use 'free recall'. This is a simple technique to get additional benefit from their lessons. A day or so after a lesson they think of the situations we talked about and say any sentences they remember out loud. The attempt to call to mind what we worked on will enhance their retention, and is far more effective than re-reading notes, or trying to memorise vocabulary lists or grammar rules.

Some students like to take this further by writing down some of their sentences.

BEWARE OF STUDENTS' BELIEFS …

Students do not come to the class as specialists in language learning, and many do not know what one must do in order to learn a language.

- Many believe that if they learn all the vocabulary and the list of irregular verbs by heart, they will have done what needs to be done.
- Others believe the foreign language will just 'come to them' as their first language seems to have done. They believe languages are 'picked up': you choose the language you wish to acquire, go to classes, do what the teacher says and the language should somehow just appear in you.
- Others have been told that communication—getting the message across—is sufficient, and accuracy doesn't matter—the previous teachers of the 'fluent bad speaker' made the mistake of believing that speaking a language should be judged by the learner's capacity to communicate. They come to class wanting better, but don't realise that their way of working has created the problem.
- Others believe that it is necessary to suffer if one wants to learn. They do not think they have spent their time properly if the lesson was a pleasant experience. They cannot imagine that it is possible to enjoy oneself and learn a language at the same time.

Students who come with any of these beliefs are hindered from doing what is necessary to learn the language properly.

POST-PARATION

Since the students are as responsible as the teacher for the content of a Silent Way class, it is not possible to prepare one's lessons in the way that this is usually done. Instead, Silent Way teachers use post-paration.

Post-paration takes place after the class rather than before it, and involves thinking about what happened and what could have been improved. Usually, I reflect on each student, dwelling on those who have had a problem of some sort, and I think through solutions which I will try out in the coming lessons.

Sometimes a student can remain in my mind for years. I remember a certain Doumi I worked with in the early 1990s. He was in a class of twenty students that I was teaching to read. The other nineteen learned to read in a few days, but not Doumi. I never found a way of getting him to realise that the syllables *Dou* and *mi* were each made of two sounds, a necessary awareness for learning to read in French. Since

> *'Only when one works on oneself do changes happen. So we must make students work on themselves as a matter of course.'*
>
> Gattegno (1976)

then, I have collected many ways of provoking this awareness of sounds as against syllables. I would now be much better equipped if ever I meet another Doumi.

Not all cases are as haunting as that of Doumi. Usually I think about what we might do in the following lesson, always keeping my mind open to what the students might introduce. I think about how I might build on what was done during the day; for example, whether I should now allow the students to forge ahead, or launch the next lesson in such a way that they will consolidate certain points. Rather than preparing the next lesson, I use reflection on today's lesson to prepare myself to better subordinate my teaching to their learning in the next one.

Post-paration prepares me rather than the lesson. It's how I grow as a teacher.

HOW DO I KNOW IF I HAVE DONE A GOOD JOB?

I judge the quality of a lesson I have just given by asking myself questions of the following type.
- Were the students mentally present and engaged all the time? If students are not present, no learning can take place.
- To what extent did I hold myself to my true function as a teacher? To what extent did I become 'sick to teach'?
- How many awarenesses could have been provoked, and how many took place?
- How many ogdens were spent and was the number quite small?
- How often did the students take the initiative?
- Was enough time spent by students getting the necessary practice?
- Was the work done in such a way that the students had access to the spirit of the language?

MAKING LEARNING A LANGUAGE A JOYFUL EXPERIENCE

Learning should be a joyful experience. Look at the small children around you and see how happy they are when left to their own devices with a good challenge. No young child shows signs of suffering as they learn their mother tongue.

Language learning can be joyful and effective. This book tells you how to make it so.

'We can see that teachers and students have two very different functions. The latter are dedicated to acquiring a language, and they must feel that they are in fact exchanging their time for that acquisition. The former do not have to work on the language while teaching, but only on the students: on what they are doing or not doing, on their progress towards mastery of every item being worked on, and on offering them exercises or suggestions that lead to the required mastery.'

Gattegno (1976)

BETWEEN THEORY AND PRACTICE

*'Each of us has been by far the best teacher
each of us has ever had'*
Caleb Gattegno

4. Keeping teacher talk brief

Three core ideas guide how teachers respond to students: provoking awarenesses; intervening without interfering; and using silence while not being mute.

PROVOKING AWARENESSES

As we saw in Chapter 1, Gattegno proposed that we learn by becoming aware. Awareness is what allows us to live our lives, to educate our perception, our muscular movements or indeed anything else we do or live. As Gattegno pointed out so often, 'Only awareness is educable'.

He also proposed that the role of the teacher is to provoke awarenesses, using the word *awareness* as a countable noun. All the techniques presented in this book, everything that is said, the whole system of teaching, is designed to provoke awarenesses.

TO INTERVENE WITHOUT INTERFERING

Gattegno pointed out that a teacher should not interfere in the students' learning process, but can intervene when she sees the possibility of provoking an awareness. It is not always easy to know in the moment whether one's next action will reveal itself to have been an interference or an intervention. Silent Way teachers try to keep this question alive within themselves.

USING SILENCE

The moment a teacher stops speaking, or significantly reduces what she says in the classroom, her attention is released from generating input and she is freed for other tasks. What does she do with her time? Her most important activity is observing her students, watching for clues to what they are thinking, and where they are at in their learning. When she sees a problem developing, she thinks about how she can intervene, perhaps by setting up a situation with rods as an example, by pointing on a chart, by making a gesture, or by actually saying something.

At the same time, space is made for the students to talk: they are the ones who are learning the language and they should do most of the talking.

My silence is essential.

Silence establishes my role and the students' roles in the class without anything needing to be said: they will be speaking, I will be the 'quality control' for what they say.

It is a constant reminder to me that my role is not to transmit knowledge, not to give explanations. My role is to create linguistic situations for students to explore and learn from, and then give them feedback on their attempts.

It means that the students will speak. They will not be inhibited by my display of expertise that makes their efforts seem so inadequate in comparison and therefore discourages participation. Once students are speaking spontaneously they reveal their current strengths and weaknesses in every sentence they make: what they can say belongs to their know-hows, what they can't say will be the subject of the work that follows.

It forces me to use gestures when possible. These are always preferable to speaking; they are less intrusive, can be understood when the students and I don't have a common language, and they remove any temptation to say too much. I do sometimes speak, to show from my tone of voice that I am not becoming impatient or upset by the mistakes they make. I may speak in the students' language if I know it or in English, if the students can handle it. But even without a common language, the same effect can almost always be achieved using gestures.

My cousin once provided her students with a supply of paper and asked them to experiment with making and flying paper planes. Everyone set about the task with enthusiasm and soon they were launching their creations. Many planes were plunging to the ground, but new designs quickly took their place.

My cousin was an expert at making paper planes. After some time, she made one and threw it. It flew right across the room, swooping up and down elegantly. Everyone thought her plane was admirable; but everyone lost interest in making paper planes themselves. The group's will to experiment had disappeared.

It means that it is largely the students rather than me who trigger the introduction of new language and new situations, sometimes through the mistakes they make, sometimes through their creativity and playfulness and, particularly for intermediate and advanced classes, simply through their urge to express themselves.

It forces the students to explore what they themselves must do with precision and ease in order to be able to speak the language well. This exploration will only take place if I remain silent. As soon as I provide a model, students will be drawn into trying to copy me, instead of generating it from within. It's not what I do that's important—we know I can already speak the language—it's what the students do that matters.

It forces me to regularly reflect on the clarity of my work, and this changes my preparation completely. I strive to find unambiguous ways of presenting each linguistic step. If ever my job is not well done, the whole class is immediately plunged into silence; no student can say anything. If a Silent Way teacher strays ahead of her class she quickly discovers it, whereas with explanations, the teacher can easily get far ahead, leaving her students behind.

Many students who have learnt using the Communicative Approach have had teachers who gave more importance to the message than to the form. The students have a sense that their English is unsatisfactory.

If I do not insist that they pay attention to the language, then they will not make the progress for which they have come to the class.

BUT I'M NOT MUTE

A teacher must be completely at ease with silence before she can consider herself to be a Silent Way teacher. She may speak in class, but what she says will be quite different from what she used to say and said for entirely different purposes. She doesn't model and she doesn't explain.

The few words she does say serve to:
- manage the class;
- give feedback;
- give hints or indications for what the students should try.

The phrases on the following pages, or similar ones, help students to discover for themselves how the language functions and how best to work.

Say it again	• If I am not sure exactly what the student said—if he mumbled, or several students spoke at the same time—I need to be sure of what was said before I can give feedback. • Sometimes I have an intuition that the student will be incapable of repeating what he has just said. I want to make sure he has sufficient control to be able to say it again. When he tries to do so, I can learn a lot about his degree of certainty. • Some students find it surprisingly difficult to say the same thing twice, even saying a sentence four or five times believing that they are saying the same thing when in reality the sentence changes each time. If the student is not aware of what he is saying, there is no point in correcting him. I make it clear that he has to be able to say exactly the same thing a second time. This moves his attention from the meaning to the form and may solve the problem. If it doesn't, the sentence may be too complex for him just now and I change it. I make sure he succeeds before moving on. • Sometimes a student makes a slip of the tongue. For example, he gets the word order correct, but when he starts working on the pronunciation something else goes wrong. My tone of voice is usually enough to draw his attention to the fact that there is a mistake. • Sometimes I want other students to hear clearly what has been said, correct or not.
Show your sentence on the Word charts [Alternatively I can silently offer the 'blunt end' of the pointer to a student and indicate the charts]	• Sometimes I am not certain whether the student is using the wrong words, or the right words with bad pronunciation. If he points the words correctly, it is clear to me that he has a problem with the pronunciation. If he points the incorrect words, I know the problem relates to the construction. I can only give appropriate feedback when I understand the problem. • Sometimes, a student cannot manage to say a sentence orally, but can point the sequence of words on the charts. Just pointing the sequence of words halves the the task. Once that is done, saying it orally can be tackled. • When one student is pointing, the rest of the class is not idle. They can follow what is happening at the front of the classroom. They can check whether they agree with what is being pointed. They can help the student who is pointing. Students quickly get into the habit of helping each other, often quite subtly, giving clues rather than providing answers, just as I would, and they take pleasure in doing so.

More energy! *Less energy!* *Tighten it!* [or an appropriate gesture]	• Reduced sounds—the schwa family—are the most common sounds in English, and the language does not sound correct if the energy level of the weak syllables that contain them is too high. • The easiest way for the students to get into this aspect of pronunciation is to work on the varying levels of energy required, rather than thinking of pronouncing different vowel sounds. • Sometimes, particularly with short (lax) vowels, my French students use vowels which are not crisp enough, in a sentence like *Give it to him*. In this situation, I might say, *Tighten it!*
Show it again *Point to it again* *Start again* *Do it again* [or an appropriate gesture]	• Sometimes a student points sounds, words, or a sentence very slowly—he is clearly unsure of what he is doing and the sequence loses coherence. I get him to point it again, until he can do so with more confidence. • Sometimes it is necessary to point again when another student wasn't looking at the sequence, although this is quite rare. Usually students only look away when they know they do not need to watch. • If a student is inattentive, I might ask him to point a sequence again. My aim is not to punish or humiliate him, but to make him aware that learning requires him to be present. Nobody ever learned anything while thinking about his last holidays or his next meal. The physical act of pointing the words often helps him to re-engage with the class. • *Do it again* is useful when a student has acted in such a way that the relationship between what he did and what he said is not clear. For example, if a student says *I'm going to take a rod* while his hand is already on the rod, the distinction between *I'm going to take a rod* and *I'm taking a rod* is not respected. If the action described is not completely correct, other students cannot use the situation to link the action to the language needed to express it. • Often I am not the person who initiates the repetition of a sequence. Students will stand up spontaneously to point a sequence when they feel they should check something.
Softly! *Gently!* *Slowly!* *Smoothly!*	These words can be replaced with hand gestures once the students know what is expected of them. I use this type of feedback when, for example, I want the student to eliminate a jumpy or staccato quality from what he is saying. French, Spanish and Italian speakers, for example, often find it difficult to speak smoothly in English because these languages do not use the schwa family of sounds at all, or use them in very different ways. Speakers of such languages tend to put too much energy into unstressed vowels, and therefore find the flow of English difficult to produce.

Shorter *It's too long* *Be more economical* *That's possible but not necessary*	These sentences can be replaced by various gestures based on the *The fish I caught was this long* gesture—hands separated to show the length of the fish—or by using finger correction (see Chapter 7). These sentences are used to obtain shorter answers. For example, in a beginners' class, when confronted with the question, *How many rods have you got in your hand?* a student might answer *I've got six*. In everyday life, the usual answer would probably be *Six*. I want to make sure that the students realise that there are three answers to the question: *I've got six rods, I've got six,* and *Six*. Each answer is acceptable. I would use the word *Or …* to obtain all three. With a higher level group I can say *Be more economical*. If, for example, a student proposed an extension to the sentence, *The man in the picture …* to, *The man that is in the picture …* I might say, *That's possible but not necessary*.
Say it in English!	Once a student has managed to say the words of his sentence in the correct order, I might well ask him to *Say it in English!* If my students have already studied English for several years at school, this shocks the class. They think that he has just done exactly that. They soon become aware that correct word order alone does not guarantee that his sentence sounds English. I want the general impression to be that of an English sentence. The pronunciation, the rhythm and the intonation must be English as well as the words.
Change it *Something different* *Try something different*	Occasionally a student becomes locked into what he has said. When I ask him to change it, he is unable to do so. (He may say it again and not even realise that nothing has been changed.) This is usually a sign that he has ventured too far into his unknown; he is out of his depth. He will be finding the situation very tiring. For him, the sentence may have inadvertently become a chunk that he can do nothing with. When a student is locked into a sentence, until he changes something—anything—I can do nothing to help him. Changing something usually helps 'unlock' him.
Say it again, don't change it	• Students often need to practise their sentence a few times, especially if they had problems constructing it. The words are correct but they need to say it several more times to achieve ease. But I don't want it to drift, it must be the same each time. • Students don't always realise that when I ask them to repeat their sentence, it is not necessarily because the sentence is wrong. *Don't change it* makes them aware of this. I am not there to catch them out. There are reasons other than mistakes for repeating a sentence.

Put them together	I say this when I'm working with a student who can't manage to get a long sentence together. Using finger correction (see Chapter 7), I get him to divide the sentence up into sense groups. Once he can say each of these smaller chains of words, he can usually link two of them, then a different pair, and so gradually progress to the stage where he can say the whole sentence in good English. I use *Put them together* for each of these pairs, or a sweeping gesture with my other hand over the fingers involved.

Sometimes I see that he cannot link the whole sentence together, but I do make sure he can join a few of the chains.

I never want students to have the impression that they are saying unanalysed chunks of language—simply chains of words in the right order. I want them to be aware of the meaning while they are speaking. The way my lessons unfold ensures this: they construct the sentences before learning to say them smoothly. |
| *Problem*

One problem

Three (four …) problems

[Said with a smile …] | The word *problem* tells a student that something must be changed in what he has just said. It doesn't tell him where the problem is, nor what he should have said. What the student does then tells me a lot about his understanding of the issues it raises.
• He might be able to correct his sentence by himself immediately, because his mistake was merely a slip of the tongue, or a fossilised error he is aware of and is trying to dissolve: a mistake he can catch after he has spoken, but not yet before.
• Or the student may show me that he has no idea what the problem might be. I see this because he changes one or more elements which were correct and thus reveals that he was unsure of them too. Occasionally, when I ask him to say his sentence again, and then again, it might dissolve into a terrible mess and will have to be completely reconstructed. It sounded quite good, but was partly built on sand. He needs to start again from what is solid ground for him.
• Perhaps he needs another example so that the English way of constructing this meaning becomes clear. My response must be adapted to the nature of the problem and my observation of him since the beginning of the course.
• The expression, *One problem*, gives a little more information. The student knows how many changes he must introduce, and his reaction gives me valuable information about how solid his criteria for correctness really are.
• In the case of *Three problems*, he knows that the sentence will probably have to be reconstructed. This might well be a task for the whole class. I only have to lift my eyes and look at the other students for them to start making suggestions.

I need to establish when other students can or should intervene to help a student correct his sentence. He will best retain those sentences he has corrected himself because he will have developed criteria in the process, but the time this takes has to be balanced against the needs of other students. If they are learning vicariously from his work, fine. If not, I need to be judicious about the time I give him. |

Is that true?	Suppose, in a beginners' class, a student says *My rod are blue*, and a second student, holding a red rod, wants to help by telling him what he should have said, and says *My rod is blue*. I would respond by asking him if what he has said is true. He should be talking for himself. There is a reason for this. I create situations and get students to make sentences which express them, and these associations of situations and sentences must be clear and unambiguous for every single student in the class, especially the weakest ones and those who are furthest from the action. But a sentence is unambiguous only if it corresponds exactly to the situation. Each person who speaks must respect the visible facts before him.
Are you sure?	I say this quite often, but I don't usually say it to imply that a sentence is wrong. I say it because I want the students to become aware of the strength of their own criteria and to stop depending on me to know if what they say is correct. It makes the student stop, look closely at what he has just said—examine it word by word—and then be able to say, *Yes, I'm sure*.
Is it a question?	If a student is saying something and at the same time implicitly asking me whether his sentence is correct, he will use a rising intonation pattern. *Is it a question?* draws his attention to the rising intonation he used when falling intonation would have been more appropriate for the meaning he wanted to convey.
Not now! *Not yet!* *In a minute!* [or making a gesture with one's fingers as if to throw a light object out of the window]	Sometimes, a student tries to follow an idea which has come to him, but which does not fit in with what the class is doing at that moment or which will take us beyond what I know some students can currently handle. I have a choice: I can follow his lead if his 'leap in the dark' is not too difficult to work on, or I can come back to what the class was doing. These sentences indicate my choice not to follow him. Students readily accept my decisions because they know they can speak whenever they want to, they know their suggestions and queries are usually followed up, but they are also aware that I know where their exploration might take the class and if I refuse to follow their lead, I will have a reason for this. Occasionally, if I make the wrong decision and we get bogged down, I simply stop everything and tell them we'll deal with it another day.
That's correct, but it's not true	Sometimes a student produces a sentence in which the mistake lies in the fact given, rather than in the grammar. *Warsaw is the capital of Hungary* would be an example. I say, *That's correct, but it's not true* to inform the student that what he said is unacceptable not because of the language but because of the content.

BETWEEN THEORY AND PRACTICE

Now say the sentence again. Start from the beginning.	Sometimes, a student makes quite a long sentence and the problem I need to work on is towards the end. Once it has been fixed, I ask him to start again from the beginning. Firstly, so that he reconnects with what originally moved him to speak, and the words he says become an expression of this once more, and secondly, so that the thread of the conversation is re-established for the other students.
Let's go back to José	Similarly, a student might make a sentence which I have had to work on at length. I then get the students to recreate the context by starting the Class Conversation (see Chapter 23) again from several sentences before it was interrupted. It is not unusual for work on solving a complex problem—and the others that may well arise in this process—to take up to fifteen or twenty minutes. When I go back to the student who will relaunch the conversation, in this case José, I may have to give him the first few words of what he said earlier. I may ask, or need, the class to help me with this. Even an interruption of twenty minutes is possible without the thread of the conversation getting completely lost.
Or … Another possibility …	- I want to develop the native-like capacity to think of several different ways of expressing a thought. A student constructs a sentence, and I encourage him to construct a second and then a third stating a similar idea. For each there are slight differences in meaning or register. Each of them makes the exact meaning of the others a little clearer. Sometimes I might illustrate these different nuances with rods, objects or drawings, etc. - Students soon propose - themselves, test hypotheses about similar sentences and ask if this or that variant would be possible. They like the sense of rapid progress and mastery that working on nuances like this gives them.
Relax!	The work that the class does can be intense at times and this is one reason why it works so well. But from time to time, I see that a student is becoming too tense and that his tension is harming his ability to perform. At this point, I might gently say *Relax, relax!* A more general way of keeping the class relaxed is for the teacher to show that she is happy for the atmosphere to be playful and light-hearted if at the same time the class remains serious. This is not a paradox. As Noel Coward said, *Work is more fun than fun.*

Do you know what you are trying to say? *Stop for a moment. Now start again*	Sometimes, when a student has worked on a sentence for a few minutes—on the order of the words or the intonation perhaps—he loses touch with the meaning. Saying one of these sentences is enough to get him to re-evoke the situation he is talking about. He is then usually capable of saying it much better than before. Students must be able to move easily between two frames of mind: either being with the message they wish to convey or attending to the language itself and what is required to convey this message. When there is an imbalance between these two ways of being as a language learner, I intervene to bring the other perspective back into the awareness of the student.

SOMETHING I DON'T SAY: VERY GOOD!

I might say *Good* or similar words as straightforward feedback on a sentence that has just been made. However, when *Very good!* is said, it is often praise of the student, and this is antithetical to the ethos behind the Silent Way approach, which considers students to be strong, independent, resourceful learners who have demonstrated their ability to learn in countless ways throughout their lives. There is no reason to praise them for doing something in a language class which, frankly, is trivial compared to their other learning accomplishments.

I also see praise as a sign of a teacher who tries to control her class by rewarding them with praise for following her instructions. This is demeaning. In any type of class, and certainly in language classes, it often leads to students participating less and less with the result that the teacher ends up praising the student for even the most minor contributions.

It is not my place to pass judgement on anyone. I am there to evaluate the language spoken, not the speaker. This is why I don't praise students.

5. The principal materials

In this approach, the teacher uses a set of materials to help her work efficiently in the classroom. They include:

> A BOX OF CUISENAIRE RODS which are used to set up linguistic situations for the class to work on. Rods can also be used symbolically.
>
> A POINTER which is used to capture, direct and hold the classes' attention.
>
> A RECTANGLE CHART which displays a set of coloured rectangles representing the sounds of the language being learned.
>
> A FIDEL which presents the relationship between the pronunciation and the writing system.
>
> WORD CHARTS which present the functional vocabulary of the language.
>
> THE VERB TENSE SYSTEM, a layout constructed for intermediate or advanced students to facilitate work on verb forms.

The Silent Way materials are different from typical language learning materials because they are 'uncommitted'. Other materials and activities in books are usually **committed** because:

- They are designed to present specific grammatical points: the Present Tense, the pronunciation of plural <s>, or comparatives and superlatives, etc.
- The topic of conversations and role plays, and sometimes even the

'As for the [Silent Way] materials, they are Spartan in their simplicity, with everything pared away which does not contribute toward the student's development of his own inner criteria.'

Stevick (1976)

specific words to be used, are given—*my visit to London, my profession, climate change*. What the student is asked to say is not what the student actually did, does or thinks; nor what he necessarily has any interest in talking about.

The Silent Way tools are **uncommitted** because:

- The tools provide teachers with means to work on whatever problem the student has—whether it's grammar, the pronunciation or the vocabulary of the language—rather than providing a particular solution. This leaves the teacher to invent a solution for the particular student and the unique problem they are working on, but of course also imposes the obligation to do so.
- The tools are entirely neutral with respect to both the situations the teacher might set up for exploration and what the student wants to say or talk about.

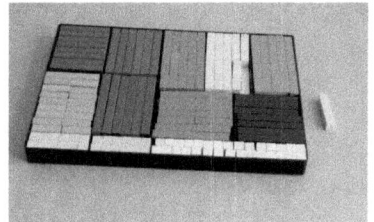

Cuisenaire rods can be used to work on many aspects of the language.

CUISENAIRE RODS

For beginners or low intermediate level language classes, the teacher will make use of Cuisenaire rods. These are pieces of wood or plastic with a cross section of 1 square centimetre, and which measure between 1 and 10 cm in length. Rods of the same colour are the same length. They are easy to manipulate and allow the teacher to construct unambiguous linguistic situations which are directly perceptible by all. For example, an arrangement might be described by the sentence, *The green rod is between the red one and the blue one.*

Students can talk about the relative length of the rods, their colour, whether they are close to each other, or far away. They can give them to each other, take them back, put them here or there, etc.

Using Cuisenaire rods to explore the functional vocabulary

The rods can also be used symbolically. A green rod standing on the table can represent Mr. Green. They lend themselves to the construction of plans of houses, towns, cities and stations. They can help to tell stories, and so on. They can also be used to symbolise grammatical constructions.

The students understand each situation before any words are introduced. Before any sentence is spoken, communication has already taken place. Thus an implicit emphasis is always placed on the fact that learning a language is not learning to communicate; communicating requires much less than a mastery of the language. Rather, it is learning how to use the language to express oneself correctly.

THE POINTER

A telescopic metal pointer is one of the most important instruments in the teacher's arsenal[1]. It extends and amplifies one of the oldest pedagogical tools in human history: pointing with our index finger.

Using the pointer allows the teacher to very precisely direct the attention of the class to whatever she wants them to work on. The human eye and our mental attention is inevitably drawn to whatever is being pointed at, creating the shared attention which is necessary for teaching.

The teacher can use the pointer to point from sound to sound on the Rectangle chart, from word to word on the Word charts, from spelling to spelling on the Fidel, or directly at objects in the classroom. She can give emphasis to a word or a sound by how vigorously she points. She can use it to indicate the melody of a phrase. Pointing can be used to draw everyone's attention to precisely where there is a mistake or to get the class to speed up or slow down.

The teacher can also use it as a diagnostic tool by handing a pointer to a student and inviting him to point. What he does, and how confidently or hesitantly he does it, reveals a lot about the criteria he has, or doesn't have.

Like speech, pointing is ephemeral, leaving no visible trace. This means that students have to hold the sequence in their minds as the sounds or words are touched and the pointer moves on. They cannot flick back a few pages, or glance in their notebook to find a phrase to refresh their memories. So using a pointer instantly raises the level of presence demanded of students.

It can also slow things down, forcing students' attention onto the details, greatly enhancing what they retain.

Pointing is visual and helps the teacher say less.

THE RECTANGLE CHART

The teacher uses a phonemic chart hung on the wall. It presents a set of coloured rectangles on a black background. The rectangles represent all the sounds of English. Some rectangles have two colours representing the diphthongs and the affricates. The same colours are also used on the Word charts and the Fidel.

[1] *A bamboo garden stake of about 70 cm in length serves the purpose equally well.*

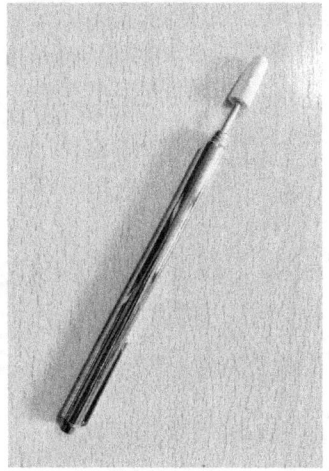

A telescopic pointer.

Scan to watch a video about using a pointer and charts

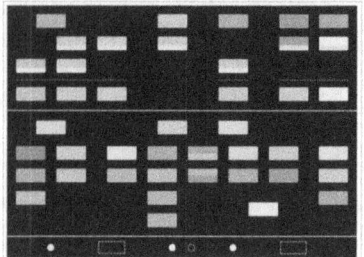

The British English Rectangle chart

On the Rectangle chart the vowels and diphthongs are in the top section and the consonants in the middle.

The reduced sounds—the schwa /ə/, the schwi and the schwu (and in American English, the schwr)—have been separated out from the vowels and placed at the bottom of the chart, in an area reserved for unstressed sounds. They are not shown as rectangles but as small dots; this shape and size reflecting the fact that they are both very low energy sounds and very short.

These dots are also found on the Word charts under all the words which have strong forms but can be, and usually are, said with their reduced forms (e.g. /əv/ rather than /ɒv/ for *of*).

The area for unstressed sounds, at the bottom of the chart, also contains two dashed rectangles. These are used to indicate full vowels that are unstressed, like the vowel in the second syllable of *window*.

At the start of a course, the teacher works with the class to learn the sounds of the language. At the same time, they will also learn how the colours and the sounds correspond. Once the class is sufficiently familiar with the sounds, she can get the students to produce any sound, word or sentence by pointing on the chart, without saying or writing anything. It takes surprisingly little time for students to become familiar with the chart but much longer, of course, for them to be able to pronounce every sound well.

The teacher can also use the chart to:
- introduce new vocabulary;
- give precise feedback on students' pronunciation;
- indicate stress, rhythm and flow,
- as a diagnostic tool to reveal students' thinking.

The Rectangle chart shows the inventory of the sounds of English. This means that students know that the sounds of everything they say must be chosen from what they can see. When in doubt, they have to choose: this one or that one? This sharpens their awareness of the sounds of the language.

Knowing that there are only a limited set of sounds to master, many of which they already know, is reassuring for students.

Scan to download a guide to the layout of the Rectangle charts.

The layout of the chart gives the students clues about the place and manner of articulation for each sound and this helps their exploration of the sounds and their mouths.

The Rectangle chart means that pronunciation and writing can be dissociated. Students whose native language uses the Roman script aren't presented with spellings which they might be tempted to read with sounds from their own language. Students of languages that use other writing systems don't have the hurdle of learning to decode a new script at the same time as they are learning the spoken language. For both, colours are less offputting than artificial scripts such as the IPA.

English spelling is so complex that the written form gets in the way of learning to pronounce. The Rectangle chart separates the two.

WORKING WITH COLOUR-BLIND AND BLIND STUDENTS

People often ask me how I manage with colour-blind students. I have taught hundreds of classes and there were certainly colour-blind students present on many occasions, but no one has ever said to me that he couldn't work with the charts for this reason. These students do see some colours and they see the ones they are 'blind' to in varying shades of grey. They are in their world of colour which might not resemble yours or mine, but which they have lived within all their lives and know intimately. They also exploit the position of the rectangles to distinguish them.

I have also worked with blind students. This does require adaptations. If the class needs to work with rods, then I make sure that all the students can recognise the rods by their length. I work on this with the whole class by spending ten minutes at the very beginning of the course getting them all to hold several rods behind their backs and guess the colour of one after the other from their lengths using touch. Sighted students generally find this an enjoyable activity.

Two students working together using the Fidel.

When using finger correction, I respectfully extend the fingers of the blind student and either touch the fingers myself or ask one of his neighbours to touch them so that the student understands the problems that anyone in the class is having when finger correction is being used.

THE FIDEL

The word Fidel comes from the Amharic language of Ethiopia. It is the name given to a table presenting the relationship between the writing system and the sounds of this language. Amharic was the first language Gattegno put into colour, in the 1950s, and he continued to use the same word for all charts of this kind.

The British English Fidel

Scan to download a guide to using the Fidel.

The layout of the Fidel reflects that of the Rectangle chart. It groups together all the possible spellings for each sound. Like the Rectangle chart, the Fidel is synthetic in nature: all the choices are always visible. It is sometimes called the Spelling chart.

The Fidel allows the students to investigate the relationship between the spelling of words, or series of words like *There are a lot*, and their pronunciation. This is especially important for languages like English where this relationship is complex. Once the student has found the chain of sounds on the Rectangle chart, he knows which areas to look at on the Fidel and thus finds himself with a limited range of possibilities for the spelling of these sounds. Although there may still be many possible choices, there are only those choices present in that area. As well as this, the letters on the Fidel are written in two sizes and the answer will usually be found in the larger letters. The large letters cover between 90 and 95 per cent of the spellings for any one sound. The small letters cover irregular spellings. Thus the student's work is narrowed down and his criteria refined, leaving him to work on the genuine issues in the sound/spelling correspondence of the language.

For example, the different ways of writing the sound /i:/ are found in the red area of the Fidel: *e, ee, ea, ie, ei, i, ey, ay, oe, eo* and *ae*. Of these, *e, ee, ea* and *ie* are written in larger letters. The other letter combinations, used for words spelled in unusual ways, like *people* or *amoeba*, are written in small letters. The student must find a suitable grapheme within the red area; he already knows from his work on the Rectangle chart that the red graphemes represent the correct pronunciation. Now he can consider which of the large letter combinations is the most likely. (If it were an irregular spelling, the teacher would give it to him.)

Over time, students gain familiarity with the correspondences between spellings and sounds in English, gradually building the kind of mental model they need to read and write confidently.

THE WORD CHARTS

The Word charts contain the functional vocabulary of English: the prepositions, pronouns and conjunctions, certain adverbs and adjectives, and the verb endings, colour coded to reflect their pronunciation. They also contain some of the commonest and most useful words: for example, common verbs, colours, the numbers, the days of the week, etc.

These charts allow the teacher to work on how the function words are used—essentially every aspect of the grammar needed to express every kind of relationship—without herself speaking. She can simply point on the Word charts either to provide students with the sequence of words they need to say or to offer corrections.

There are two types of Word charts. The Silent Way Word charts, created by Caleb Gattegno, which are for use with beginners, and which present words in an order which introduces the functional vocabulary to the class for the first time. The Silent Way Word charts are hung on the wall one by one as the class takes its first steps in English.

The Pronunciation Science (PronSci) Word charts (see Appendix 4) are for non-beginners. They present the same set of words but organised on a different principle.

Non-beginners may need any word at all when they speak, so the full set of PronSci charts will usually be put up on the wall from the start.

Word Chart 1

Scan to download a guide to the Word charts.

It is useful for everyone to be able to find words without slowing the class down, so on the PronSci Word charts, the words are organised by parts of speech so that students and teachers can locate them easily: all the pronouns are on one chart, all the auxiliaries on another; three charts have the most common verbs arranged in alphabetical order; there is an adjective/adverb chart, etc.

You will find colour pictures and detailed guides to the content and use of the British and American English Rectangle charts, Fidels and Word charts at www.pronsci.com/support.

The PronSci charts allow teachers to use Silent Way techniques with people who have already studied English at school. They are also the ones that teachers should use if they only want to use charts for teaching pronunciation while using a non-Silent Way approach for grammar.

Whichever set of charts is used, Silent Way or PronSci, the teaching techniques remain the same.

WALL PICTURES

In 1965, Gattegno published a set of ten coloured wall pictures which are striking in their simplicity. Eight of them use only one colour, though in several shades. They do introduce students to a certain amount of new vocabulary, but this is not their main value. Each picture is an invitation for students to exercise their imagination in making sentences about it.

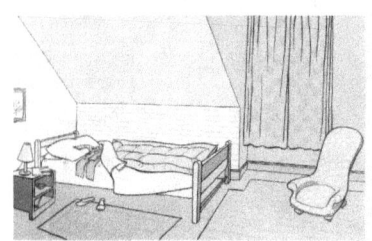

One picture is that of a bedroom, in shades of yellow. A group of beginners might simply describe the picture. A class of intermediate students might respond to a statement by the teacher who simply says, *My bedroom is not like this*. Advanced students might speculate about why the person who got out of bed didn't put his slippers on, whether we are looking at a scene in the morning or the evening, or anything else they might be inclined to wonder about. If the teacher remains silent, someone will have something to say.

Another picture, in shades of blue, is that of a man sitting in a rocking chair, smoking a pipe and reading a newspaper. Who is he? What do we know about him? What do we not know about him? What might students choose to say about him, beyond simply describing the scene?

A third picture is that of a cat walking through a door. The only colour in this picture is orange. We don't know which room the cat is leaving, nor which one it is entering. Or is it going outside? Once the objects visible in the picture have been named—there are only about fifteen of them—what is there to say about this scene if one is being purely descriptive? Very little, and that is the point. The class must start to speculate.

Like other Silent Way materials, the wall pictures have an uncommitted quality. Because of their paucity of detail and the fact that they never show the defining moment of a story, which has either happened or is to come, the pictures become a springboard for a wide range of responses.

A Silent Way teacher will experiment with and collect other wall pictures and similar materials. Simple 'before and after' pictures can work well for lower intermediate students. Two pictures of the beach, one in the early afternoon, and the other several hours later, allow work on verb forms and complex sentences. For example, *Although the sun has not yet gone down, most of the people on the beach have already gone home"* or, *The tide has now come in and destroyed the sand castles that the children built.*

However, in my experience, it is quite difficult to find pictures as useful as Gattegno's. Pictures created for language classes usually show too much. The more detail there is in a picture, the more there is to simply name and describe. Such pictures tempt a teacher to give students long lists of vocabulary with which they only weakly engage. Posters, paintings, photographs and other pictures are typically visual experiences, created to be looked at and moved by, but not to be commented on.

RICH TASKS

The wall pictures are an example in the language classroom of what are called 'rich tasks' in mathematices.

As Gilderdale and Gilderdale and Kiddle (2014) describe them:

> Rich tasks have a range of characteristics that together offer opportunities to meet the different needs of learners. On its own a task is not rich, it is how the task is used in the classroom that may make it rich. With this in mind it might still be useful to list some of the characteristics that make a task rich.

Rich tasks:
- are accessible to a wide range of learners

- draw learners in with an intriguing starting point or intriguing initial discoveries
- offer opportunities for initial success
- challenge learners to think for themselves
- offer different levels of challenge (low threshold - high ceiling tasks)
- allow learners to pose their own questions
- allow for different methods and a variety of responses
- offer opportunities to identify elegant or efficient solutions
- have the potential to broaden learners' skills or deepen their mathematical understanding
- encourage creativity and imaginative application of knowledge
- have the potential for revealing patterns or leading to generalisations
- encourage collaboration and discussion
- encourage learners to develop confidence and independence

Not all rich tasks will do all of these things but they will certainly manage a number of them when used in a way which values discussion, insights and critical appraisal. It is for the teacher to look at a task and recognise its potential, and present it in a way that offers a rich experience for the learners.

THE VERB TENSE SYSTEM

With intermediate and advanced students I work on the English Verb Tense System. The aim of this work is to give the students a feel for how English uses the different verb forms. Things like: *I work, I have been working, I had worked* etc.

I do this in several stages. I start by drawing a set of eight boxes on a large piece of paper, then I gradually lay out models of the different indicative forms in each box using Cuisenaire rods. Thus when the system is complete, whenever a student works on a specific verb form he does so within the context of the whole system.

I ask the students to start exploring how the forms are used by making true sentences about their lives. For details, see Chapter 19.

Using this technique I can work on every aspect of the English Verb Tense System in great detail without ever using the grammatical names for the forms—Present Perfect or Past Perfect Progressive etc. It can all be done visually. As well as this, all the work is done orally, so that the class has the experience of saying many true sentences, that they themselves generate, in a short amount of time. This work naturally leads into the Class Conversation (see Chapter 23).

The author working with a class using the Verb Tense System

6. Using a pointer

Pointing directs students' attention where the teacher wants it to be. It is such an important technique that it is worth a teacher spending time practising how to do it well.

POINTING ON THE CHARTS

Pointing at rectangles or words on an individual set of charts on your desk or picking them out on your computer screen is not the same as standing to one side of a chart and using a 75 cm pointer, with the class watching. Before you use the charts with students, you will need to practise pointing all types of sequences until you can point easily and with confidence.

Put the charts on a wall, stand to one side and practise pointing sequences of sounds, spellings and words:

- Glance at the Word charts, choose a word, point it on the Rectangle chart and then the Fidel, and then check that you chose the right colours. Then challenge yourself with longer words and phrases.
- Pick words at random and point their sounds on the Rectangle chart.
- Vary what you do: speed up and slow down; shorten and lengthen your pointer; move closer to the charts, and further away; point from the other side. Practise until you can handle any word or phrase with confidence.
- If students are to 'read' a sequence, your pointing must be precise. The tip of the pointer must touch the chart cleanly. Then the pointer

A student using a pointer

is lifted off the surface and moved smoothly to the next rectangle or word. It should not skid on the chart and it should not be waved around between touches.
- Notice that I use the word *touch* not *tap*. The pointer is not used to hit the chart. The tip of the pointer comes to a perceptible stop on a rectangle or word before you move it on. For larger classes, the time you need to remain with each touch has to increase slightly.

General advice about pointing for teachers and students

The person pointing should stand to one side of the charts so that the whole class can see what is being pointed. As the teacher, you should not forget to set a good example!

If a student takes too long to point a string of rectangles or a sentence, he should be asked to point the whole sequence again until it is smooth. If this is a problem, see *'Blind' pointing*, below.

Once you have put something into circulation, you should expect that students will be able to find it again on a chart. If they ask you to point it again, ask if anyone in the class can do so. Wait a few moments. Someone usually has the sequence, or at least part of it, but may need time to be sure enough to come out and point it.

It only takes a few seconds for you to indicate that a student's pointing was too messy, by letting your body and arm go limp and slipping and slapping the pointer here and there all over the chart while rolling your eyes, or by moving your head with the movement of the pointer while looking seasick; students get the message.

You can invite students to help each other in pointing, offering them each their own pointer, unless you need to check something about a particular student's understanding. However, don't allow other students to call out instructions to the person who is pointing.

When you point, you don't speak. You should expect the students to read the sequence under their breath while you are pointing, and to say it out loud only once you have finished.

When a student points, it may be appropriate for him to speak as he does so, or it may not. Similarly, it may be appropriate for the class to read aloud as he points, or to have to wait until he has finished before saying the phrase, or even to remain silent. There are no hard and fast rules. It depends on what you want the student(s) to achieve.

Choose pointers which have silver or white tips rather than black ones, because they are more visible.

You will need several because you will sometimes ask several students to work on the charts at the same time, and they should all be given pointers.

Pointers are tools, not toys. Don't let students play with them.

To signal that you are about to start pointing a sequence, it can be helpful to tap the wall audibly a couple of times with the pointer to draw the students' attention to the new activity.

Even confident students find pointing difficult when they are close enough to a chart to point on it. If a student is struggling to find things that you think he knows, ask him to step back a few paces so that he sees the view of the charts that he is more familiar with. You can invite another student (or even a third) to come up to help. Give them their own pointers. Interesting questions often emerge when this is done.

Sometimes you will hesitate in the middle of pointing a sequence, unsure of what to touch next. When this happens (and it happens to everyone), move the pointer off the chart completely until you decide what to touch next. It is then often best to complete the sequence, 'apologise', and indicate that you will point the whole sequence again from the start.

Pointing and 'reading' sequences aren't the same

When you point a sequence, you know what you have in mind. For your students, 'reading' a sequence is more challenging than reading text:

- The students' eyes can never flick forward to anticipate what is to come.
- Their eyes cannot flick back to remind themselves of what has already been pointed. They have to keep the sequence in their minds as it unfolds.
- There is no opportunity to read in chunks, in the way that words on a page are chunked.

These challenges are part of what makes pointing such an effective pedagogical technique. The extra mental effort it demands of students enhances their retention of the language.

You need to be sensitive to your students' ability to read sequences: aware of the challenge but aware, too, that their ability will rapidly improve.

Following the pointing of a sequence of sounds or words requires presence and generates a certain healthy tension. However, if the students become restless or anxious they may be unable to stay with what is being pointed. This is a sign that the sequence is being pointed too fast or is too long for their current capacities.

'The pointer can be brandished as though it were a birch rod or it can be used like a conductor's baton, to order people around in an imperious way.

But it can also be used deftly and gently, as a way of keeping the student in contact with the work at hand, while at the same time keeping the teacher as far out of the picture as possible.'

Stevick (1980)

As the teacher, you will soon realise that you are better at pointing sequences than reading them, and your students are better at reading than pointing. To experience this, go to the back of the room and try to follow a good student pointing a long sequence. You will find this more difficult than you might expect.

THE ACT OF POINTING ENHANCES RETENTION

Obviously when launching a new sentence, I have to point. I am the only one who can do so. However, if something needs to be pointed again, it is usually better to have a student do this because that helps students to internalise new sentence structures. When a physical movement is associated with a pronunciation, spelling or sentence, the kinaesthetic trace in the student's body helps him to stabilise the sequence in his mind. Students retain both the place of words on the charts and their order until they know these well enough not to need the charts to say them.

DIAGNOSING PROBLEMS

Pointing on charts is also a diagnostic tool. In a simple example, a student might say something that I hear as *They are thirty days in June*. What did he mean to say? Is his problem grammar or pronunciation? If he now points incorrect words, the problem relates to grammar. If he points the words correctly, then his problem is pronunciation. I know how to begin correcting.

Inviting students to point is often a good way of diagnosing their problems precisely: it makes their thinking visible.

When I get a student to point, I discover to what extent he controls the sentence and exactly where his problems lie. He doesn't have to spell, write or pronounce his sentence as he points, so grammatical problems are more clearly revealed. When he has finished pointing, he says the sentence, and pronunciation problems become apparent.

Just as important, as a student is pointing, I also discover something about his inner state: his doubts and certainties are revealed by his demeanour and the way he moves the pointer—smoothly or chaotically, in a well-thought-out sequence or in a series of tentative taps.

Getting a student to point a sentence with a problem unpacks it for everyone. It gives the student a better chance to self correct, and gives me greater insight into his difficulty.

Getting the rest of the class to help

If a student cannot point the sentence, I usually offer the handle of a pointer to the rest of the class, inviting someone else to come and point. The reactions of the other students are useful indicators. How willing are they to try? It is usually in my interest not to ask the most proficient students to point the sentence, as I need to find out where the weaker students are at. So I will ask one of them to do the job. From their willingness to try, I will know more clearly whether the sentence is too difficult for the whole class, or for the weaker students, or for one student only. At the end of the process, the student who had the initial problem should be able to point the sentence correctly.

Students using their index fingers to point

If the class collectively can't point a sentence I have launched, then I know that I have made a mistake: I have launched something too difficult for them at the moment. I make a mental note of what I did, and resolve not to do it again! This is a case for post-paration, a reflection on the work I did in classs after the class is over.

POINTING WITH A 'LASER FINGER'[2]

I use the 'laser finger' technique with a class of children or a very big class when I have an intuition that the whole class would make the same mistake as the student who is pointing. I ask everyone to point with their 'laser finger'. Without moving from their places, they extend one arm out as far as they can, stretch out their index finger, and point the words at the same time as their fellow students. This helps create stronger visual images in all their minds, enabling them to better fix the sentence and therefore to retain it more easily. They quickly learn the location of the words on the charts and in what order they should be said. More important, they can also find the sentence some time

[2] *Alain L'Hôte, a primary school colleague, developed this technique in his Grade 1 class with pupils learning to read.*

later, since using their 'laser finger' heightens their presence to the words they are pointing. I can usually see if everyone is pointing to the right place and, if not, I can work on the error which has been revealed.

'BLIND' POINTING

Occasionally, I become aware that a student is really struggling. If I ask him to point the sentence, it becomes obvious that he has no idea how the various elements, most of which he in fact already knows, are put together with whatever is new to form the new sentence. He is lost.

In such a case, it is important for the student to sort the sentence out in his mind and give it meaning. When he has done this, he will be back with the rest of the class.

I ask him to stand squarely in front of the charts. (This is not the usual position for pointing; usually the whole class needs to see, so the person pointing stands to one side.) I get him to place his pointer on the first word and then to close his eyes and point the rest of the sentence from memory with his eyes closed—'blind' pointing.

The first time I ask a student to point blind, he will be taken aback, and quite unable to do so. I say *Watch*, point the sentence myself and then ask him to do so with his eyes open. He now pays more attention, knowing that he will soon have to rely completely on his mental images to find the words. Usually I see a noticeable improvement but it may be necessary for me to point the sentence once more and for him to point two or three times with his eyes open before he can point blind. As he points the words, I should get the impression that he knows where they are. It doesn't matter if the pointer touches the charts a few centimetres away from some words.

If he is successful then I am sure he has the sentence. If he can't do it after several attempts, then I know it was out of his range, and possibly too difficult for most of the class. Perhaps we ended up adventuring too far for this student today. Should I have stopped the earlier exploration, rather than letting it go ahead?

The challenge of 'blind' pointing allows me to test a student's mental imagery, a good way of knowing if he has in fact created an adequate mental image of the order of the words. It is a powerful tool for helping students become more present.

WORKING ONLINE

I have spent most of my career working in classrooms, but now that I have retired this is not usually possible for me, so I have begun teaching online. Here are some of the aspects of pointing online that I have noticed.

Firstly, pointing in a classroom is a dynamic process. Most aspects of pronunciation benefit from the various ways a pointer can be used beyond simply showing a word or rectangle. Stress, variations in speed and the changes in the language they introduce, intonation and other aspects of pronunciation can all be demonstrated by the way one points or holds the pointer, and the students benefit from seeing the teacher physically manipulating it. Online, pointing loses many of these dynamic qualities; consequently, it becomes more difficult to work on the dynamics of the language. If you compare the movements of a conductor working with his musicians to the pendulum movements of a metronome, you see immediately what is lost in the online world.

Many of the problems this raises relate to the nonverbal interactions between the teacher and the students. For example, it's more difficult to get students to experience stress in their bodies in an online environment because no one can see the other people's whole bodies. Hand gestures indicating these kinds of movements are a poor substitute.

Secondly, when the person using the pointer—teacher or student—is not experienced in the art of using a mouse, its movements can be difficult to control. They might run out of room to move it; they might move it involuntarily while considering their next move; they might misjudge the distance it has to travel; any number of things can complicate pointing online. We have a lifetime of experience moving our arms and can point using a physical pointer with high precision; we don't have comparable experience in using a mouse.

Thirdly, in the classroom, the pointer makes a noise when it touches the chart; it is this noise that indicates to the students that the pointer has landed and that what it has landed on is therefore included in the string being pointed. In the online world, the pointer makes no noise and this can cause confusion. To remedy this, I have adopted the habit of making some kind of noise when landing on a rectangle or word. I use *tac, tac, tac, …* for example, but others count—*one, two, three, …* —as each word is pointed, or have a visual mouse-click highlighter set up.

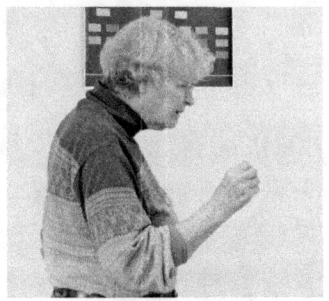

It is much easier to get across the dynamics of the language in real classrooms. We have to be inventive to find ways of doing this when working online.

Another consequence of the online environment is it isn't possible to tap more vigorously on the wall to indicate stress.

Fourthly, I can't extend and collapse the cursor as I can with a real telescopic pointer, and this hampers me when I want to indicate a length of time. For example, if I'm working on *this week*, I can't simply extend the pointer to show the length of time involved.

Some hints for working online[3]

I need to make sure the students can see what I want them to see. They will need to zoom in or out to adjust the size of the charts to their screen, but they also have to be with the class. I check this every time I move from one type of chart to another.

It is counterproductive in an online environment to get students to speak at the same time as each other. I can't hear well enough to give feedback if two or more students speak at the same time.

To signal the end of a series of words or sounds, I move the pointer outside the chart, pause an instant and then move it back in to begin the next word.

The student's camera can be used in selfie-type mode if I want him to adjust tensions, or perhaps the position of his lips.

I can ask the students to switch off their microphones for a few seconds to practise, then switch them back on in order to give them feedback. This saves time, especially when I'm working with a group online.

[3] *My thanks to Nicoleta Surdu for the discussions we have had on this topic.*

7. Correction

Chapter 1 explains how we learn skills and the model of learning that underpins my teaching—students learn to speak English through trial and error, feedback and practice. They learn from the experience of using the language to express meanings. This, rather than rules, is the base data from which their minds construct criteria for the language and is the foundation for ease and confidence in speaking.

The purpose of correction is for students to build correct criteria rather than simply to say the correct words in the right order.

Note that I deliberately wrote *the purpose of correction* rather than *the purpose of correcting*. This is a vital point. I work using feedback, hints and guidance to get the students to correct themselves and each other. It is in the process of working towards a correct sentence that students develop and refine their criteria. Learning takes place by means of the process.

A WORD ABOUT PRONUNCIATION

Later chapters deal with working on pronunciation—sounds, intonation and flow—in detail. However, here it is sufficient to say that pronunciation is different from other aspects of language in one important way. It takes time for students to train their muscles to pronounce sounds and words accurately. So while the grammar, word order and word choice for every sentence should be worked on until it is correct, this is not usually possible for pronunciation.

'In my approach I do not correct learners; I only throw them back onto themselves to elaborate further their criteria and to use them more completely.

I take upon myself the burden of controlling myself so as not to interfere. By doing so I give time to a student to make sense of "mistakes" (which are precious indicators of the discrepancy between what is said and what should be).'

Gattegno (1963)

So teachers have to judge what work to do on the pronunciation of each sentence moment by moment. A reasonable rule of thumb is that the student's pronunciation should be improving, and the teacher judges that he has achieved as good a result as he reasonably can at this stage of his learning to pronounce.

DO THE MINIMUM

The less the teacher does, the more the students do. The teacher needs to judge what is the least she can do to get the students to correct themselves. It is better to start by doing less and seeing what the students can do themselves, and only offer more help if they need it.

So when someone makes a mistake I do not simply give them the correct answer. To begin with I only give them the information that a mistake exists in what they have said. If the speaker cannot find it, I silently ask the class simply by lifting my eyes. If no one can find the mistake, then I indicate where it is in the sentence using my fingers. I only give the correction itself as a last resort, if no one else can produce it. Each step of this process keeps the question alive.

Soon I have to intervene less and less as the students begin correcting each other. This is an important step, since they can only do so when they have developed criteria for evaluating sentences themselves.

My role is not to 'teach' in the usual sense of the word. I am there to make the students more aware of the language, and more aware of themselves learning it. I am there to help them gain criteria.

THREE KEY NON-VERBAL TECHNIQUES

As far as possible, I use non-verbal techniques to get students to correct. When it is appropriate, I do use my voice, albeit sparingly, and Chapter 4 provides examples of the things I might say. But teacher talk is a potent spice, a little might enhance your work but too much will certainly spoil it. Here are three key non-verbal techniques to use. These techniques are designed for working on speech since that is the priority in my classes.

> FINGER CORRECTION which provides a quick and efficient way of enabling the whole class to see where there are problems in the sentence.

Scan to watch a video of a teacher working with a class on the order of adjectives and using the 'do the minimum' principle.

POINTING ON THE CHARTS which provides a visual way of getting students to realise which alternative word is needed. The pointer can also be used to give feedback on sentence stress, rhythm and flow.

THE AEROPLANE GESTURE which signals there is a problem. It can also mean that the sentence is almost right, but can be improved a little.

FINGER CORRECTION

The basic principle is to hold up one's fingers and the students 'place' one word on each finger. Thus I can:

- hold up fewer fingers or more fingers than the student says to indicate the right number of words in the sentence.
- hold up the number of fingers the student says and fold down one to indicate which of his words needs to be omitted or I can add a finger to indicate where an additional one is required.
- show contracted forms—*it's*, *they're*, *who's*—by closing the gap between the fingers carrying the two words.
- wiggle a particular finger or point to it to show where a problem is.
- group fingers together to indicate breath groups.
- indicate that a suffix is inaudible or missing from a word by 'lengthening' the end of the relevant finger. (I make a small space between the index finger and thumb of the other hand and 'add' this to the relevant finger.)

It is not necessary to explain finger correction to the students. They quickly grasp the different conventions involved.

Finger correction does not generate any sense of failure or shame. It maintains the students' presence. It sets a public challenge that can be solved by the whole group, and not just by the student who revealed the problem. It gives each sentence a certain permanence in time, without the sentence being written. It allows the teacher to remain silent while helping the students to find the required answer.

Finger correction stabilises sentences in students' minds until they are sure of them. They work out the correct content of the sentence using the fingers as placeholders. They 'read' the sentence using their mental imagery to 'lift' the words from the fingers. They know that they can come back to 'reading' the sentence if they have to.

Finger correction allows me to intervene very precisely in a sentence, stopping it exactly where the correction is necessary. It can be used in many different ways to address various types of mistakes.

How to hold one's hands

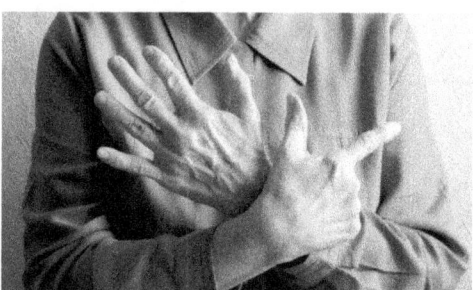

Hands crossed

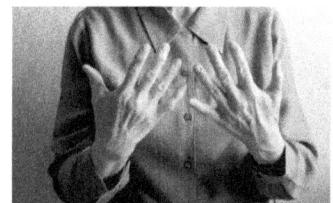

Palms facing teacher

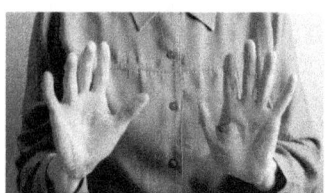

Palms facing students

Personally, I prefer to work with my hands crossed and my palms facing me, because when I want to remove a word by folding the finger carrying it, the finger actually disappears. Other teachers prefer working with their palms facing the students.

The students read the fingers from their left to their right, so I must work from my right to my left. I prefer to begin each sentence on the little finger and fourth finger of my left hand (touching these with my right index finger), because when I want to show contractions such as *I'm* these fingers close together better than a thumb and index finger combination.

When the sentence has more than five words, I cross my hands at the wrists and either wiggle the additional fingers on my right hand or touch them with the index finger of my left hand. The second time the students read the sentence from my fingers, I might get one of them to do the touching.

An example: a word too few

Suppose we are working on the sentence *There are seven days in a week*. From one student, I hear *There are seven days in week*; he has forgotten the word *a*.

I raise five fingers on my left hand and the thumb and index finger of my right hand, these seven fingers representing the seven words. The remaining three fingers are folded and therefore hidden. I ask the student to say the sentence. When he gets to the end of it, he finds one finger untouched. The ease with which he corrects the sentence now gives me precious information. I discover how sure he was of what he said.

For example, when he discovers the mistake, he may be able to correct himself spontaneously. It was only a slip of the tongue; he says it again, I hear the certainty in his voice and the problem is solved.

Or, surprised, he begins the sentence again, carefully checking every word, searching for what he has left out. After a little thought, he finds the mistake, corrects it, and ends up with a word for every finger. In this case, it was not a serious mistake needing further attention. I ask him to say it again, he does so easily, I hear the certainty in his voice, and the problem is solved.

A student pointing on the teacher's fingers.

In another case, the student may have no idea which word is missing. He knows there is a mistake in his sentence, but where? I have several strategies to help him.

I invite him to say the sentence again. When he is about to say the word *week*, I wiggle the last two fingers to make him aware that there are still two words to be said. Now he can correct himself. To consolidate, I get him to say it again, perhaps several times. When I hear the certainty come into his voice, the problem is solved.

However, he may have no idea at all which word should be included there. I lift my eyes to the class, inviting the others to provide the word which is missing (and I indicate my displeasure if they say more of the sentence than the word we need). Someone says *a*; the student recognises it as the word needed and places it on the right finger. I invite him to say the sentence again, and when I hear the certainty in his voice, the problem is solved.

However, if none of the students can fix the sentence, then I know that my earlier teaching was defective. If they are unaware of the structure, they cannot correct it. I might have worked too fast on this structure, or introduced it prematurely. I certainly have not given students enough time to come to grips with it. I know I will have to do this work again, perhaps differently from the first time.

Long sentences

If a student makes a sentence with more than ten words in it, when he reaches the eighth or ninth I simply move my first hand to the other side of my second to give myself a 'third' hand; I can do this again if necessary, in order to present every word of the sentence on my fingers.

Finger correction for liaison

Fingers help one to think

In the sentence *There are seven days in a week*, the pronunciation of *there are*, /ðərə/ will often be a problem. Non-native speakers are misled by these words because the second syllable corresponds to all the letters <re are>. Using two fingers and the Rectangle chart, I can show the existence of the two words; I can then separate them one from the other using the segments of my fingers and show exactly what sounds on the Rectangle chart correspond to each segment.

The first beat /ðə/ corresponds to the letters <the> of the word *there*, the sound /r/ corresponds to the <re> of *there* but begins the next syllable, and the word *are* is completely reduced to /ə/, in this second syllable. The combination of fingers and Rectangle chart solves this problem well.

— *What do you have here?* I show the first phalange of the first finger.
— /ðə/
— *And here?* I show the first phalange of the second finger.
— /rə/
— *Exactly.*

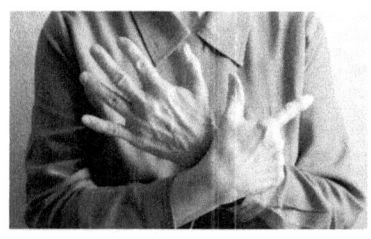
Finger correction for sense groups

Once he has pointed the sounds of the words on the Rectangle chart in order to start this process, now we place the words on my, or his, fingers and then on the Word charts and/or the Fidel.

Grouping fingers to produce sense groups

Once the number of words being said corresponds to the number of words in the sentence, I can group my fingers to represent sense groups. For *There are seven days in a week*, I create three groups of fingers: the first group corresponds to *There are*, the second to *seven days* and the third to *in a week*. Once everyone can say each individual group well, we can put two groups together: *There are seven days* followed by *in a week* and *There are* followed by *seven days in a week*. Finally, we put it all together and everyone in the class can say the whole sentence fluently.

Personal use of fingers

Students use fingers themselves as soon as they become aware of how fingers can help them to organise their thoughts. It is not uncommon to see students reflecting privately on a sentence, using their fingers to help them hold the sentence as they work. A few moments later, they launch what they have been working on.

Personal work

SYLLABIFICATION

Using fists

Students are often uncertain how many syllables there should be in a word. I use fists—either my fists or the students'—to count them. I ask everyone to fold their hands into fists. Then I ask them to place one fist on top of the other and exchange the top fist for the bottom one with every syllable counted. The syllables are sounded out loud so that I can hear if a sound has been misplaced in a syllable or if a syllable isn't being reduced. It takes time to swap their fists around and therefore each syllable is clearly separated from its neighbours. A sentence like *There are a lot* becomes limpid: /ðə rə rə lɒt/.

Using one's fists in this way has advantages over clapping or tapping on the desk. Clapping is never coordinated, so it is impossible to know who is making a mistake even though it is clear that mistakes are being made. Fists slow the process down to the point where I can follow

Scan to watch a video on how to work with students on syllabification and stress

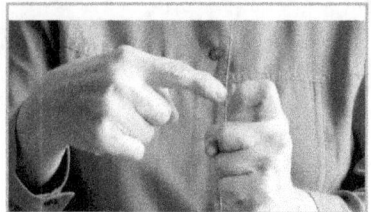
The 'hook'.

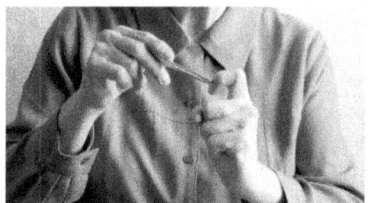
Finger correction <va>

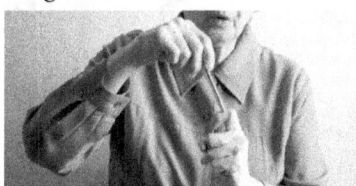
Finger correction <ri>

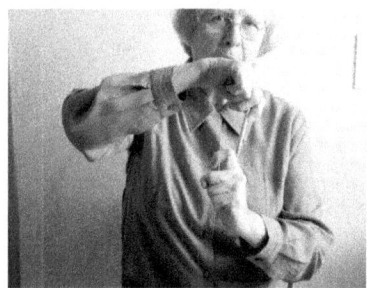
Finger correction <e>

Finger correction <ty>

everyone. It is very clear what each student is doing, who has got it right and who hasn't.

One syllable per segment of a finger

I may use a single finger to refine the pronunciation of a difficult word. Often a word is difficult because the students do not know how many syllables it has and they are unsure of the exact content of each syllable. In particular, many English words are shocking for speakers of Romance languages because they find the spoken form unrecognisable despite the written form being familiar.

Words like *January* and *February* are also difficult because students can't decide how the sounds correspond to the letters and how they are distributed over the different syllables. These two words sound indistinct to a foreign ear. These kinds of words have given English speakers a reputation for 'swallowing their words'. It is therefore important to deal with this problem in depth.

Imagine that we are working on the pronunciation of the word *variety*. I want to take the word to pieces, syllable by syllable. I clench my left fist, extend the index finger of the hand, and then fold it to make a hook, showing it in profile above the other folded fingers with all its segments visible.

Then, using a closed pointer—rather than my finger because this keeps the hooked finger as visible as possible—I place each syllable of the word on a segment of the finger: /və/ on the segment with the fingernail, /raɪ/ on the next one, /ə/ on the third one leading to the knuckle and last of all, I place /ti/ on the back of my hand, on the part lined up with the index finger.

Now that each segment represents a syllable, I can work on them separately to make sure that the pronunciation of each is exact. To do this I first get the students to try to guess the content of each syllable, pronouncing them one by one. For this particular word, they are usually surprised that it has four syllables; they were not aware of the third one at all. I indicate the stress by touching the second segment a little harder with the pointer. When the class is clear about the content of each segment, I stretch out the finger and sweep it with the pointer from the nail to the knuckle, and the students pronounce the word, linking the syllables to each other.

In this way, I can make them practise a word bit by bit, then put the bits together. The pronunciation of these difficult words improves rapidly.

I explain how I deal with *January* and *February*, and similar problems, in Chapter 14.

THE AEROPLANE GESTURE

Supposing a sentence is launched, and among those who say it I hear a discordant voice, a student who does not have the word order of the sentence. What should I do? To begin with, I must always determine the nature of the problem. Is it a real mistake or merely a slip of the tongue? I hold out my hand horizontally, palm to the floor, fingers spread out and then slowly 'waggle the wings' as if my hand were a small plane—the 'aeroplane gesture'. I use this gesture to signal that there is a problem. It can also mean that the sentence is almost right, but can be improved a little.

The aeroplane gesture

In a big class, I might need to ask the students to repeat the sentence in order to locate the person who made the mistake. I use the aeroplane gesture to prompt him to say his sentence again. Sometimes this is enough on its own for the student to correct himself.

I use the aeroplane gesture a lot with more advanced classes where students can usually fix their own problems if prompted to.

THE UNEXPECTED

What I have said about correction up to here sounds very organised, and it is. However, the unexpected will happen from time to time, and here is a case in point.

> One day, I was working with a class of French teenagers who had between five and seven years of school English, but had very real problems with the language.
>
> Someone in the class had produced the sentence,
>
> I am going to the station
>
> and the rest of the students were now working on it. One of them was having such difficulty that I was mystified. He was incapable of keeping the words in any order, and clearly saw no logic at all in the English sentence.

In French, I asked him if he knew what he was trying to say. He said that he did and he translated the sentence into French,

> Je vais à la gare

Something prompted me to ask him how many words he was saying in French. He took a few seconds to count them and answered *Two*. I was speechless for a few seconds. Finally, I said, *Ah, when I count, I find more*. He counted again and then said, *Mmm, ... Three*. I said that I still found more. He counted again, and said, with conviction this time, *Ah! There are five*. I put the French words on my fingers and this confirmed that there are indeed five words in the French sentence. He then said the sentence in English easily.

This experience made me aware that a student can have made the functioning of his first language so automatic that he is unaware of the individual words he is using. He is not thinking in words at all, but in ideas: (1) *Je vais* and (2) *à la gare*. This is what my student had counted. We all think in groups of words naturally—and it is highly efficient in our native language—but most of us can re-enter the process of expression at the level of words with ease. This student, though, only started doing so once it was brought to his attention. His English improved quickly once he had had this awareness.

Just as teachers of reading know that not all young children can spontaneously break words down into sounds and have to be taught to do this, we should realise that not all students spontaneously reach the individual words within a sentence even if they are literate and, of course, do so when they are writing. In a language class, they may remain at the level of the ideas expressed. If they are trying to correlate single English words with French chunks representing ideas, as I think this boy was, it will be disastrous for their language learning.

PRONUNCIATION

'It is obvious that a neglect of the basic foundation [the emission of sounds] leads from a shaky contact with the language in the beginning to a continuing uncertainty into the future.'

Caleb Gattegno

8. Below the superficial

Gattegno pointed out that although language is used for communication, its more primitive use—and a more insightful way of looking at it when considering learning a new language—is for expression.

In Chapter 2, I wrote about what I have learned in the light of this idea by observing myself speaking and writing English and French. I explained why I believe that language is not simply 'for communication' but more fundamentally allows us to express ourselves. I made the point that to master a language requires more than the simplistic view of 'getting the message across'. I explained what this implies for teaching languages.

But there is more to say about language as a means of expression. In the spoken language, voice itself has a fundamental role. In teaching foreign languages this is not taken into consideration, perhaps because teachers know that it is an entirely personal expression of who the student is at any particular moment. It too carries his thoughts and emotions, but it is not the domain of teaching

However, those using the Silent Way know that the people in the classroom are people before they are students. To learn to speak this foreign language 'from the heart', they should learn it as an authentic expression of who they are in the moment from the very beginning. This will speed up the learning process.

This chapter will start by bringing together some observations about the voice before looking at learning the sound system of English which, as we will see, is more than simply getting students to make sounds. There are other components which must be put into place if our students are to reach a high level in their pronunciation, a level where how they sound resembles how a native speaker would sound.

THE NATURE OF SPEECH

Speech as energy

Speech is, like all sound, a distribution of energy over time. However, speech is produced by human bodies using human energy, and the speakers of any given language use the sound-making potential of their bodies in ways that are distinctive for that language. Each language sounds correct only if the person speaking it respects the way native speakers use their energy to produce it.

Many pronunciation problems can be worked on more readily if they are thought of as particular uses of the speaker's energy. When students are asked to think in terms of energy, they usually achieve better results than when they are only asked to think in terms of particular features of pronunciation; this leads them to lose sight of the whole.

Finding a way to change the energy one is using to speak a new language is a more holistic approach to any pronunciation problem. This keeps students in contact with the whole task and at the same time, aware of what part of it they are working on at any particular moment.

The voice

It is the quality of the voice which gives one the sense, when listening to a speaker, of how coherent he is at all levels in what he is saying.

Our voice is the vehicle of our inner climate, our emotional state. Anger, disappointment, fear, anguish, joy, pleasure—these emotions and others are present in our voices and heard by our listeners.

> In 1988, I was visiting Japan for the first time. A few minutes after we arrived at my Japanese friend's home, the phone rang. I had no qualms about listening intently to the conversation as, with my fifty hours of Japanese, I knew I would not understand anything more than a few words here and there, and certainly not the meaning of what was being said.

> At one point, after a long silence, my friend said just one word, *Hontō?!* The surprise in her voice was palpable, and I understood immediately what she had said—*Really?!*

Thinking about this incident later, I became more aware of the role of voice as against that of intonation in language. In this case, they were clearly in step, but the voice certainly carried a good part of the message. The voice is primary; it carries the emotion, and the intonation pattern will only add to what the voice is expressing.

Voice and emotion

Many emotions come in several 'flavours': love for one's lover will produce a quite different voice quality from the love one expresses for one's child or for one's mother. The surprise produced by the sudden revelation that a party has been organised in one's honour is quite different from the surprise generated by a suspicious noise at four in the morning and accompanied by fear. In this case, the speaking voice will betray not only the presence of fear, but also how fearful the speaker feels.

A 'gushing voice' is created by letting air gush out through the glottis in quantities beyond what is necessary and normal in speech. This is the 'sexy voice', famously used by Marilyn Monroe when she sang *Happy Birthday* to President Kennedy. We can produce a 'big voice' which is devoid of anger but indicates to children that boundaries have been reached and that anger might soon follow. There is a 'steely voice' that some teachers use when being sarcastic. Many other 'voices' can be produced by any speaker, whatever the language. These are human uses of the vocal tract.

Emotions do not need to be extravagant in order to be present. Few utterances are emotion-neutral. Almost all have some emotional quality to them, however faint, simply because the human expressing himself is involved enough in the situation to have wanted to speak. Speaking costs energy and is undertaken for a reason.

We can know from experience that the voice we are hearing can be trusted to reveal the state of the speaker. In cases where we think the voice we are hearing is inconsistent with the intonation pattern used and the words expressed, we know intuitively that we should trust the voice to reveal the real emotions of the speaker, rather than the words. We are hearing a lie.

How do we meet language?

Clearly an infant can associate the voice that speaks to him lovingly with the feel of the hands that cradle him at the same time; the voice which speaks in anger with the anger in the hands that handle him roughly at the same time; the voice that speaks to him while bathing him, perhaps telling him what is happening to him, with the more businesslike hands that are washing him. Even very young children have access to the emotions in the voices around them.

What babies experience is an integrated whole. Before they can make sense of the words, they hear in the voices speaking directly to them and around them strength or tenderness, intense or relaxed qualities, etc. These elements contribute to the 'timbre' of the voice. The timbre in speech is concerned with the human changes which are generated by the emotions of the speaker, while intonation—as I will be using the word, not including tonality and tonicity—is concerned with pitch changes demanded by the language.

Intonation

By the end of his first year, an infant has some of the sounds of the language he will learn. He can also produce the most common intonation patterns in his environment, though we cannot yet say how much meaning the child attributes to any particular pattern. However, many people attest to the 'speeches' given by one-year-olds who make long 'statements' using some of the sounds and intonation patterns of the language, but no recognisable words.

A small child can do this because he readily perceives intonation patterns. These are the most accessible part of the language because they don't need to be understood in the same way as words do, but only to be noticed. Intonation patterns are 'music'—organised melodic structures of sound in time. Intonation is used constantly by the people in the environment and the watchful infant can easily pick it out of the sounds and noises around him. Intonation is the most primitive part of language, the closest to the emotional aspects of what the speaker is saying.

Words, sentences and use of grammar come later in the child's development. They are the cognitive parts of the language, requiring to be understood by the child before he can construct them in himself as functioning language. Only when all these levels have been integrated can the child be considered to speak the language, at the age of about three or four.

Where humans and their language meet

A spoken sentence should be coherent from the deepest level, the emotion in which the sentence is grounded, to the shared levels of word meanings and grammar. At the deep level of feelings, the emotion produces the voice quality, the timbre. The intonation pattern required by the language overlays the voice with the most basic of the linguistic parameters, and the words and the structures, chosen because they conform with the underlying idea being expressed, are superimposed on the other levels. This structuring creates a coherent utterance, by which I mean an utterance in which all levels, personal and linguistic, express the speaker as he is in the instant.

At a primitive level then, the human speaker and the language he speaks meet each other at the intersection of timbre and intonation: timbre determined from within, intonation determined by the language community to which he belongs.

Implications for language teaching

Intonation is one of the aspects of language learning most affected by teachers' use of textbooks. Students are asked to make sentences in which they have no emotional involvement, and therefore cannot correctly 'embody'. They speak about whatever the authors consider important for them to learn—characters visiting a new place, or asking each other for the time or, at a higher level, negotiating or signing a contract—but the sentences they make are divorced from the students' themselves. Words can be learnt by heart, sentences can be said or written, but intonation needs to be generated by the speaker in touch with his ideas in their pre-worded state and with his emotions. Erroneous intonation patterns produced by even quite advanced students often betray a lack of grounding in their experience of what they are saying; what is said is not properly embodied in and by the speaker.

When language is taught from textbooks, few students know what to do to make the language come alive in them, to take it in and make it theirs.

Working on voice, melody and intonation

Since intonation is the most fundamental linguistic element of spoken language, it should be present from the beginning of learning to speak

Scan to watch a video of some students extending the work they have just done in class.

Notice the intonation patterns they produce when they say the word 'but'—the natural consequence of the emotions the situation generates.

The language really does come alive in these students.

> 'To require perfection at once is the great imperfection of most teaching and most thinking about teaching. Since we can only attain approximation of the goal from people moving towards it, we must develop techniques of teaching that are molded onto reality and take into account what is going on in the learners all the time.'
>
> Gattegno (1963)

a new one. This is one of the reasons why I base all the work done in class on the direct experience and lives of the students.

In the introductory lessons to English pronunciation, I do not aim for the students to reach perfection immediately—it would be foolish to even try to obtain this—and intonation will be worked on throughout the course. During the first few hours, my aim is only to arrive at a point where the students are aware that they can control the pitch of their voices. From the beginning, the students need to learn to convey grammatical meaning by their use of intonation.

The students talk about what they perceive and experience, then their own lives, and when talking about themselves they always tell the truth. They are encouraged to live intensely what they are saying. There is no need to do more than this—but to do this much is essential.

THE SOUNDS OF ENGLISH

English is different from many languages in that there is an astonishing tolerance of differences in the pronunciation of vowel sounds across accents. These vary so much from place to place that a foreign speaker can sound native-like if he has any coherent and complete set of vowels that he pronounces consistently and if the energy distribution of the language is correct, i.e. if the stress and reduction patterns sound English. He might even be identified by the unsophisticated listener as coming from 'somewhere else' in the English-speaking world. What he says sounds English and is easily understood although it is clearly not from the immediate locality.

Some examples:

> One afternoon many years ago, I was in my classroom about to start the lesson when a colleague came in and whispered *Can you give me some chalk?* and I didn't understand what she said. She picked up a stick and left the room. Ah, 'chalk'! I heard an /ɑː/ where I would have said /ɔː/.

This is a very considerable difference in pronunciation for what is supposed to be the 'same' word. This incident set me thinking. Although the vowel sounds used by my colleague were different from mine, her American accent did not bother me. I seemed to be able to compensate for it without really thinking about it. I became more aware of the variety in the pronunciation of vowel sounds in different accents of English.

One afternoon I was working on pronunciation teaching with an American colleague, and he happened to point the name of a third colleague, Sonia, on the Rectangle chart. I was astonished to see that he pointed /əʊ/ where I would have pointed /ɒ/. He was just as astonished to discover that I would have pointed it differently from him.

What really surprised me, though, was that although both of us were interested in pronunciation and often reflected on the sounds of English and how to teach them, and although we had spoken about Sonia very often over a period of more than twenty years, neither of us had noticed that the other used a different pronunciation for her name.

My colleagues from the North American family of English accents assure me that they cannot tell an Australian accent from a British one. On the other hand, I asked a Canadian colleague if she could tell whether a speaker was American or Canadian. She said she could, very easily, and gave me a set of clues which informed her. One was the Canadian pronunciation of *about*, similar to mine of *a boat*. What surprised me most, though, was that I hadn't noticed this before she told me.

These sorts of observations brought me to realise that the exact vowel sounds English speakers use count for much less than I had imagined.

THE STRESS & REDUCTION SYSTEM

It is the way English speakers use the stress & reduction system which holds the English language together across multiple dialects and accents. Here are a few of the reasons why I think this is true.

Mistakes in stress are noticeable

Many words like *'con tent* and *con 'tent* or *'pro ject* and *pro 'ject* have two stress patterns depending on their parts of speech, but such pairs are usually consistent across the American and British families of speakers. If I encounter someone who uses one pattern for any word where I would use another, I notice. I am aware, too, that my immediate inclination is to consider it to be a mistake, rather than a regional difference in pronunciation.

Few words have two accepted stress patterns

It is uncommon for English words to have two different stress patterns while having the same meaning. The language contains tens of thousands of words and those like *laboratory* or *kilometre* are exceptional. This suggests to me that the stress pattern of a word is at least as fundamental to its identity as its vowel sounds.

Mistakes in stress make understanding difficult

It is far more difficult for me, a native speaker, to understand a non-native speaker if he makes a mistake in placing stress in a multisyllabic word than if he makes a mistake in the sound of a vowel. The example I sometimes use in class is *elevator* with the stress moved to the second syllable, meaning that two of the other three syllables change (their vowels reducing to schwa), making the word unrecognisable.

The distribution of energy

I have met any number of non-native speakers of English whose English is good, but who have retained a foreign accent. I have met a very small number of people who speak the language with a perfect or near-perfect accent. What these few have mastered are the energetic qualities of spoken English. It seems to be much more difficult to master these than the grammar of the language or the vowel sounds. (However, it should be said that students—and their teachers—are usually unaware that this, too, is part of the challenge of learning a language.)

I knew a non-native speaker whose English was excellent although he learned it quite late in life. I once listened to a tape recording of this person speaking English and was amazed to discover on the second and subsequent times that I listened, that he had made several grammatical mistakes in just a few sentences, mistakes which I hadn't noticed the first time I listened. He even left out words. But his use of the energy of the language—the placement of stress, the rhythms and intonation patterns—was convincing and the other problems seemed to have faded into the background and vanished. Obviously I was not listening for the kinds of mistakes he made.

Rather than only concentrating on getting vowel and consonant sounds, I try to make my students aware of the way energy is distributed in the spoken language. If our students want to sound like native speakers, we need to work on this aspect of the language, too.

In the context of motor control, a "forward model" predicts the sensory consequences of a motor command, while an "inverse model" calculates the motor commands needed to achieve a desired sensory outcome. I.e. a forward model predicts what will happen based on an action, while an inverse model determines what action to take to achieve a desired result.

A DOUBLE SYSTEM

Babies and young children start putting into place a double system of sound production and perception very early. The baby has first to recognise that he is in fact responsible for some of the sounds he is hearing. Once he has had this awareness, he can begin creating the first of the systems, what configuration of his mouth is giving the sound that he hears himself making? Can he do it again? In babbling he works on this. Later, when he picks out a new sound from his environment, what does he have to do with his vocal system in order to produce it? When he has an answer to both of these (unstated) questions for all the sounds in his language, it can be said that he has built a complete inventory of sounds. He will need to do this same job for any new language he meets later in life.

Scan to download the article on Articulatory Settings by Honikman.

ARTICULATORY SETTINGS

Every language has a specific, default position used by native speakers. This position is called the articulatory setting for that language. It is the position adopted by native speakers as they are about to speak, the configuration they adopt for their speech articulators: the mouth and tongue, the lower jaw, etc.[1]

English uses an unusual position, compared to most languages, which radically affects both how the language sounds and the ease with which a speaker can utter the sequences of sounds the language requires.

The placement of the tongue

French speakers and speakers of many other languages tether the tip of their tongue behind their lower front teeth. From this position, the hump of the back of the tongue can easily reach the positions required for the back vowel sounds. The blade of the tongue moves up to the alveolar ridge for the front consonants. French is spoken with considerable tension in the lips, which are extremely mobile, often thrust forward in a rounded position. The lips are moved by facial muscles which non-native French speakers have to develop. In teaching French, I must make students aware that for each syllable, the vowel should already be in place as far as possible before the preceding consonant is begun. This will make French sound French.

During English speech, native speakers spread the back of their tongue to tether it against the upper back molars and keep the very tip of their

[1] B. Honikman, Articulatory Settings, in *In Honour of Daniel Jones. Abercrombie et al. (eds.), London: Longman, 1964*

This position might seem strange until one realises that it is very close to one of the new-born baby's first gestures, that of sucking. To suck, one has to create a pressure seal under the roof of the mouth using the tongue. This position is very similar to that of the articulatory setting of English, and so very natural for a young child to adopt.

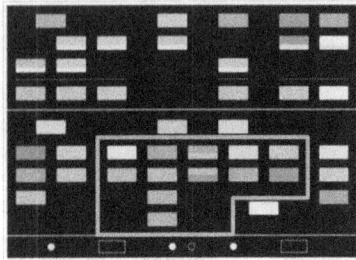

The central section of the Rectangle chart with consonants produced with the tongue close to the alveolar ridge marked.

A rough sketch on the board can help students identify what's in their mouth.

You can read more about the theory behind the articulatory approach in: Messum and Young (2021) Teaching students to pronounce English: a motor skill approach in the classroom, *RELC Journal*.

tongue close to the alveolar ridge, the ridge which is a little behind the upper teeth and just in front of the palate. This has been called the 'butterfly position': the back of the tongue widening out to form the wings of the butterfly, leaving its centre slightly lower, like the body of a butterfly suspended between the wings. It creates a channel for air to run over the tongue. From this position, the tip of the tongue can easily be flicked upwards to touch the alveolar ridge or forwards towards the upper teeth, touching them with minimal effort. Usually the tongue and lips are quite relaxed. When the tongue is touching the alveolar ridge, the slightest pulse of air is enough to blow it away. The relaxed tongue and lips of English and its pulsatile style of breath control explain why some English consonants are aspirated when they begin a stressed syllable.

On the Rectangle chart, the central section in the area presenting the consonants reflects this aspect of the articulatory setting of English. The consonants in this area of the chart are all pronounced within a few millimetres of each other, using various pressures of the tongue against or close to the alveolar ridge to create each sound.

SENSITISING STUDENTS TO THEIR TONGUE

When the students have worked on the relevant vowels and consonants for about half an hour or so, I get them to make sounds like /tɑː/, /sɑː/, /nɑː/ or /dɑː/, /zɑː/ and all sorts of combinations like /ɑnz/, /ɑts/ or /ɑːnt/. As they speak, I ask them to feel what they are doing with their tongue in relation to their teeth and to the alveolar ridge.

I draw a sketchy side-on diagram of a face and mouth like the one on the left and ask the students to show me where their tongue is for each of these combinations. Or I might use one hand to represent the roof of the mouth, with my nails representing the teeth. My other hand then can indicate what the tongue is doing.

During speech we can rarely see what happens inside the mouth, so I need the students to be able to feel what is happening when they speak. I want each student to focus his attention on his mouth and tongue, and become more aware of their movements.

If I speak the students' language, I might say:

> Rub your tongue vigorously across the top of your lower teeth until it hurts a little. You can now feel where it is for about twenty seconds.

Place your tongue against the cutting edge of your top front teeth. Rub it up and down the teeth for a few seconds. Can you feel where the horizontal edge of the teeth becomes the vertical surface of the back of each tooth? Now move your tongue up onto your gums. Can you feel the junction between the teeth and the gums? Move it up and down over this junction several times.

Now pull your tongue back just a little until you come to a bump. The roof of your mouth goes up more vertically here. Can you feel this? Rub your tongue back and forth over the bump. This bump is essential in pronouncing English well because most of the consonants are made in contact with it or close to it.

Move your tongue further back. Can you feel your hard palate? Can you feel where the hard palate stops and the soft palate begins? There is no bone behind where you are now touching.

We can't usually move our tongue further back than this.

You may encounter students who are unfamiliar with cross-sectional drawings.

If so, hang a large piece of paper on the board. Invite one student to stand looking sideways in front of the board. Have another student shine a torch so the first student's shadow is projected onto the paper. And then a third student draws round that shadow with a black marker.

I would get the students to do this exercise several times, and I would start the next few lessons off by doing the same exercise again until the students know how to activate sensations in their tongue by rubbing it on their teeth, and can therefore feel where it is when they move it elsewhere.

SPEECH BREATHING

In all languages, speakers place their speech on the outgoing stream of air. They mould the air with their speech organs in order to create the sounds they want.

For most languages, the column of air is created by pressurising the lungs in a uniform, continuous way. For an adult speaker, the same seems to be true of English (and of other West Germanic languages) but when the system is taxed (in loud whisper, for example), a different underlying control mechanism is revealed; the one that English-speaking children had to adopt in order to learn to speak the language.

This way of controlling the breath can be described as 'pulsatile'. Children use contractions of their abdominal muscles to create pulses of air, each pulse carrying one stressed syllable together with all the other syllables belonging to that foot. Each pulse creates a stressed syllable and each

Scan to watch a video of this process of sensitisation.

This example was part of a French class but the sensitisation process is exactly the same.

But note the postures adopted to speak French and English are totally different.

stressed syllable is carried by its own pulse. The system of speaking on pulses of air is the corporal basis for stress and explains the accompanying reduction system, the schwa family of sounds.

Any syllables between one stressed syllable and the next are pronounced on the air remaining in the pulse. I.e, they are reduced to the point where they can be produced by the aerodynamic resource that remains available to them.

The distinctive way of controlling the breath used by young English speakers naturally creates the distinctive energy distribution of the language. If a non-native speaker gets this right, he will sound English even if no native speaker would pronounce the sounds of the words used in the same way as he does.

For a young speaker, one danger of the pulsatile system of English speech breathing is that each pulse puts him at risk of losing too much air from his limited resource of air volume. (His lungs are much smaller than those of adults, but he uses similar amounts of air to speak on.) Thus, the 'short' or 'lax' vowels of English are always checked by the presence of a following consonant, the role of which is to cut off the flow of air. Otherwise, the size of the opening of the vocal tract for the lax vowels is too great to allow a strong pulse of airflow to be maintained for any length of time.

Since most languages are spoken on a steady pressure of air rather than on pulses of pressure created by the abdominal muscles, most of my students will need to learn how to use their abdominal walls to create pulses as English-speaking children do. I will need to make them aware of their breath control and to help them to reinvest in these muscles. This can be done with practice, and gives them an authentic basis for the stress and reduction system of the language. Some may decide not to invest the further time to make this automatic, but it should be their choice, not mine for them.

How can speech breathing be taught?

A (SPOKEN OR UNSPOKEN) DIALOGUE

I might stand, arms akimbo, with my hands placed at the level of my belt, just below my rib cage, fingers spread as much as possible around my waist. I gesture to the students to do the same. I get them to snort—with their mouths closed they have to feel what they are doing when they expel air out through their noses in short, sharp pulses generated by the muscles around their abdomen.

Next I show them that I want them to pant, mouths open, while feeling their abdomen move as they do so. Once they can do this, they can be asked to place a sound on each impulse, /ɑ/, /ɑ/, /ɑ/, /ɑ/, for example, sensing the movement of the abdominal muscles expelling the air.

Then, when they are a little more at ease, they can gradually make more complex groups of sounds, introducing rhythms. The actual sounds worked on depend on what the students have done before this begins. What follows is an illustration only.

arm, **farm**, *a* **far**mer, *the* **far**mer's **car**, *the* **far**mer's **car**pet, *the* **far**mer's got *a* **dark car**pet

arm, *to* **arm**, **ar**mour, *an* **ar**moured **car**, **the far**mer's **ar**moured **car**

put, **out**: **cat**, *the* **cat**, **put** *out the* **cat**, *she* **put** *out the* **cat**:

/aʊ/, /aʊ/, /aʊ/, /aʊ/, **cow**, **now**, **thou**sand, *a* **thou**sand, *a* **thou**sand **cows**, *a* **thou**sand **sounds**, *a* **thou**sand **scoun**drels

/æ/, /æ/, /æ/, /æ/, **cat**, **cat**tle, *the* **cat**tle, *some* **cat**tle, **head** *of* **cat**tle, *he's got a* **hun**dred **head** *of* **cat**tle, *etc.*

The most efficient way of working on this is to consider that it is a question of energy.

I sometimes introduce the control of breath for English as shown in the side column and for the rest of the course, at appropriate moments, I will give micro-lessons on speech breathing lasting from a few seconds to a few minutes.

Teachers will certainly want to investigate this system working in themselves. This can be difficult to begin with, as the system was made automatic in childhood, and it is not easy to regain access to automatisms established so many years ago. We are all high-level performers, Olympic athletes, in this area, having honed our speech breathing so that it works to perfection with the least possible energy expenditure, and we have used it for so many years.

A good way to start connecting with one's speech breathing is lying on the floor on one's side or on one's back. This position restricts the movement of the ribcage and makes the abdominal movements easier to detect. As one gains in expertise, the movements can be felt standing and then sitting.

THE STRESS & REDUCTION SYSTEM

A lot of attention is usually given to stress in teaching English, but much less to reduction. But stress can only be salient if the rest of the language is relegated to the background in some way. The low energy background against which stress emerges in English is created by the different schwa sounds which native speakers use. Therefore, I teach stress and the schwa family of sounds as a single 'Stress and Reduction System.' If my students correctly distribute the highs and lows of their energy over words and sentences, what they say will sound English.

JC Catford's A Practical Introduction to Phonetics *is a good guide to this work.*

To sum up, young native English speakers produce stress by means of their pulsatile speech breathing. The energy they use to create the pulse is concentrated in the stressed syllables. The low energy schwa sounds allow other words to fit into the intervals between the breath pulses, and to ride on the stressed syllables free of charge, so to speak.

The schwa family—the key to English pronunciation

The most common of the low energy sounds of English is the schwa itself. It is to be found, for example, in the first syllable of *about* and in the last of *comma*.

TWO KINDS OF SCHWA

There are two kinds of schwa:

- A schwa at the end of a word like *butter* is definitely a sound in English.
- The second type of schwa (called an 'open transition') occurs between two consonants. For example, in pairs of words like *please* and *police*, the transition from the first consonant to the second differs. For *please*, the positioning of the /l/ is already underway during

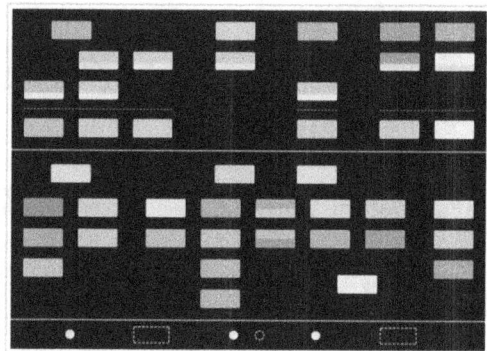

Vowels and diphthongs

Consonants

Schwa sounds

The British English Rectangle chart

the production of the /p/—they overlap—while in the word *police*, the /p/ is completely finished before the /l/ is begun. The result in the second case is a schwa, but it is more the side effect of the movement than an independent intentional sound. This 'open transition' schwa is the key to obtaining good pronunciation with students.

SCHWI

Schwi is to be found in the first syllable of words like *between* and *behind* and in the final syllable of *happy*. Clearly the sound /i/ at the end of the word *happy* is not the same as the sound in the first syllable of *between*, but both require little energy to produce, and certainly less than the full vowels /iː/ and /ɪ/.

SCHWU

Schwu /u/ can be found in words like *influenza*.

SCHWR

Schwr in American English is a schwa with a retroflex /r/.

PRONUNCIATION

Coaching stress and reduction with the Rectangle chart

The Stress and Reduction System has been made visible on the Rectangle chart. The schwa family is placed at the bottom: coloured dots for the schwa, schwi and schwu, and a black circle for the open transition. We also use this area to indicate unstressed full vowels using the dashed rectangles.

Positioning unstressed sounds at the bottom of the chart reveals the stress pattern of words at the same time as the sounds. Stressed syllables are pointed with an upward motion, and unstressed syllables (usually those containing reduced sounds) are pointed with clear downward movements.

In the conventional approach, the schwa family is taught as vowel sounds like the other vowels, starting with examples to be listened to and copied. This defeats the purpose: students end up putting too much energy into them so that they can hear them properly, which means that they stop being reduced sounds. The whole point is that they should be low energy and unclear.

To start with, I teach my students to reduce syllables using only schwa—aiming for maximum reduction—until the system of complementary stress and reduction is well installed. Only later do I ask them to distinguish between the various schwa sounds, refining the reduction system as needed.

The sidebar shows examples of pointing words on the Rectangle chart.

Varying levels of reduction

When my students are ready, I can begin to coach them in distinguishing one level of stress and four levels of non-stress. They will need to distinguish these levels using several criteria.

> STRESSED SYLLABLES: These will be the salient feature of each breath pulse. This

---

How can the stress and reduction system be taught?

POINTING VOWELS ON THE RECTANGLE CHART

The vowel in all stressed syllables is pointed in the upper section of the Rectangle chart. This is the area used when the vowel sound can be most clearly identified.

The first syllable of the word *above* is a schwa, using the yellow dot at the bottom of the chart. The /b/ is dark green, in the consonants. The <o> carries the stress and is therefore pointed in the full vowel rectangles in the top section of the chart. It is pointed by touching the yellow rectangle representing /ʌ/. The <ve> is pointed by touching the olive green rectangle in the consonants.

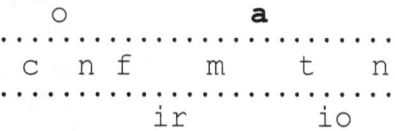

In the word *confirmation*, the first syllable is pronounced using the sound /ɒ/, with secondary stress and is pointed in the vowel section. The second syllable is a schwa, the third carries the primary stress (pointed with more emphasis), and the fourth is pointed schwa.

	Syllable?	Full vowel?	Pitch change?
/	✓	✓	✓
~	✓	✓	✗
...	✓	✗	✗
•	✓		
,	✗		

I introduce the stress and reduction system to intermediate and advanced students using this 'noughts and crosses diagram'.

For a full set of examples, see the Guide to the PronSci English Rectangle charts, parts 1 and 2.

means that they will be louder and longer than other syllables, and they often carry a pitch change. The vowel sound they contain will be clearly audible and easy to identify. When writing on the board, I put a slash (/) in front of such syllables.

All unstressed syllables are pointed in the lower section of the chart.

In syllables containing OTHER FULL VOWELS, the syllable will not have its own breath pulse and will not stand out from neighbouring syllables, but the vowel sound will be easy to identify. I put a tilde (~) under such syllables.

SCHWI, SCHWA AND SCHWU are never stressed, and their vowel sound is produced with low energy. I use a small circle under the syllable.

THE BLACK DOT is used for open transitions, where there is no vowel sound, full or reduced, in the syllable at all.

THE APOSTROPHE is used in writing, to show when a word has been so completely reduced that it no longer has its own syllable. A contraction like *I am* becoming *I'm* is an example of this.

Occasionally I use a metaphor to help my students understand the relationship between stress and reduction in English. I ask them, *If you want to feel the sensation of height, would you go to the middle of a plateau at four thousand metres altitude or to the edge of a cliff at four hundred?* They agree that the edge of the cliff will create the sensation of height more than the plateau, that absolute height is less important than relative height. Stress works in the same way. If we want to create a sensation of stress, then we must create the 'cliff' and the 'valley' below. It is the role of the schwa family of sounds to create the valleys.

Pointing unstressed full vowels

The Rectangle chart includes two dashed rectangles in the bottom row. These are used to point unstressed full vowels, as in the second syllable of *window*. I gesture 'dragging down' the vowel from its normal rectangle to one of the dashed rectangles. This signals to students that they are to say the full vowel sound but with low energy.

WHAT I AM AIMING FOR

By the end of the course, I want my students to have integrated the following things about English, and to be able to think about them conceptually and use them in practise:

- Words and sentences carry stress patterns.
- Stress is generated through a pulsatile movement of the respiratory system, best felt as a contraction created by the abdominal muscles.
- Native speakers normally pay more attention to stress than they do to vowel sounds.

In these introductory lessons to English pronunciation, I do not aim for the students to reach perfection immediately. It would be foolish to even try to obtain this. Rather, the aim is for each student to know what he should be trying to do with himself when he says each of the sounds in English. All the students should have an idea of what the sounds of English are like and the kinds of movements necessary to produce them, even if they can't actually manage to say all of them every time they try. They should know what they are aiming for. This job takes between two and five hours with older children and adults. These hours spent at the beginning of the course will save a lot of time later on.

'Since all learning is in time and is progressive, we need not request perfection (which in any case is unattainable) but only be concerned with steady improvement.'

Gattegno (1976)

HOMEWORK LINKED TO PRONUNCIATION

I know that the muscle movements necessary to speak good English will take more time than I can devote to developing them in class. So about seven or eight hours into the course, I begin to give pronunciation homework. This homework is designed to lengthen the time spent exploring the sounds of the language and their production. If I speak my students' language, I might say to them:

> *Go for a walk alone in the park, and try to say aloud all the sentences we worked on today. Do what you need to do so that your mouth enjoys speaking English. Feel yourself using your muscles to speak in English.*

or

> *Go for a walk in the park, and talk to yourselves in your native language; try to give yourself a strong English accent. Notice what you do to make yourself sound English. Then speak English doing the same thing. How does it feel?*

Scan to watch a playlist of videos on how to teach three of the key topics covered in this chapter: the Articulatory Setting, stress and speech breathing and reduction

I want students to get a sense of what they do with themselves when they speak English rather than simply imitating the sounds they think English speakers say.

A NEED FOR CHANGE

Surveys consistently show that students want to improve their pronunciation, but that teachers are reluctant to teach it. Teachers say that they lack confidence and consider that they need more training.

This may well be true, but I would suggest another reason why teachers do little work on pronunciation: when they do, they realise that what they are doing is a waste of students' time, and they therefore decide to spend class time on other activities. This is perfectly reasonable. The conventional pronunciation activities seen in textbooks are indeed largely a waste of time. They are based on the idea that students will learn new sounds by copying models. This comes up against the major problem that students' expertise in hearing their L1 prevents them from hearing new and similar sounds in L2 with the accuracy needed to reproduce them. (A problem known about even before Trubetskoy coined the evocative term 'phonological sieve' in the 1930's to describe the way that students hear L2 through the 'sieve' of their L1.) The listening exercises that try to address this problem are largely ineffective.

However, taking an Articulatory Approach to pronunciation teaching does work. After all, pronouncing a new language involves making new actions with your speech articulators, so coaching these skills is the logical way to improve them.

Teachers are willing to spend time learning about English grammar and about how to teach it. The same should be true of pronunciation, and indeed this was the case in the first half of the twentieth century, up to the time of the 'communicative' revolution. The Communicative Approach prioritised 'getting the message across' over any notions of accuracy, and work on pronunciation seemed to have little or no place in this. As a result, several generations of teachers and teacher-trainers were de-skilled, and there is little expertise on pronunciation within the general body of English teachers.

To help with your teaching of English pronunciation, I would suggest that you find a good, specialist pronunciation dictionary (the Longman one, edited by JC Wells, includes helpful notes on important features of English pronunciation) and that you sensitise yourself to how your mouth works in sound production in English and other languages. One way to do this is by working through the many exercises devised by JC Catford in his *Practical Introduction to Phonetics*.

To equip yourself to teach pronunciation well using the Articulatory Approach, there is no substitute to now watching yourself grapple with learning the pronunciation of an L2. If you are not currently learning an L2, start now!

9. Putting theory into practice

Historically, pronunciation has been taught using some form or other of 'Listen and Repeat.' The teacher gives a model—either saying the example or playing a recording—and asks the class to imitate what was said. Unfortunately, whatever the immediate performance of the class, this teaching approach gives poor learning results. As we saw in Chapter 1, imitation isn't the best way to teach pronunciation: if a student can make the gesture for a sound after hearing it, he already knows how to make it. If he can't, I have to actually teach him how to do it. I will do this by coaching him rather than by modelling the sounds for him.

Throughout any course, I will not model anything I want my students to say. I may show them the shape of the mouth by mouthing the sounds I want to put into circulation or by using a drawing of the mouth, or I may make gestures, but I will not actually say anything that I want them to repeat.

WHY NOT MODEL PRONUNCIATION?

It is a mistake to model.
- When I ask a student to listen, I ask him to put his presence in his ears. But we don't pronounce with our ears; we pronounce with the muscles of our mouths and this is where his attention should be. I need the student to explore his mouth and change the way he uses it. If I model the pronunciation of a word or phrase, there will be no exploration, only an attempt to copy what I have said. His attempts to imitate undermine my aim which is to get English into the muscles

- of his abdomen, chest and mouth.
- When a student listens, he does so with the mental filters of his own language, and what he hears may or may not be faithful to what was said.
- After a maximum of about twenty seconds, the sound image a student has heard will have faded from his mind and he is left with nothing to work with. If my overriding aim is for him to increase his sensitivity to his muscles, then rather than giving him a sound image, I need to give him feedback on his various productions.
- If I model, the students might end up believing that there exists only one correct variety of English pronunciation, mine. All the other varieties might therefore seem wrong, and this simply is not true. On the other hand, using the Articulatory Approach I can easily give students an entry into several pronunciations of the language, all of which are perfectly acceptable. For example, it's in their interest to become aware of the differences between American English and British English.
- Teachers who are not native speakers of English are sometimes self-conscious about their accent. Even if this is not justified, one advantage of the Ariculatory Approach is that she need not speak. She certainly has criteria for pronunciation, even if she doesn't always pronounce perfectly herself. She can effectively bring these criteria to life in her students even if she doesn't speak. It's perfectly possible to bring students to the point where they have better pronunciation than their teacher.

I will, however, frequently use the students themselves as models. I will ask them to say a sound that they have just said successfully once more, so that the others can hear it clearly. Being a model myself and using students as models are two very different things. The other students know very well that the one who is now serving as a model may only have managed to pronounce the sound well by accident. His time in the limelight is fleeting; no one can count on him to provide the sound again in a few minutes' time.

In fact, students are often unable to produce a sound correctly even after they have just done so. This reminds everyone that the job of exploration must continue. Consequently, my overriding goal of keeping everyone exploring and experimenting is not undermined by using students as a model whenever appropriate.

'Because of the fact that no model has been offered, students know only what they are doing and see that some of the things they do make them capable of improving their performance. They cannot deny their own progress, collectively. They often enjoy the feeling that the group dynamics has brought them opportunities to be more effective faster.'

Gattegno (1976)

LISTEN FIRST OR PRODUCE FIRST?

Since our ear is an unreliable guide to the sounds of a foreign language, it is problematic to attempt to use our hearing to train our pronunciation. It is also rather inefficient: first one has to educate one's ear to hear new L2 sounds reliably, and only then is one in a position to work on the challenge of production—the job of modifying the way the muscles of the mouth move.

Nevertheless, many people believe that it is necessary for a student to be able to hear a sound in order to be able to pronounce it, because otherwise how could he know what he is aiming for. It's true that a learner's productions must be evaluated, but Gattegno realised that he doesn't have to be the source of the evaluation. Instead, it is more efficient for the teacher, as his expert coach, to take this role.

Within the production-first paradigm of the Silent Way, students hear themselves as they speak. If they are being encouraged to move their muscles differently, then they are at the same time training their ear to hear slightly different modulations of the sound produced at each try. When they reach a satisfactory level of production for a sound, they have also gained the ability to hear it. Both jobs can, and should, be done at the same time.

STARTING OUT

This chapter describes how I work with beginners in English. For students who already have some English, I work in a different way, doing little work on the pronunciation of individual sounds in any detail unless it is necessary (see Chapter 22).

The way of beginning the work that I am about to describe is just one of many possibilities. The choices I make at any time are guided by the successes and failures of my students. If they find a particular sound easy, we move on. If a student has trouble with a sound or a chain of sounds, we work on it until it becomes easier.

It takes time, perhaps the whole length of the course, to reach a good level of pronunciation. We therefore begin with a major effort on pronunciation for a few hours, then continue the work in dozens of micro-lessons lasting from a few seconds to a minute or two whenever necessary until the end of the course.

I use the rough sketch of a cross-section of a head to guide students to explore their mouths.

Scan to watch a video of this process of sensitisation. This example was part of a French class but the sensitisation process is exactly the same. Note the postures adopted to speak French and English are totally different.

MEANING CAN WAIT

For beginners, meaning would be a distraction at this point. I want the class to be focused on this one thing—sound production. So for now, we simply work on sounds and chains of sounds. Introducing meaning would throw the students into a mindset of memorising words, and this would be a distraction from the precise work they should be doing on their sound-making system. I want the students to be learning to produce the sounds and rhythms of English and to control their breath as native speakers do. Everything else is extraneous at this point.

OFF WE GO

On the board I draw a very simple cross-section of the mouth, showing the lips, the teeth and the alveolar ridge. I do this quickly so that no pretence is made of it being well done. The drawing only has to be recognisable. When I need to use this picture, I place my hand, or point, to indicate what my tongue is doing.

I run my pointer over the drawing, silently asking the students to feel the roof of their mouth. Following the pointer, they slowly run the tip of their tongue from the biting edge of their upper front teeth, up the teeth to the gums, moving back until they get to the flat part behind the teeth. Then they come to the alveolar ridge, then to the hard palate and further back, the soft palate. I can encourage them to do this slowly simply by how I move my pointer or my hand over the drawing. I particularly want them to notice the alveolar ridge, so I move my pointer from the flat part just behind the teeth to the hard palate and back, several times, exaggerating with my pointer the sensation of the bump as they move their tongues back and forth over the ridge.

I show with my hand held against the drawing how the tongue is hollowed out a little in the middle, with the two sides lifted and tethered against the molars. This position is the 'speech-ready' position for English. The tip of the tongue is entirely free in its movements and is very relaxed. It hovers just under the alveolar ridge. It can flick upwards, forwards or backwards for all the sounds made in this area of the mouth. The fact that it is so relaxed means that a puff of air is enough to blow it off the alveolar ridge in an aspirated /t/. I work with the drawing and my hands, indicating what I want the students to feel.

I know I will have to come back to this idea of the 'speech-ready' position and work on it more as the course progresses.

PRONUNCIATION

THE RECTANGLE CHART

I hang the Rectangle chart on the wall.

I find it useful to begin with the easiest sounds, those which exist in almost all languages. At the beginning, I only want to establish the rules of the game, so I avoid starting with the difficulties. However, I soon begin work on those sounds which will require the most practice. I want to give the students all the time they need over the length of the course to experiment with these sounds so as to reach a good level of facility in their speech. I want speaking English to become easy.

What takes place during the first few hours has the same function as babbling in babies. We all did it in our cribs when we put into place the feedback circuits necessary for learning to speak our first foreign language, our mother tongue.[2] Now we do it again for English.

I don't want the students to memorise either the colours or the places of the rectangles on the chart. This is not why the work is being done. The students may well retain the places of some or all of the rectangles, as well as the sound each triggers, because each sound comes up many times, but they do not do this through a deliberate act of memorisation. In fact, if I realise that a student is trying to memorise the chart, I always ask him to stop, though he will probably be unable to stop himself from doing so—'memorisers' find it difficult to change this habit. But I make the request and I reiterate it. The correspondence between the sounds and the colours is established by use and familiarity, not through memorisation. A few students never learn the correspondences between the colours and the sound on the chart; if they do their 'mouth gymnastics' conscientiously, I'm happy with their work.

The first vowel /ɑ:/ as in PALM

I begin with the rectangle in the vowel section of the chart corresponding to the sound /ɑ:/. I choose this sound because all the languages in the world seem to have it or something like it, and its production never poses a problem—one simply opens one's mouth and makes a sound and this is the sound that usually comes out. The students will be able to make the sound easily and will therefore be free to put into place the conventions of the pointing games we will be working with.

I touch this rectangle and say the sound once; the students need to know what game we are playing. I make a gesture which invites them to say the sound. Then I touch the rectangle once again; they are to

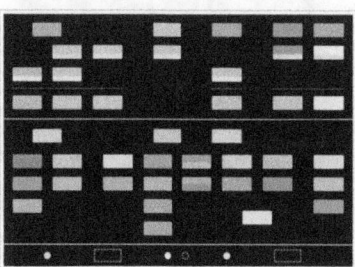

The Rectangle chart—all of the sounds of British English

[2] *For more on how children learn to speak, see* The Universe of Babies, *by Caleb Gattegno, 1973.*

For convenience, the phonetician John Wells created a list of words chosen for their lack of ambiguity from the point of view of the pronunciation of the vowels they contain.

By convention these words are written in capital letters e.g. PALM *here. The complete list appears at https://en.wikipedia.org/wiki/Lexical_set*

> 'The Rectangle chart is used only for work on pronunciation and all related areas like intonation, stress, melody. When I work with it, I am not necessarily concerned about whether my students understand what they are saying. Their full attention is focussed on the work they have to do with their throats, lips, tongues, including their learning how to breathe in new ways. The beauty of an instrument like this lies in its utter simplicity: I can pin it up to a wall and begin my work, with no other fuss. Because I can make students utter some sounds through visual clues, I am freed from having to utter these sounds or sentences for them. I can remain silent.'
>
> Bartoli (1981)

Scan to watch a video of the process of using one student who gets something right to help the others

make the sound. In these thirty or so seconds, two conventions are established between the students and me:

> ONE: They know we have associated a sound with a coloured rectangle.
>
> TWO: They know that when a rectangle is touched, they should say its sound.

They also know that /ɑː/ is associated with this purple rectangle. Now we can introduce a game.

Working on sequences to produce rhythms

I touch the rectangle twice and they say the sound twice using the same rhythm as I used when I pointed. Next, I point twice, followed by a pause and then a third time, and they say the sound three times using the rhythm indicated. If I accelerate the pointing, they will speak using this rhythm.

Students often begin saying what I am pointing before I have finished; if so, I signal to them to wait until the end of the pointing before speaking. This will quickly give us two more conventions:

> THREE: The students should follow the rhythm I suggest with my pointing.
>
> FOUR: They must not begin to say the chain until I have finished pointing it.

I can also ask the students to come out and point—people like doing this. I get them to point different chains of this sound, while their classmates say them. In this case, it is useful to put into place a rule that when students point, *Give us whatever rhythm you like, but no more than five touches.*

When I am satisfied that the sound is right and the conventions established—two or three minutes of work at most—we can go on to a second sound.

The second vowel—/iː/ as in FLEECE

For the second vowel, I usually choose /iː/. This sound is very common in languages and should not pose any significant problems.

This time I will not have to say the sound. I need only touch the red rectangle and then, indicating my lips, stretch them to encourage everyone to say it; someone in the class will say something similar to what I want. I ask him to say it again and the class uses him as a model. I might intervene so that the sound is produced slightly longer or shorter. I can hold my hands almost together and then spread them further and further apart to prompt a variety of durations, later homing in on the correct length. I will then do the same job on rhythms as I did on the previous sound, first touching only /iː/, then combining /iː/ with /ɑː/ and varying the sequence of sounds.

Working on intonation

Now I point to the /ɑː/ rectangle and draw an upward sloping line in the air with the pointer. The students say the sound with rising intonation. Those who are not sensitive to the pitch of their voice will find this task difficult or even impossible. I work on this for a few minutes and then pause and return to it later. We have time.

Teaching pronunciation without modelling the sound—showing the mouth shape plus feedback and coaching is sufficient.

In this way, a further convention is introduced:

> FIVE: English has rising and falling intonations. I will use gestures or point intonation in the air to guide students towards the correct pattern.

The significance of this job must be emphasised. We have just introduced English as a language musically alive with rhythm and pitch, yet the students have said only two sounds. They have used /ɑː/ and /iː/ to experiment with variations in these parameters. I continue this work for only a few minutes. This lesson is not the last on pronunciation, and I will come back to intonation as often as necessary as we work on the next sounds. I do, however, want these students to be aware of their problems. If they cannot master moving their voice up or down as we work on it today, I might smile and shrug, indicating, *Don't worry. You'll manage tomorrow.*

We are now ready to introduce additional sounds, integrating them into the basic rhythmic and intonation patterns. Even counting the work done on intonation, the lesson began only five to ten minutes ago.

The third vowel—/uː/ as in GOOSE

A good choice for the third vowel is the sound /uː/, which is dark green on the chart. It is quite distinct from the other two already in circulation, and something like it is also common in languages around the world, though with a variety of pronunciations.

Scan to watch the author introducing sounds to a class of French speakers.

This sound is more likely than the previous ones to be poorly pronounced, as it is a vowel that is further back in other languages and often rounded, while in English it is pronounced more towards the front of the mouth and with unrounded lips. This is the first time that a real job might have to be done to obtain the desired sound, even if this job is not difficult.

I point to the dark green rectangle, and mime the sound, advancing my lips just a shade. But I don't say it, so the students can only find it by guesswork. Everyone has a try, and at least one student is likely to provide something similar to the required sound.

Many will round their lips. I pat my lips flat with my fingers to indicate to them that they should not do this.

I indicate which student manages to pronounce it best and which students have to change radically in order to reach the sound. I try never to actually say it.

Once the job of exploration has been undertaken by everyone and they know the nature of the sound they are trying to produce, even if it's not perfect, I can go on to another sound. For example, I might introduce glides between /ɑː/ and /iː/ or between /ɑː/ and /uː/. These sounds will suggest the diphthongs /aɪ/ and /au/ which are quite foreign sounds for many students. The aim here is to put the students in contact with movements that are different from what they are used to. I do this for a few minutes. I am looking for exploration, for contact with the unknown.

In working this way, the students have taken the first steps towards putting into place the double system (see Chapter 8) which will eventually allow them to catch their own mistakes. Each student possesses this system for his own language and must construct a new system from scratch in this new language. Poor pronunciation is assured if he applies the criteria of his mother tongue to the language he is learning.

The students need to hear any sound said by both male and female voices, clear and muffled. During this work, variety is important.

I need not rush, time is on my side. Reaching the sounds is but one of several aims. At this stage of the work, my overriding aim is to get the students to reinvest in their mouths, putting their presence in muscles they have not consciously used for years. So it is actually beneficial if no one manages to reach perfection immediately. For the work they are doing now, exploration is more important than quick results.

The first consonant—/m/

The word *consonant* means *sound with*. Consonants should always be said with a vowel to ensure correct pronunciation, even if some can be produced in isolation. Physically, the plosives like /t/ and /p/ can only be pronounced properly with a vowel.

The first consonant I introduced is /m/, situated in the consonant section of the chart and coloured bright orange. This consonant is by far the easiest: it is only necessary to close the mouth and make a noise, and /m/ is produced. I touch /m/ then /ɑ:/, then close my lips and open them, mouthing the syllable /mɑ:/.

The introduction of /m/ allows us to use syllables such as /mɑ:/, /mi:/ and /mu:/ and also /u:m/ /i:m/ and /ɑ:m/ and then /mɑ:mi:/, /mi:mɑ:/, /mu:mu:/, and many others. Small 'sentences' become possible.

Usually at this point, I introduce the idea of reversal. I touch the purple rectangle with the tip of the pointer, then looking fixedly at it, theatrically 'transport' the sound to my middle finger and virtually place it there. I do the same for the sound /m/, 'lifting' it from the orange rectangle and placing it on my index finger. I might need to do this twice the first time the students are exposed to it. The palm of my hand is facing the students. I indicate that I want them to speak. They say /mɑ:/. Then I turn my hand around so that the palm is facing me; in this way I show the inversion I want to hear. Some of the students say /ɑ:m/ and the others hear this, see my gesture and understand immediately.

I want my students to think in terms of transformations from the very beginning. Hand gestures like this will be important later.

The second consonant—/t/

The sound /t/, represented by a fuchsia-coloured rectangle, is a good choice for our second consonant. It allows some real words in English to be formed: *tea, tar, toot, tart* and combines easily with /m/ to make words such as *meet, team, mart,* etc. Sound combinations which resemble words can also be used.

Using the drawing of the mouth, I show that the tip of my tongue touches a place on the alveolar ridge. Someone is likely to find the sound I am looking for. However if a student proposes /l/, I might decide to work on /l/ before /t/, since someone has put it into circulation. The order of introduction of the sounds is not important. As I

> 'Silence is a precise technique used in this approach and it is a very important one. Because I remain silent, my students become more daring and take more risks. Through hand gestures, facial expressions and other techniques. I guide my students towards the utterance of the correct sounds, intonation, stress, word grouping and so on. The atmosphere of my classes has definitely changed since I became silent. Students take their mistakes and blunders with far greater lightheartedness. Everything acquires a game-like quality in which things are not just right or wrong but rather explored. Their throats are explored, their hypotheses, and other students' hypotheses, too.'
>
> Bartoli (1981)

said at the beginning of the chapter, this is one possible progression, not a rigid sequence.

I go on and introduce the third consonant.

The third consonant—/p/

This consonant allows us to work on an essential aspect of English, speech breathing, because speech breathing is very apparent with this sound. The students need to become aware that their lips and cheeks must be very relaxed—so relaxed, indeed, that the lips can be blown apart by the pulse of air generated by the abdomen. To begin with, then, I ask the students to stand, arms akimbo, and to snort: to expel air through their noses using pulses of air generated by the movement of muscles in the abdomen. Snorting is the easiest way I have found to make them sensitive to their abdominal muscles.

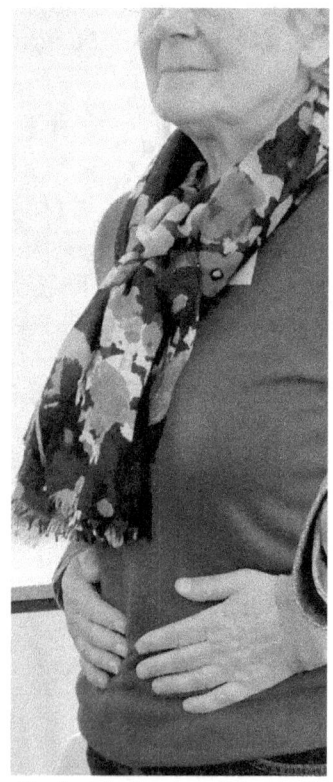

Student feeling her abdominal muscles at work.

Once the students feel more or less at ease doing this, I ask them to use the same muscular movement to produce /piː/. Without actually making a sound, I point to /piː/ on the chart, mouthing the first sound. Some will guess /p/, although occasionally, someone might propose /b/. I choose to continue with /p/ because the work I want them to do is more obvious with this sound. I demonstrate that my lips are very relaxed, exaggerating even, so that it is easily visible.

We change vowels in order to try other combinations: /piː/ /pɑː/, etc., then /piːp/, /pɑːt/, /pɑːm/ etc.

Now we are in a position to come back to /t/ and work on it in a similar way. In the students' L1, /t/ is likely to be made using a firm contact between the blade of the tongue and the alveolar ridge. For English, students should check that their tongue is in the speech-ready position and then simply raise the tip to the alveolar ridge for the /t/ closure. They should make the tongue as relaxed as the lips and cheeks were when making a /p/. I want the students to get a feel for the way the tip of the tongue can be blown off the alveolar ridge by the air pressure pulse behind it. This creates authentic English aspiration naturally.

However, I never spend too much time on this at this point because to reap the full benefits of this work, we need to introduce the schwa.

The introduction of the schwa /ə/— the last sound in COMMA

By now, the students should know how I expect them to function in class and we can begin work on the heart of English, the *schwa*, and with it, the *schwi* and the *schwu*, though these two will receive less attention to begin with.

The schwa is represented by the small yellow dot located at the very bottom of the Rectangle chart. The schwi is represented by the pale pink dot to its left, and the schwu by the pale green one. Pink and green reflect the 'families' of these sounds. The pink dot is exactly below /i:/, while the schwu dot is exactly below /u:/. Schwi includes what is sometimes called the 'happY' vowel and the so-called 'weak /ɪ/'. Schwu appears, for example, when *to* precedes a vowel: *to India*.

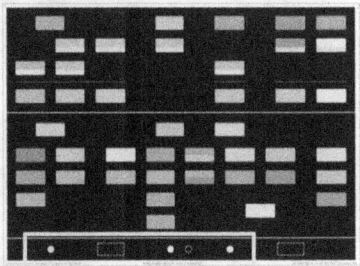

The Rectangle chart—the schwa family of sounds.

The small size of these three dots and their position at the bottom of the chart indicate that the sounds they represent are much shorter than the others and have little or no energy. None of them ever carries any form of stress.

The sounds in the schwa family are very common but the schwa itself can be almost imperceptible to foreign ears. When foreigners complain that English speakers 'swallow their words', the schwa is to blame. It is this sound which creates the rhythms so characteristic of English. It must be mastered if one wishes to acquire good pronunciation.

Working on schwa—the energy of English

During the work described below, I get the students to work consciously with their abdominal muscles so as to obtain the stress patterns created by the juxtaposition of the stressed syllables and the unstressed schwa, thus incorporating speech breathing into the work.

I indicate by pointing on the Rectangle chart, and if necessary, by using my hands, which syllables should be stressed and which should be reduced.

When I use my hand, I might lift one hand to the level of my shoulders for accentuated syllables and lower it to my waist for reduced syllables, that is, all the syllables which contain a schwa. The students quickly realise that the 'high' signal corresponds to a stressed syllable, and therefore to some combination of several parameters: an increase in energy or in length and/or a change of pitch. The 'low' signal corresponds to an unstressed syllable and, therefore, to a fall, or even a collapse of energy. I will use these gestures during the whole course.

I now ask them to say the sound in isolation. I use my fingers to indicate that it has to be very small. The job now is to add this sound to the combinations that we've just worked on.

BACK PUSHING

Back pushing usually helps students to experience the rush of air out of their lungs when I push them hard on their back.

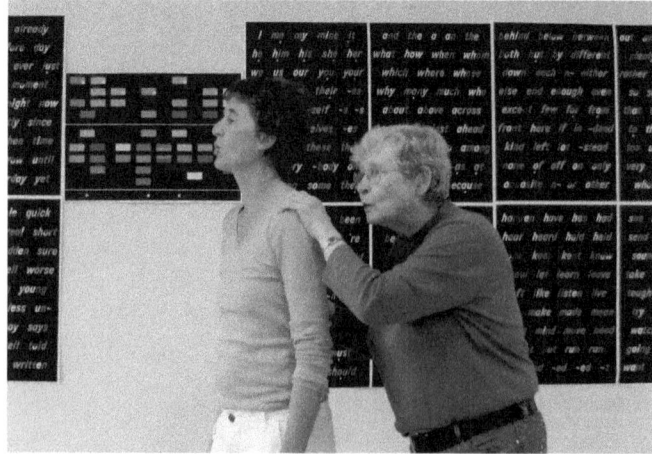

MAKING CIRCLES

I stand facing the student and take their hand. As they speak, I make wide and powerful circles with their hand. The stress is always marked from the bottom upwards.

This gesture seems to have the effect of emptying their lungs to some extent, and usually produces a heightened sense of the balance between the strength of the accentuated syllables and the low energy of the schwa family.

The signs introduced here—a dot and a slash—can later be transferred to writing. When I write sentences on the board with the intention of working on pronunciation, I mark each schwa by putting a dot under the written vowel of the syllable and each stress by putting a slash above and to the left of the syllable.

I use a tilde ~ for secondary stress. I place this below the syllable.

For example:

Peter, Peter Palmer, apart

/.   /.   /.   ./

tar, tart, a tart, a tartar

/   /   ./   ./.

I mark the stresses and reduced sounds as indicated—the small dots represent the schwa, as on the charts, and the slash represents the stressed syllable.

I show *tar* and *tart* with natural descending intonation—the students usually use this of their own accord—then *a tart* for which the first beat is low and the second high/falling, and finally *a tartar* with the stressed syllable high for *tar-* and with two low schwa sounds, *a* and *-tar*.

Using the small number of sounds available, I now lead my students through a series of words and phrases, gradually building up the number of syllables, thus increasing the number of stressed syllables and of schwas around them. I get them to stand, arms akimbo, and use their speech breathing to create the pulses of air on which these words are spoken, each pulse giving a stressed syllable, with all the syllables containing schwa sounds being produced on the rest of the air.

In their experiments, they soon realise that their mouths and chests do not always do what they want them to, that they remain captured by their mother tongue. It's challenging and often quite funny when they feel that their bodies do not immediately obey their mental instructions. It usually requires many attempts before they can take conscious control of these habits. In this first lesson, perfection is not required. They only need to begin to internalise the rhythms of English together with the muscular gestures which generate them, and we have lots of time—the whole course is there before us, with the many micro-lessons it will contain.

We might continue with

mart, martyr, a martyr with the rhythms shown here:

/   /.   ./.

I work in the same way for everything that follows.

Scan to watch a video on teaching stress and speech breathing.

| me, | meat, | meter, | a meter, | a meat-eater |

/   /   /•   •/•   •/ ~•

Since English is a language whose rhythms are as important as its sounds, we are now working on the key to good pronunciation in English. The students must look out for the stressed syllables and use them when they speak, but more especially, they must also learn to reduce the sounds of the schwa family.

It is better to treat a few sentences in depth early in the course to establish a real understanding of the rhythms of English and the way these are generated by speech breathing, rather than skimming superficially over many examples without reaching an understanding of the problem. Until the end of the course, they will need to work on speech breathing, and stress and reduction at the same time so that these come together naturally.

HELPING THOSE WHO FIND ENGLISH BREATH CONTROL DIFFICULT

Some students find the breath control of English difficult. Here are two techniques which I have found usually help them.

BACK PUSHING. I place myself behind a student who is finding it difficult to say a sentence that sounds English. I put the flat of my right hand on his back, I put my left hand on his shoulder to steady him, and then I ask him to say the sentence again. As he utters each stressed syllable, I push him firmly in the back so that the air rushes out. The first time, students are very surprised and laugh, but they soon feel the movement, and then when they have a problem with a sentence, they often spontaneously stand and turn their back to me to be pushed.

MAKING CIRCLES. Sometimes, I stand facing the student and take his hand. I shake it gently from left to right a couple of times to make sure the whole arm is relaxed, then ask him to say the sentence. As he speaks, I make wide and powerful circles with his hand. The stress is always marked from the bottom upwards, as an up-beat which starts at the bottom of the circle, rather than as a down-beat (as stamping would require), so that the main thrust of the gesture is upwards.

Panting

This gesture seems to have the effect of emptying his lungs to some extent, and usually produces a heightened sense of the balance between the strength of the accentuated syllables and the low energy of the schwa family.

Another way I ask students to work is to imitate a dog, panting slowly on a warm day. I ask them to do this, then to snort on each pant instead of simply breathing in and out. Then I ask them to place a syllable on each panting movement, *hah, hah, hah*, and to feel what is driving the movement. This helps them to feel the breath pulse being produced for each syllable. Then we can place a suitable sentence on each pulse—*a hundred and fifty, four hundred and sixty*—reducing all the other syllables as much as possible.

STUTTERING

In English, I say to the class, stuttering as I speak, *Dddo pppeople in your cccountry ssspeak lllike this?* They nod. I want them to become aware of the sound that is caught between the consonants when one stutters. I ask them to stutter /t/, /p/ and /m/ and put these into the words we already have available: *ttteam, pppalm, mmmost*; each now has three syllables, only one of which has a true vowel in it.

The introduction of /f/

This sound is useful now because it will enable us to work on the schwa in context. Once the students can produce /f/ easily, I get them to stutter it, and then backchain two stutters of /f/ into *An offer for Fred*.

Then I can ask them to 'stutter' an /f/ into a /t/. (Strictly speaking, this is not a stutter, but it is analogous to it.) We can write the combination as /f.t/. On the chart, I touch the /f/ several times as they stutter, but then show them that I will point the black dot between each consonant when I am 'stuttering' from one to the next. If I go directly from one consonant to the next, without using the black dot, then the sounds overlap, creating a consonant cluster. *Police/please* and *terrain/train* are examples of words distinguished by 'stuttering' and overlap, or open and close transitions in technical terminology.

We then work on *Tea for two* and *two for tea*, using this very reduced form of *for* as a stutter instead of the full version of the word. Once the /n/ has been introduced we will come back to this, join the two, and add the next lines of the song: *Tea for two/ and two for tea./ Tea for you/*

Scan to watch a video on using stuttering to teach students to make reduced sounds

and you for me. Usually students who have already studied English do not recognise the words they are saying, even if they know the song.

They can now compare how they used to say these words with what will be an impressively authentic new rendition that they themselves are able to produce.

The students have now started to experience the otherness of English: its breath control, its articulatory setting and now its system of reduction. They are truly entering into a <u>foreign</u> language, but they are doing this through learning motor skills. This they can do. They can be confident of success, as they would be if they were taking up playing a new sport or a new musical instrument.

The introduction of /s/

Putting the sound /s/ into circulation allows new combinations. To obtain this sound, I pull my lips back a little to show my teeth and make a little movement with my fingers beside my mouth to evoke the turbulence that is one characteristic of this sound. I might also touch the alveolar ridge on the drawing. Someone usually gets it, although from my gesture /z/, /ʃ/ or even /ʒ/ might appear. I could accept the first or second and start with one of them, but /ʒ/ is too uncommon to make it a good choice at this point.

Supposing that /s/ is chosen, the series in the sidebar is now possible with what is available. Series like these help to highlight the role of the schwa and the way it is inserted into words and sentences.

> **INTRODUCING /s/**
>
> *see, seem, seat, a seat, a seater, a two-seater...*
>
> *tea, team, a team, steam, a steamer...*
>
> *are, art, mart, a mart, smart, smarter, a smart mart, a smarter mart...*

AFTER THIS...

A teacher should not set out to follow the description given above to the letter. She should let herself be tempted into introducing other sounds if it feels natural, perhaps by integrating the students' names into the lesson and pointing *Leila, Anna, Marie, Masa, Ali* or *Mamadou* on the Rectangle chart. This is all beneficial.

The pedagogy behind the Silent Way allows teachers to give themselves as much flexibility as they like. But it also precludes them from establishing lesson plans, except at a very general level. The teacher's role is not to teach a planned lesson but to remain 'glued' to the reality of the class, to follow the students as they learn. It would be impossible in a book like this to address all the pronunciation problems which might come up, and there are always students who have specific unexpected problems.

Therefore, I now leave the 'step-by-step guide' and only give a more general idea of what might be done sound by sound, without taking into account what has been done previously. The indications given below are to be incorporated into a lesson as and when they are useful. It is for the reader to 'sew' the available sounds into a coherent whole so as to make the words and sentences the class needs. This is why no two lessons are ever the same. They are invented as we go along in response to what comes up.

When working on a new sound, if no one can provide it then I indicate by gesture who is closest and whether each new try is closer to or further from the goal I have in mind. As soon as one student begins to close in on it, I can use him as a model. I ask him to make the sound again, check that his attempt is useful for us and gesture for the others to follow his example.

THE OTHER VOWELS OF THE FIRST LINE

The three vowels already in circulation are all from the top line of the chart. The other vowels of this line can be introduced quite rapidly.

The sounds /ɜː/ and /ɔː/

The sounds /ɜː/ (NURSE—peach-coloured on the chart) and /ɔː/ (NORTH—dark brown) require some attention, especially for speakers who are used to rounding their lips for similar sounds in their L1. The English language uses very little labialisation (pushing one's lips forward in a rounded position). When I am showing students what sound we are dealing with, I might push my lips forward just enough for them to see what sound they should be aiming for. I then use a gesture to show that the lips remain more or less flat for English. These vowels can be linked to the consonants already in circulation to make new words.

THE FOURTH LINE OF VOWELS

The vowels in the top line are all unchecked or 'long' vowels. Those in the fourth line are checked. (Checked vowels are always followed by a consonant—*sit*—while unchecked vowels can finish a syllable—*see*.) Checked vowels need to be controlled by the con-

---

> **INTRODUCING**
> /ɔː/ AND /ɜː/
>
> *More, morse, mortar, mortars, a mortar...*
>
> *Sort, a sorter, taut, tauter, storm, a storm.*
>
> As other consonants are introduced, more combinations become possible. The schwa family of sounds is used constantly. For example, in the following sentences, the word *is* would be pointed using a schwi.
>
> *Saul is tall, Paul is short.*
>
> In the sentence *Paul is shorter than Saul or Maud*, only the three names would be pointed in the top section of the chart. I would point the word *or* in the upper vowel section then 'drag it down' virtually to the schwa section to show that the vowel is pronounced, but not stressed.
>
> *Paul talks to Maud on the lawn. Maud yawns and falls. Poor Maud!*
>
> *Sir, stir, terse, a stir, a stirrer...*
>
> *Term, a term...*
>
> As we move forward, I introduce as many sentences as possible which give students access to the schwa family of sounds.

sonant that follows them, so they should always be followed by a consonant even when they are only being practised.

The sound /ɪ/ as in KIT

This sound will be very useful, and can be introduced early. It allows us to use *it, it's* and *is* (once /z/ is available) and so gives us the possibility of creating more varied sentences, sentences which are more elaborate than those used during the first half hour of work on this chart.

The sound /e/ as in DRESS

This sound should not be a particular problem, as many languages have it or another which is similar. It may require 'tuning' to sound English.

The sound /æ/ as in TRAP

This sound is uncommon in other languages, and can be quite difficult for students to find and produce if their articulatory setting is incorrect. The phonetic symbol gives a good indication of what to aim for: an /a/ with a strong dose of /e/. Since it is also a good starting point for one of the diphthongs, it is worth spending a little time to make sure students can make it correctly.

While the students are working on this sound, I often introduce a gesture with which I can accompany it so as to trigger it when necessary. I place my hands on either side of my mouth as if I were using a loudspeaker and then sharply move them a few centimetres away from each other, encouraging the students to open their mouths more and separate their lips. Later, when the /æ/ rectangle will be linked to /u/ (schwu) one to create the diphthong /aʊ/, I will use the same gesture at the beginning, but I will bring my hands round together again to indicate the closing induced by the schwu at the end.

It can be useful to hook one's index finger over one's nose and one's thumb under one's chin, so as to appreciate with one's fingers that the sounds /ɪ/, /e/ and /æ/ require the mouth to be more and more open. One only need lower one's jaw to move from /ɪ/ to /e/ and again from /e/ to /æ/.

The sound /ʊ/ as in FOOT

This is not usually a difficult sound. It can be obtained starting from the green /uː/ sound, and then tuning it so that it is shorter and sharper.

Some students might have a tendency to round their lips and this is to be discouraged.

The sound /ɒ/ as in CLOTH

This sound is not rounded as similar sounds are in many languages. The lips remain more neutral. It is considered to be a short sound in English but in American English it is often longer than other sounds in this line.

This sound is unusual in that the British English pronunciation is very different from that used in American English which is much more open. The difference between these two types of English will be dealt with later in this chapter. This sound can be reached by starting with /ɔ:/, opening the mouth wider and unrounding the lips even more.

The sound /ʌ/ as in STRUT

This sound is not usually a problem, since it can be reached as a shortened version of the purple sound /ɑ:/, the first sound introduced. /ʌ/ sometimes becomes a problem for some students when its spelling appears, since the most common spellings are the letters <o> and <u>. We find it in words like *come*, *love* or *month*, and also *cup*, *Sunday* and *Monday*.

Many students find the <o> spelling for this sound counterintuitive, but in the work being done here—simply learning to say the sounds—problems linked to spelling do not yet exist.

THE SECOND AND THIRD LINES—THE DIPHTHONGS

A diphthong is a vowel sound which begins in one place and glides in the direction of one of the schwa family of sounds. As soon as one of the starting vowels is in place, work can begin on the diphthong(s) which use that vowel.

Diphthongs involve movement. Many students find it difficult to make sure that their diphthongs do move from the starting position, whichever it is, towards one of the schwa family of sounds.

Students also need to develop a sense of the energy balance the diphthongs require. The energy of the diphthong is always on the first part. They are shown on the chart as rectangles predominantly made up of their starting element and finishing with a schwi, a schwu or a schwa. This visual presentation helps students to understand that the second element must be audible, but it must be reduced. It 'trails off'.

Thus there are two challenges. One will be for students to 'glide towards' the final sound, resisting the temptation to say only the first one, even when speaking quickly. The other challenge, just as important, will be to get the energy balance right between the first and second elements.

I have several ways of indicating this change in energy. For example, I can close my fingers energetically into a fist and then open them, letting them sag. I can hold my wrist up and then let my hand drop as I take out the muscle tone. I can 'collapse' upon myself as if I have been hit in the stomach, indicating the lowering of the muscle tone. There are many visual metaphors for what the mouth does, but the students have to translate this into the physical actions necessary to get their mouth muscles to produce the desired effect. My best tool here is feedback: using gestures, I constantly let them know whether they are moving in the right direction.

The first line of diphthongs contains those which glide towards schwi—thus /aɪ/ as in PRICE, /eɪ/ as in FACE and /ɔɪ/ as in CHOICE— and towards schwu, /aʊ/ as in MOUTH and /əʊ/ as in GOAT. These are called the 'closing' diphthongs because the gliding movement tends to close the mouth.

Note that these five diphthongs are all either words or expletives in their own right: *I, eh?, Oi!, Ow!, Oh!*

The centring diphthongs

There are three centring diphthongs—diphthongs which finish with schwa—/ɪə/ (NEAR), /eə/ (SQUARE) and /ʊə/ (CURE). With the centring diphthongs, the loss of energy in the second half of the sound is particularly noticeable. I use the hand gestures described above to indicate this.

The triphthongs

Last come the triphthongs. These are made up of a vowel followed by a first sound from the schwa family, either schwi or schwu, and then a second which is always a schwa, the weakest sound in the language. The triphthongs are not represented on the Rectangle chart because the balance between the different elements is more easily acquired if they are broken down into their constituent parts. Again, I let my hand go limp for the schwa parts of these sounds to show the changes in energy between their various constituents.

OTHER CONSONANTS

The sounds /r/ and /ʃ/

The problem students have with the sound /r/ stems from the fact that the front of the tongue has no firm contact with the mouth and so it is difficult for them to locate the sound. Students are often tempted to try to make contact somewhere in order to sense something tangible.

The tip of the tongue is situated just behind and below the alveolar ridge, leaving space for air to pass. The sound /t/ is produced just a little in front of /r/ and can be used as a starting point. If I produce a /t/ on the back side of the alveolar ridge, and then pull my tongue back horizontally, letting the /t/ explode very, very slowly, I go through the position of /r/. The sound /ʃ/ is also produced in the same area.

Both /ʃ/ and /r/ are often associated with /t/, the first in the sound /tʃ/, the second in the consonant cluster /tr/. This in itself indicates that /t/ is a good place to start when looking for either of the other two.

The sound /n/

This sound is usually easy for most people though some may find it difficult to pronounce /n/ at the end of words if their language only contains open syllables.

The /n/ allows me to introduce the repetition of words, using *and* reduced to /n/ as English speakers so often do. It should be brought in quite early. For example, *steeper and steeper* pronounced /stiːpərənstiːpə/. Such sequences allow me to show several schwa sounds in close succession, useful practice of schwa at the same time.

In English, syllable-final /n/ is sometimes pronounced without letting the tongue move from its previous position, thus combining it with the preceding consonant. This occurs in words like *Edinburgh* or *sudden* where the previous sound is /d/. When /d/ has been produced, the tongue remains in place for the /n/, exploding the /d/ into the /n/.

It is not necessary for students to use this combining /n/ when they speak, but the surest way for them to learn to hear it is to have the experience of saying it.

RE-AWAKENING SENSITIVITY

If I speak my students' language, I say something like this:

> *What does your tongue do when you speak your language? How does it move? Feel it!...Feel where it is. When you stop speaking, where does it come to rest? Where is the tip now?*

> *Make an /s/.* (I would of course point to the rectangle, I wouldn't say the sound.) *Can you feel a little turbulence just behind your lips? For me, the turbulence hits my lower lip very close to the front of my mouth, just where the dry part of the lip joins the moist part.*

> *Can you feel the turbulence? Does it feel the same for /ʃ/ and for /s/? Is the turbulence in the same place? Now make a /θ/ sound. Where is the turbulence?*

> *Now make a /s/ sound again. Move your tongue back a little so there is no turbulence, and now lower your jaw a little. Leave room for the air to escape, and make a sound. What sound are you making?*

> *Now, make a /ʃ/ sound.*

> *Try now to put a /z/ behind this sound. What do you get? And behind this one? And this one? What can you feel? Can you feel the difference?*

Depending on whether they have managed to keep their tongues tethered against their back molars or not, the sound they make will be an /r/ for some students, an /l/ for others, or perhaps a different sound for still others. I will use one of them as a model, then another and another...to obtain these sounds from most of the students, then from all. The emphasis always will be on what can be felt.

I get them to compare the sensations they feel with /iː/ and /iːz/, /ɑː/ and /ɑːz/, for example. Then we might go on to /sɑː/ and /ɑː/, then all the sounds they have worked on up to now. I guide them through these exercises to re-awaken their sensitivity to their mouths. They have to feel the sensations, the 'textures' of the sounds, the levels of muscular energy, the degrees of flexibility, etc.

CONSONANT CLUSTERS

By now, we have more than enough consonants to work on consonant clusters if students find them difficult. Sequences of sounds like /st/ and then /str/ at the beginning of words can be difficult for people from some linguistic backgrounds.

I use /t/ as a starting point because it requires contact with the alveolar ridge and is easy to find. Starting from /t/ with the tip of the tongue placed midway between the alveolar ridge and the line where the teeth and the gums meet, I ask the students to create a very slight distance between the tongue and the ridge by blowing air to open up a space. In English, the tongue is relaxed compared to how it is held for many other languages and can easily be blown away from the alveolar ridge by pulses of air. Some of them find /θ/ immediately. Then, instead of blowing it away, if they move the tip of their tongue back very slightly and hollow it out, they will soon find /s/. I get them to feel the thin stream of air which hits the inside of the lower lip and cools it slightly. I ask the students to lick the inside of their lower lip so that the cool air is easy to detect. We go on to /ʃ/, feeling what it requires. The turbulence created is not the same for /s/ as for /ʃ/.

Now we can work on combinations. The /tθ/ at the end of a word like *eighth* can be learned relatively easily. They only have to make a very soft /t/ and gently blow it open. Similarly, starting from /t/ they can pull their tongue back a little and produce /tʃ/, feeling the pulse of air as they do so: /tʃ/, /tʃ/, /tʃ/, /tʃ/, like the noise people make to imitate a steam train starting to move away. Once they have laughed at this, I get them to re-engage with their mouths so as to work on the sensitivity they need. The /ks/ followed by /tθ/ at the end of *sixth* is fun to work on: the four successive consonants /kstθ/ require a high level of sensitivity. Although some native speakers don't use the /t/, I would instead ask the students to try and produce the sequence, just for practice. In the plural, this word is even more challenging!

All this work demands heightened sensitivity rather than exaggeration. We are fine-tuning, using tiny movements of the tongue, the smaller the better. The students need to discover the economy of movement these various gestures require.

MORE ON SPEECH BREATHING

To enable students to feel what happens when English is spoken, I ask them to stand and place their hands on their abdomen. Then I ask them to snort, to blow air out through their nose while leaving their mouth closed. This requires considerable muscular action of the abdomen which can easily be felt. We work on this for a moment and then I introduce words.

I choose a short sentence and ask the students to say it in their normal voice: *It's a quarter to ten*. Then I ask them to whisper it. When we whisper, the muscular movements necessary for speech are more obvious than when using normal speech. They can usually feel the muscular action of the abdomen necessary to produce the whispered sentence.

Now I ask them to use a stage whisper. This is the whisper that actors use when they have to make sure that what they whisper can be heard by everyone in the audience, no matter how far they are from the stage. This requires considerable effort on the part of the abdominal muscles and is easily felt.

I then introduce a cycle which makes evident these three levels of effort when saying the sentence. When students return to normal voice, I ask them to try to feel the subtle movements their abdominal muscles are making.

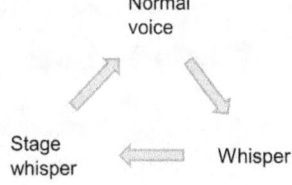

Students gradually learn to feel the movements of speech breathing used when native speakers speak. Then they will need to practise it until it becomes automatic. This may well take more time than the duration of the course, so learning to control their breath this way when speaking English is left in their hands.

THE IMPORTANCE OF THE ARTICULATORY SETTING

I always notice an improvement as soon as the articulatory setting for English is put into place. In Japanese, for example, the tip of the tongue is placed against the gums below the lower teeth, and the blade is against the teeth themselves, so that the tongue is bunched up in the front of the mouth and has lost a lot of its mobility. This articulatory setting explains why Japanese people change the /s/ sound to /ʃ/ in front of the vowel /i/, for example, or palatalise the sound /n/ before /i/. It is unnatural to say /si/ from this articulatory setting. It is also awkward

Scan to watch a video on articulatory settings.

to produce a consonant cluster. The tongue is not mobile enough to make the tiny movements that English requires.

Therefore the first thing to do is to make sure that students with articulatory settings which inhibit their pronunciation of English find the articulatory setting necessary for the language. They need to gain much more freedom for their tongues, so as to feel the tip of the tongue free to flick back and forth if they want to make the various clusters common in English. For example, the cluster /str/ requires only a few millimetres of movement around the alveolar ridge. The sequence /tʃt/ at the end of a word like *watched* becomes much easier if the articulatory setting is correct.

Students need to redevelop their sensitivity to their mouths, and to their tongues in particular. Until they have done so, they will have problems. But it is not hard to do and with a little time and practice, they rapidly achieve better results for pronunciation, which is encouraging.

The introduction of /h/

Some languages do not possess this sound, and speakers find it very difficult to learn, as they do not consciously control the opening and closing of their glottis (which is just behind their Adam's apple) and to be able to control this is imperative for reaching mastery of this sound.

It is possible to make things easier for them by getting them to feel what is called an 'effort closure'. I ask students to stand up and try to lift a very heavy object—a table which I am sitting on, for example—while watching what they do to their breath. The reflex in this situation is to block the column of air coming out of the lungs by closing the space just above the glottis using the false vocal folds. Students notice that they have stopped breathing, and I inform them, either in words or by using gestures, that this is because they have closed their airway. I ask them to open it and close it several times so that they realise this is under their control. I want them to be able to do this deliberately. When the airway is open, air passes out of their system unhindered. In everyday life, the airway is open because we breathe.

I ask the students to make a sound—/ɑː/ for example—and to be aware that they are saying it with the glottis closed at the beginning. The result is a rather abrupt onset, without /h/. Then they say /ɑː/ with the airway open. In this case, the result will be /hɑː/. They must do this very gently and very slowly in order to feel what they are doing and hear the changes in the sounds. When they can do this, they know what they are aiming for.

If students are to gain control over their glottis and then automatise this, a lot of practice will be necessary. It is useful to come back to this sound for several weeks, to virtually lift the table once or twice each day, to say /ɑː/ and /hɑː/ several times, in order to feel the airway opening and closing, and to say a few words with and without the /h/ sound. Gradually it becomes easier. After the first introduction to this sound, it is better to come back to it often than to spend a lot of time only once. What is certain is that without practice, no progress will be made.

The introduction of /ð/ *them* and /θ/ *thin*

Even though these sounds do not appear in many English words, they are very common because the words they do appear in are used so often. The words *there* and *their*, as well as the phrase *they're* which is so similar, and the group *the, this, that, these* and *those* are the most common words for /ð/. Many foreign speakers consider these sounds difficult. Both can be worked on at the same time.

There is no one right way to produce these consonants but students have often been taught to do more than is necessary. The tongue need not protrude out of the mouth between the teeth. For most speakers it stays behind the upper teeth almost in the same place as for /t/. Here again, the work is all about sensitivity, and not exaggeration. The movements have to be felt and internalised. The more seriously this work is done now, when the sounds are introduced, the less it will be necessary to come back to them later. As was done with /h/, /θ/ and /ð/ will however require a few minutes' attention every day for a few days.

For one way of producing /θ/ and /ð/, the tongue can be placed almost touching the flat area behind the teeth, leaving just enough space for air to flow over the surface of the tongue. Students have to take the time to explore their mouths and tongues slowly and deliberately, listening to the differences any tiny change creates.

When the students can feel and hear these differences more easily, I can come back to an exploration of more complex combinations, like /tθ/ to get ready for words like *eighth*, and then *month*, where the introduction of a /t/ helps pronounce the following sound.

/ð/ THEM AND /θ/ THIN

They, there, they are there. There they are! They are theirs. Theirs are there. Here they are. They are here. In the last three of these sentences, the word *are* is reduced to a schwa.

Think, sink, I think they're sinking. I think they're thinking.

This thing is theirs. That's their thing.

a hundred 'n' ten, a hundred 'n' ten to the tenth.

THE REDUCED FORMS

A long and careful job also needs to be done on the reduced forms of common words, and the reductions to be made when they are in certain contexts. During the hours spent on the Rectangle chart, these reductions are worked on without any reference to meaning. They are simply combinations of sounds that are common in English.

For example, in running speech *There are* is pronounced /ðərə/ in two beats, and later, will perhaps be shown on the board as either /ð•r•/ or th•r•, depending on the class, each dot representing a schwa. Once several examples have come up, the teacher only needs to ask (silently!) the question *How will you say this?* The students should be able to find the answers. This kind of work is done throughout the course, as and when it is necessary.

Some sequences provide an opportunity to come back to this work on the tiny movements of the tongue used when saying strings of consonants in phrases like /ə hʌndrəd ən ten tə ðə tenθ/ or, illustrating the schwa more clearly, /• hʌn dr•d •n ten t• ð• tenθ/. The tip of the tongue hardly moves from the alveolar ridge except during the sounds /ʌ/ and /e/; it is blown away by the puffs of air making the /t/ sounds; it produces the /ð/ of *the* and then rebounds to the ridge for the second /t/, the /n/ and the final /θ/, having moved only a millimetre or so from the end of the second syllable to the end of the phrase. I can illustrate this using the drawing of the mouth on the board. I place my fingers, which represent my tongue, on the alveolar ridge, move them away a shade then move them back for the /t/ which is the beginning of the next syllable. This is reminiscent of the stuttering work done before. I spend some time on this, in order to bring students to understand that pronunciation is about micro-movements, not about exaggerations.

AMERICAN ENGLISH: THE SCHWR

In different varieties of English—American, Australian, British, etc.—the vowel sounds can be rather different without causing problems. This is the case because English is united as one language not by the pronunciation of the vowel sounds but by the stress and reduction system. If the stresses are produced well and the schwa family of sounds are suitably reduced, the language will sound correct.

However there is a major difference between the British family of English dialects and the American and Canadian dialects. This is the use of the

Scan to watch a playlist of extracts from a conversation between the author and a colleague about teaching English pronunciation.

schwr sound in American English, the sound used by Americans at the end of words like *further, either*, and many others which contain the letter <r> at the end of a syllable.

On the American English chart, the third line of the the vowels contains the diphthongs which finish with schwr. The second line shows the other diphthongs. The schwr is pale orange to indicate its similarity with /ɜː/, and it is placed vertically below /ɜː/ and /r/ on the chart, in the schwa family section.

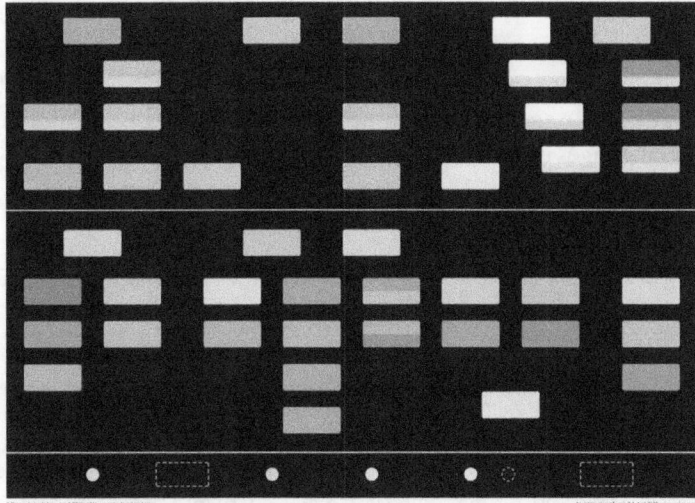

If students have difficulty producing schwr, I ask them to rub the sides of their tongue against the cutting edge of their molars until it hurts a little. This enables them to feel where their tongue is and what it is doing for about twenty seconds. I ask them to say a prolonged British /ɜː/, feeling where the various parts of the tongue are in their mouth and what they're doing with their tongue. Then I ask them to draw its body back slightly, and then curve the tip up towards the roof of the mouth before making the sound. Depending on how far they lift it, they will produce an increasingly strong schwr.

OTHER STRATEGIES FOR WORKING ON SOUNDS

Teachers have used many other strategies for students to discover how to pronounce the sounds on the Rectangle chart.

I might work with the names of the students. I can ask each student to point his name, I tune it to become its English version, and the student becomes the 'keeper' of the new sounds his name requires.

When the majority of the rectangles have been worked on, I can ask students to come out and point to words they know in English. Even beginners know many, though they are sometimes surprised to find out the origin of the words. This exercise is an excellent way to get students to understand the pronunciation changes English imposes on words like *Paris* or *Dublin*, *Scotland* or *Poland* where at least one syllable will contain a schwa or other reduced sound.

Using my hands, I might evoke a scale being played on a piano, then launch *do, re, mi, fa, so, la, ti, do*. (The scale in English is not exactly the same as the scale used in some European languages and perhaps other languages elsewhere.) This scale, if it is brought in early enough, allows me to add several new sounds during the phase of exploration of the Rectangle chart.

And work on the numbers, as described in the next chapter, can have begun by now, married into work on pronunciation.

If you are a native speaker of English, you may find that the discussion of Articulatory Settings has given you a new entry into the pronunciation of some other language that you speak.

If so, I suggest that you choose a performance piece (see the end of Chapter 22) in that language and devise some practice cycles that you can use to work on it. Note that the most common articulatory setting for languages includes the tongue tip lightly touching the back of the lower front teeth most of the time. But you will need to do your own research and experimentation for the language you choose.

10. Numbers

During the initial work on pronunciation, working on numbers and counting gives beginning students practice in pronunciation, melody and flow with what can become quite long utterances. This is important work to consolidate what they've learnt up to that point.

They gain the experience of using the language in a domain where meanings aren't problematic and where the teacher can minimise the amount of items that have to be memorised.

Furthermore, they make an early start on an aspect of the language in which it is extremely difficult to reach comfortable functional ease. Taught as items of vocabulary, numbers are rather dull; taught as a system, they give an early sense of satisfaction to students that they are on a road to mastery in English.

I construct a layout in stages. This is what it will look like at the end of the work.

			,	,	,	,	,		
	1	2	3	4	5	6	7	8	9
	11	12	13	14	15	16	17	18	19
	10	20	30	40	50	60	70	80	90

100								
	200	300	400	500	600	700	800	900
100								

832,646,981,321,764,324

THE NUMBERS UP TO NINE

I write the numbers 2, 4 and 6 on the board in their final place in the layout. I point to 2, then I show the sounds for it on the Rectangle chart. I do the same for 4 and 6. I get the students to repeat the words in chorus, varying the order of the three numbers as I point. The aim is for the students to learn the names of the numbers in isolation, rather than learning the series 1, 2, 3 …

It is surprising how many non-beginners can only recall the name of, say, eight, *by starting at* one *and counting up under their breath.*

I want the students to be able to name each number individually, without reference to any of the others although, of course, they must also learn to count up and down.

When the students are at ease with these three numbers, I add a fourth. Often I choose the number 8, because many students still need practice with the diphthong in this word, or 7, because it has two syllables and gives me the opportunity of bringing in stress and reduction. Then I might work on 9, and immediately after that, on 5, because these two have the same vowel sound. I get the students to practise the numbers we already have, adding the others to the line one by one until all nine numbers are on the board, as shown below.

    1   2   3   4   5   6   7   8   9

I mostly point to them out of sequence, but sometimes I point to them in order. As the students gain in ease, I accelerate my pointing. I adjust the speed of my pointing to the maximum speed the class can cope with at any time. By the end of this process, they are capable of saying these numbers as well as I can.

This stage might have lasted ten or fifteen minutes with beginning students.

Check the spelling

I hang the Numbers chart on the wall and, by holding out the pointer, ask the students to look for the words they have just learnt. They should be able to do this easily. I ask three students to come to the front, one to point to the numbers on the board, one to point on the Numbers chart and the third to point each number on the Rectangle chart. The colours give them all the clues they need.

THE NUMBERS UP TO NINETY-NINE

Skipping one line and writing on the third, I put a 0 exactly under the number 6 in the 'units' line. I point to the suffix *-ty* shown on the Numbers chart, associating 0 with *-ty*. Then I virtually slide the number

eight	five	two	four
nine	one	six	seven
three	fif	nin	ten -ty
thirteen	twelve		-teen
eigh	eleven		nought
twelf	twenty		forty
and	zero	thirty	-th
a	hundred	oh	-ieth
thousand	million		-h

The Numbers chart

6 down to its place, just to the left of 0, and I write 6 in this place—60. The students should say *sixty* spontaneously. Then I add 70, then 80, 90 and 40. I get the students to work on these five numbers until everyone can say them easily, speeding up my pointing as the students develop fluency.

A class working on the pronunciation of the numbers.

Now, starting again from 60, I get the students to say the word *sixty* and then I slide the pointer from 60 up to 6 on the top line so that they say *sixty … six*. I point the two numbers quickly, to indicate that the students must say them together—*sixty-six*. I work on all the possibilities from 61 to 69, pointing to the 60 on the bottom line and the unit on the top line. The pointer jumps from the bottom line to the top line, bouncing back and forth to vary the unit.

Then I work on the other four tens (40, 70, 80 and 90) in the same way. I get the students to say all these numbers counting up and counting down—99, 98, 97, 96 … 92, 91, 92, 93, 94, 95, etc. Then I vary the order, because I don't want the students to depend on counting the whole list to get to any particular number.

I put a tiny horizontal line below 5 in the units line. This line stops the 5 from being slid down to the lower lines, showing that the passage from 5 to 50 is not automatic. I show the pronunciation on the Rectangle chart and then add 50 in the tens line exactly below 5. I get the students to work on all the numbers from 51 to 59, out of order and in order, always following my pointer.

I do the same for 30, and then for 20. By now the students can say all the numbers from 1 to 9 and from 20 to 99. I work in the same way as before, so that they gain in ease and fluency for all the combinations between the two lines of numbers.

To finish off, I add 10 at the beginning of the tens line. This is the state of the board at the end of this stage:

$$1 \quad 2 \quad \underline{3} \quad 4 \quad \underline{5} \quad 6 \quad 7 \quad 8 \quad 9$$

$$10 \quad 20 \quad 30 \quad 40 \quad 50 \quad 60 \quad 70 \quad 80 \quad 90$$

They check the spelling

Once the pronunciation seems to be acquired, the students look for the words on the Numbers chart. They find them easily, because the colours help them. If there is a doubt about the spelling of a word, I get them to point to it on the Rectangle chart and then look for the same colours on the Numbers chart. I do not point myself. If I have to take the pointer, I know there was a problem with my presentation. I will have to think about it during my post-paration and work out what I did wrong.

An exercise for developing familiarity with tens[3]

When counting, young students often have a problem going from one set of tens to the next. For example, they can count very quickly from 21 to 29 but they pause at the transition from the 20s to the 30s.

This is why I might get them to count up and down around the change of tens. Thus … *26, 27, 28, 29, 30, 31, backwards! 30, 29, 28, 27, forwards! 28, 29, 30, 31, 32, backwards!* etc.

I can start wherever I like, in the 40s, 50s, 60s, etc.

THE -TEEN LINE

Just below 6 on the first line and slightly to the left, I write the number 1, and on the Rectangle chart I point the sounds for *-teen*. Then, I virtually slide the 6 down from the top line to its position on the right of the 1 on the second line. The students might spontaneously say *teen-six*, which is a pretty good guess! Now I have to show them that these two elements must be reversed. I place two fingers just under the number 16, one finger under each element, *teen* and *six*, making it clear which words have to be switched. Then I turn my hand around back to front. The students say *sixteen*.

---

[3] This exercise comes from Maurice Laurent. He taught at the International School in Geneva. He used it for young children learning to count in their first language.

I go on with 17, 18, 19, and 14 and then work on their fluency.

Next, I point to the horizontal line under *5* in the units line (to indicate that for this number again, the process is not automatic); I add 15 in the teens line and ask the students to guess. Usually, they can do so, since they already know *fifty*. I do the same thing for 13. I have to show them 12 and 11 on the Rectangle chart, because they can't guess these two. As far as possible, I get the students to create most of the numbers using their intelligence and intuition, but where guesswork is not possible, I simply give the word.

Here is the state of the board at the end of this stage.

1	2	3	4	5	6	7	8	9
11	12	13	14	15	16	17	18	19
10	20	30	40	50	60	70	80	90

Extra work—arithmetic

I usually decide to do some arithmetic with the class. Half a lesson can profitably be spent on this. It provides an opportunity for the students to challenge the rest of the class with their own problems. For a while, I can move into the shadows and restrict my job to checking the pronunciation (and the calculations).

I give them the words *equals*, *times* and *plus*: I point these words on the Rectangle chart and I write the symbols on the board. Now we are ready to begin.

First I give the class a series of simple calculations, for example: 4 x 3 = 12, 6 x 4 = 24 ... Then I propose a pair of apparently identical operations,

$$4 \times 3 + 7 = 19$$

$$4 \times 3 + 7 = 40$$

Often a class of children protests when these calculations are written on the board, but I say nothing and just wait. There is a certain excitement in the air. Soon someone discovers why it is possible to write these two equations. The class can hear the moment when someone cracks the problem, since the person lets out a loud *Ahhhh!*

I was teaching a group of children in difficulty at a medico-pedagogical centre, and was doing this exercise. One of the children read out the equations, pausing to show which one he was reading, I heard a fifteen-year girl at the back of the room say, Oh, that's what they're for! *(referring to the brackets)*

I was delighted to witness her sense of relief over something that had obviously been on her mind for years.

Scanning along under the numbers of the calculation with my pointer to make sure he stops at the right places, I get the student who understands to read one of the two equations out loud.

> *four times three* (pause) *plus seven* (pause) *equals nineteen,* written (4 x 3) + 7 = 19

or

> *four times* (pause) *three plus seven* (pause) *equals forty,* written 4 x (3 + 7) = 40

When he has done this, I ask him to choose one of the equations and to stop before the end. If the phrasing of the calculations is clear enough, the class will be able to complete the calculation and give the right answer. This exercise draws students' attention to phrasing.

Subtraction can also be launched with minimal vocabulary. I give 6 - 2 = 4, said *Six minus two equals four*, and the students can then construct their own examples from this information.

I get the students to look for the new words *plus, minus* and *equals* on the relevant Word chart, once the pronunciation has been acquired.

WORKING ON STRESS AND REDUCTION USING NUMBERS

Numbers and counting is an excellent way of working with the students on the patterns of stress and reduction in English. The schwa is at the heart of the problem. This little sound—the most common sound in the language, and which is so difficult for foreigners—should be practised right from the start.

Counting to seven

I get the students to stand with their hands on their abdomen, on either side of the lower part of their ribcage. Then I get them to count to seven on a steady rhythm noticing the movements that accompany each stressed word. To make these more apparent, I ask them to whisper the words and then to 'stage whisper' them. Now I get them to count to seven again, this time inserting the word *a* between each number—*a one, a two, a three, a four* etc.—continuing to attend to the movements of their abdomen and ribcage.

Additional unstressed syllables

Using *and*, I increase the number of syllables between each number. The numbers themselves must give the impression of being spoken at the same rate. Because more reduced syllables are inserted around each number, the rhythm accelerates. In these examples, the dots represent the reduced syllables and the slashes represent the stressed syllables.

   a 1, a 2, a 3, a 4 which gives as its rhythm this pattern

   ./ ./ ./ ./

   a 1, and a 2, and a 3, and a 4 which gives this

   ./ ../ ../ ../

The potato jingle

I also use a jingle that is well-known to English speakers. In this jingle, the word *potato* is pronounced quickly, with a schwa in the last syllable instead of the more common 'oh' sound. Thus the first and last syllables both contain schwa. The second syllable of *potato* is pronounced with a full vowel. The emphasis is on the number. (Young native English speakers learn to use the speech breathing which leads to the rhythms of their language by reciting jingles and nursery rhymes of this kind.)

One potato, two potato, three potato, four; five potato, six potato, seven potato, more. The word *potato* is pronounced in the singular.

   /.~. /.~. /.~. / /.~. /.~. /..~. /

This type of exercise is very helpful when learning English.

THE NUMBERS BEYOND NINETY-NINE

On the fourth line, below 6, I write 00. I get the students to say *hundred*, pointing it on the Rectangle chart. I add a 6 in front, and they say *six hundred* without difficulty. I add all the other numbers on this line. I get them to say *one hundred* for 100, but then below 100, I write 100 a second time. This will be read *a hundred*, which is the other name for this number.

Since my students are learning the British variety of English, I now draw a line just above the hundreds line and, using the Rectangle chart, I get the students to say /n/. They will say this, the most reduced form of the word *and*, every time they cross this line: *nine hundred, 'n, sixty, seven* (967). I propose many combinations by pointing to the numbers below the line, then to the line itself, and then above the line, so that the /n/ is well integrated. For 100, I get the students to say *one hundred*, but I also point to *a hundred* as a variant pronunciation.

Once the students have grasped the system up to this point, I start writing numbers on the board in the conventional way. We do as many examples as necessary to gain ease: 864, 610, 306, 42, etc. I write these here and there all over the board but, little by little, I make sure that some of these numbers follow each other from left to right. These will be used in a different way soon …

Once the pronunciation of these words has been acquired, their spelling can be worked on, using the chart as before. The job ends when the students can easily point sets of three numbers starting in the hundreds on the Rectangle chart, the Word chart and the layout on the board: *two, hundred, 'n, six, –ty, seven.*

I always make sure a few examples are pointed with both forms of 100: *a hundred*, the weak form, and *one hundred*, the strong form used to make a contrast with another number—*one hundred and not two hundred*. *A hundred* is used when no opposition is envisaged: *My grandmother is nearly a hundred years old*.

VERY BIG NUMBERS

Above the units line, at the top of the board towards the right-hand side, I put a comma. It is the symbol for the word *thousand*, which is written with a comma in English.

Working on big numbers gives students invaluable practice in pronunciation, melody and flow with what can become quite long utterances.

I choose a series of hundreds which is nicely lined up and get the students to say the three-figure group which is furthest to the right, let's say 368. I get them to say the next group to the left: say, 256. Then I bring down the comma representing *thousand*, write it between the two groups and indicate that now we are going to consider them together. The students can simply read off the number 256,368: *two hundred 'n fifty-six thousand* (pause) *three hundred 'n sixty-eight*. This should not be a problem since the only new word is *thousand* represented by the comma.

In the main table, above the units line I add another comma, to the left of the first one. It symbolises the word *million*. I add this second comma to the number we are working on, thus linking a third group of three to 256,368, which might give us 988,256,368. Then I add commas one by one representing *billion, trillion* and *quadrillion* until finally everyone can say 852,654,963,988,256,368 or any other series of eighteen figures. In fact, the students only need to know how to say any number up to 999 to say the very big numbers, and they have been saying the hundreds for some time now. The whole task is very easy, as the students simply name the different commas which punctuate the hundreds. The words *billion, trillion* and *quadrillion* are not on the Word charts, but they are not difficult to remember.

By adding the word *point*, as in *decimal point*, I can launch even longer combinations such as

159,268,357,456,963,852.14758

	,	,	,	,	,			
1	2	3	4	5	6	7	8	9
11	12	13	14	15	16	17	18	19
10	20	30	40	50	60	70	80	90
100 100	200	300	400	500	600	700	800	900

The final state of the board

THE YEARS IN ENGLISH

We now have enough of the system to learn how to say the years. Here and there on a clean board, I write two sorts of numbers: numbers up to 20, and numbers between 1 and 99. I ask the class to say them as I am writing them on the board. When the board is fairly full, I continue to add numbers, but I begin to organise them side by side, so as to put, for example, 20 just in front of 16. Then I put the side of my hand perpendicular to the board, between the two halves of the year, and roll it from right to left, getting them to say the part of the year which is visible. I hide 16 while they say *twenty* and then I roll my hand to hide 20 and reveal 16, which they say. Once everyone can say *twenty* followed by *sixteen*, I get them to speed up and 2016 is pronounced as a unit. Once they realise what they have to do, I can simply point to the year in full, and the students will pronounce it correctly.

In the same medico-pedagogical centre, we were almost at the end of the lesson when I put a number in the quadrillions on the board—five commas! They all managed to say it.

I asked if any of them could say the number in French. No one could, for good reason; in French, large numbers are expressed in powers after the billions.

One of the children raced out of the class shouting (in French), "Papa, papa! I can say a bigger number in English than I can in French!!!"

He was thrilled; he exuded such a sense of power! I was moved.

```
1498    1939    1666     9    1,749
 1798    1492    1215    1352
   1,327   1848    1058    1815
  1515    1066   73    1798    20
  13    1821    1,600    19
```

Working on dates

Now I go back to the other numbers on the board, and complete the half which is missing in each case, so as to form a year. For example, 17 might become 1798 and 48 might become 1848 or 1648. I roll my hand if necessary. We then have to work on years like 2008, *two thousand and eight,* which are irregular compared to the other years.

When we have finished working on the word *thousand* a few minutes later, I introduce a comma into a year, which gives as a result 1,956: *one thousand nine hundred and fifty-six,* while 1956 is said *nineteen fifty-six.* In the first case, it is a number; in the second, a year. We spend a few minutes transforming numbers into years and vice versa. I only have to put in the comma or take it out.

THE TIMES TABLES

Later in the course, times tables are an excellent way of practising pronunciation.

2 x 1 = 2
2 x 2 = 4
2 x 3 = 6
2 x 4 = 8
2 x 5 = 10
2 x 6 = 12
...

- There is never a problem with understanding the content. Everybody over the age of seven or eight knows the times tables in their own language.
- There is no need to memorise the content; it can be recreated at will.
- The content is very easy, so students can place all their attention on the pronunciation challenge.
- If they say the words slowly, students can watch their tongue and lips in operation. They can speed up, or slow down, very easily.
- The 2, 3, 6, 7, 9 and 10 times tables give students the chance to work very specifically on the Articulatory Setting. They can explore the feel of tethering and lateral spreading and the consequences on the position of the tip of the tongue. Does it now hover under the alveolar ridge? Does it rap against it for alveolar sounds?

PRONUNCIATION

A class of Japanese students working on their English

- The tables contain a number of the problematic sounds of English, and there are some interesting liaisons, for example when 8 appears.
- The tables are excellent for practising Stress & Reduction.

I always begin with the two times table (2 x). I begin with 2 x 2 = 4 on the Rectangle chart. There are various ways of saying the tables, but for British English I would point, *two twos are four*.

Students very often don't recognise what they are saying. I ask them to say it several times, and then write on the board 2 x 2 = 4. Seeing the numbers written, intermediate students often read the phrase as they believe it should be said, not connecting this to what they said a moment ago. I make the connection for them. This is a shock.

One immediate benefit is that they discover that the word *are* is reduced to a schwa. They practise this. Then I might ask them to guess how the following lines should be said, 2 x 3 = 6; 2 x 4 = 8. *Two threes are six* and *two fours are eight*. This can still be very difficult for them.

Different tables can be used for various problems the students might have, and most of them have something interesting to investigate. The 2 x table gives opportunities to check the articulatory setting and the rapping of the tongue against the alveolar ridge, checking that because the back of the tongue is spread, the tip of the tongue, rather than the blade, contacts the ridge. The fact that *two* can appear in the plural can be a shock. The 3 x table offers practice in pronouncing the sound *th* in rapid sequences. The 5 x table contrasts /f/ and /v/ which some

I never use tongue twisters. If I can't say things easily, why would I inflict what will be an impossible task on my students? I would be setting them up to fail, and that surely is the last thing I want them to do.

speakers find difficult. The 8 x table uses /s/ for the plural rather than /z/ like the others; the list of things to notice is long.

Many of the final words in each of the tables end in a consonant, giving students whose language only uses open syllables (syllables ending with a vowel) to work on saying the sentence right to the end. It helps that each sentence is so short.

This work is for pronunciation, not mathematics; the work should remain light-hearted and pleasant. The sentences are so simple that I can demand a high level of pronunciation.

And last but not least, students can take these exercises out of class and work on them themselves, as they will need to do if they decide they would like to reach excellence in pronouncing English.

ORDINAL NUMBERS

I know we will be needing ordinal numbers for the calendar, so I take a session to introduce them.

This is probably the first time I will use Word chart 9, where the words *first*, *second*, *third* and *times* are to be found. *Third* is difficult to pronounce, and gives us a chance to revisit the sound associated with <ir> if necessary, as well as the pronunciation of the *th* sound. Almost all the ordinal numbers will give us the opportunity to work on this sound. The main difficulties will be with *eighth*, where an unreleased /t/ sound between *eigh* and *th* will help them to stabilise their tongues and so help them to say the word, and the numbers with a ~*ty* ending where an extra schwa is needed; for example, *twenty* in two syllables becomes *twentieth* in three.

> *past present future*
> *o'clock quarter half*
> *minute hour year*
> *first second third add*
> *once plus minus times*
> *twice divided around*
> *count point equal odd*
> *left age exact even*
> *thank century right*

Word Chart 9

The numbers will need to be revisited from time to time whenever problems or opportunities arise.

WORKING THOROUGHLY

As with all the work we do in class this work is done thoroughly, building step-by-step, making sure each step is secure before moving on to the next one, and making sure the students get plenty of practice. This sets a pattern that we will use throughout the course. There is no point in working on anything without consolidating it properly—that simply wastes everyone's time and effort and leaves students feeling insecure.

MUCH LANGUAGE WITH LITTLE VOCABULARY

This chapter illustrates how much can be done with just a little vocabulary. The number system in English requires only 21 ogdens spent to learn words and parts of words, and the arithmetic described only requires spending a further 6. The students can now say any number of up to 18 digits in length, but have worked on much more: they have had practice in using new sounds, in using the stress and reduction system, in the intonation patterns of English, and they can control long strings of words in the new language.

For a high yield, the number of ogdens spent has been minimal. This is typical of the Silent Way and will be seen in all the coming chapters: intense work on the language—as multiple ways of expressing what one is seeing or living, as a new and different way of seeing the world—but an economy of ogdens spent. In the approach, a conscious choice is made about how the time of the class can best be used.

'To speak more precisely of these matters, I have introduced the word "ogden" to refer to the mobilisation of mental energy required to link permanently (i.e. for long durations at the beck and call of one's will) two mental elements, such as a sound and a shape, a shape or a sound and a meaning, a label and an object, etc.'

Gattegno (1976)

WORKING WITH BEGINNERS

'Language teaching becomes a scientific endeavour because the teacher makes things move in the proper direction knowingly and carefully through his access to continuous feedback of what the students are doing here and now.'

Caleb Gattegno

11. Using the Word charts

This chapter gives some practical advice about using the Silent Way Word charts and about class management which will be useful for the beginning Silent Way teacher.

THE WORD CHARTS

The Silent Way Word charts were designed for beginners. A set is made up of fifteen charts of two types. Twelve of the charts provide a suitable pedagogical progression for those encountering the language for the first time and the other three are ancillary charts. (See Appendix 3.)

Generally speaking, the first chart is hung on the wall and worked on until the class is ready for the second one. This continues until words are regularly needed from the later charts and it becomes sensible to hang the full set.

THE CHOICE OF WORDS ON THE CHARTS

A teacher looking at the Word charts for the first time will certainly have many questions. *Why these words and not others? What can be done with these words? Where does one begin? How does one construct a good progression through the language using this choice of words? How does one decide what a good progression is?* And perhaps, *What are the awarenesses that these words will allow me to provoke?*

```
a    rod   -s    -s    red    blue
green      yellow      orange
take  -n't  give   brown   's
and   me    it    to    this   's
he    two   them   here   too
the   is    her   white   the
there       an    other   these
that  one   are   us    those
put   him   black   there
```

Word Chart 1

'It is to be understood that an approach like this one, based as it is on awareness and on personal responsibility for learning, cannot be conceived as rigid. In order to help as much as I could in the direction of flexibility, I have included in the first few charts words of the functional vocabulary that could form groups of lessons in some degree independent of each other. The teachers can work around one or the other group according to taste, circumstances and personal philosophy.'

Gattegno (1963)

Before reading on, I would suggest that the reader take a little time to look at the words on the charts. You will realise that they largely contain words from the functional vocabulary of English—the pronouns, the auxiliaries, the prepositions— together with a few adverbs and adjectives. The main exception is the word *rod*. This noun, and the Cuisenaire rods it refers to, will allow the class to work in detail on how English speakers talk about what they perceive, how they situate themselves in space and time, and how they express personal relationships.

Now spend a few minutes making a list of some sentences that can be constructed from the words on the first chart. There are, in fact, hundreds of possibilities.

Your list will contain phrases and sentences like, *A blue rod and a yellow one. His rod's green and hers are yellow. These rods are brown and that one's blue. Take two blue rods; give one to her and the other one to him. There are two green rods there and one here.*

At one level these sentences are simple. However, the situations they describe are likely to be expressed quite differently in the students' native language, making the sentences genuinely challenging for them. Mastering this functional English is the real challenge of learning the language. Learning vocabulary takes time but is relatively straightforward and does not require a teacher. It is much more difficult to learn to use the function words of a language with precision, and a good teacher makes all the difference in this.

At the beginning stages of students learning English, I want to reduce the quantity of 'luxury' vocabulary (*lawn, flowers, teapot, one-way street, snowboard,* etc.) in order to concentrate the students' attention on those aspects of the language which require the acceptance and adoption of a quite different way of expressing oneself. To begin with, I will therefore limit myself to one single noun, the word *rod*. I will use the Cuisenaire rods to create linguistic situations which illustrate the use of the language explicitly and unambiguously.

DECIDING ON A PROGRESSION

Progression in Silent Way courses is quite different from other approaches. We work on pronunciation first, then add the function words. Then students start talking about their everyday life and finally we expand into any domain of interest to them.

WORKING WITH BEGINNERS

The Silent Way imposes no predetermined order for classroom activities, so there is no linear progression that the teacher has to follow. I make the decisions about what path the class will take in response to the work done by my students.

This freedom allows me to constantly adjust my teaching. On a lesson-by-lesson basis, I consider what the students know in order to find a good starting point for my next lesson, and then, on a moment-by-moment basis while the class is taking place, I construct the lesson in response to the students' achievements, step by step. The content of the course depends at all times on the exact level of the learners as I judge it from what they say and do during each lesson.

Most of my work will consist of feedback and the work required for correction in response to the mistakes I hear. This generally means working:

- first on the choice of words and their order,
- then on the sounds and the stress & reduction system, and
- finally, on the intonation and overall coherence of each sentence.

There is no point in repeating a sentence for pronunciation purposes before the words are correct. The work is finished when the sentence is as good as I can expect from the students at this point.

HOW A SUITABLE PROGRESSION IS ARRIVED AT

The progression used during any one course will be created in two ways. On the one hand, I know which structures the students are ready to work on, and for which structures the prerequisites are not yet in place. I put off until tomorrow what cannot be done satisfactorily today. On the other hand, the progression is also directed by what happens in the class, in the here and now. It is not established once and for all as it would be in a 'method', since I will always be adapting to what the students do and say.

So my teaching is not entirely *ad hoc*. Although I have no single progression in mind, I do have a clear idea at any given time of what constitutes possible progressions, possible fields of language to explore from the current development of the students. I also know what student proposals to ignore—even if the students lead us towards them, even if they insist—because I can see further ahead than they can and I know that such an exploration would be likely to take them out of their depth.

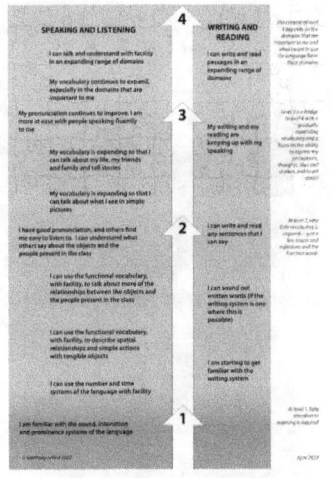

Visit this link to see the progression framework, above, in diagrammatic form and the 'bubble diagram', a tool to think about how a syllabus for a Silent Way course might evolve.

The words on the charts belong to various fields, described in detail from Chapter 12 onwards. The first field proposed on the first Word chart is that of the rods and their colours. Since I will be using rods to create situations for the students to explore and express, the word *rod* must be available immediately, as well as the colours which will provide me with variety. The imperative forms *give*, *take* and *put* together with the pronouns they require make up another field, and the words *this*, *that* and *these* form another. These fields and the others will be dealt with as coherent wholes, one by one. I will juxtapose words and structures within each field to make the precise differences between words obvious.

A STRUCTURING WHICH IS WIDER STILL—THREE THEMES

Each of these fields and all others belong to one of three more general themes. I will consciously move between these themes which I keep separate in my mind but deliberately weave together, like the three strands of hair making up a plait.

The FIRST THEME is the uses of the function words of the language—pronouns, demonstratives, comparatives and superlatives, causal words, etc.

The SECOND THEME consists of the verb tenses, their forms and uses.

The THIRD THEME is made up of the numeration system and a set of time systems.

Three strands make a plait.

I don't make the students aware that I have these themes in mind, but they guide my work.

THEME 1: THE USE OF FUNCTION WORDS

As I work through the charts one by one, I come to the various function words and put them into circulation in one or other of their uses. To begin with, the students can have only a limited feel for the use of any particular function word, but gradually, as they see it used in varied contexts, they broaden and deepen their sense of the word. Note that I am not teaching with the aim that students should add to a list of translations from their native language for each of the function words. I want them instead to gradually build up a feel for each of these words in many contexts: learning by familiarity.

The principal interaction in the class will soon be between students: giving directions to each other, asking and answering questions, etc.

THEME 2: THE VERB TENSE SYSTEM

Although verbs are presented on the charts as they are needed for the pedagogical progression, I keep the Verb Tense System as a separate theme in my mind. Learners of English have to build a comprehensive and coherent sense of how to express time and modality. I can help them to do this because I have the synthetic vision of verb forms that I will describe in Chapter 19. This encompasses tense, aspect and modality. I need to present the various forms clearly one by one and then 'sew them together' until the system emerges. To do this, I have found that I need to separate the verb tenses out into a theme, and then work deliberately through it. This allows me to keep track of where the class is in its progression.

There are several groups of words and expressions which function as 'triggers' for verb forms.

For example, the Simple Present (e.g. *I work*) is often used with the adverbs of frequency or *every* combined with words like *hour, day, week, year, summer*, etc.

The Simple Past (e.g. *I worked*) is usually used with a time marker: for example, *yesterday*, or the word *last* combined with some of the same words as *every* for the present: *last week, last year, last summer, last February*, etc.

These triggers need to be coupled with the verb forms they prompt in situations which are true for the students. Thus the words they say will be a genuine expression of who they are and what they perceive at this moment. The whole system needs to be constructed carefully and systematically as we go along so that most of the verb forms are in place when I decide to bring them together explicitly as a system (see Chapter 19.)

'Whatever language is, it is certainly a substitute for experience, so experience is what gives meaning to language.'

Gattegno (1963)

THEME 3: NUMBERS AND TIME

This theme is made up of the various numbering systems:
- The cardinal numbers used for counting.
- The ordinal numbers *first, second, third*, etc., not forgetting *last*.
- *Once, twice, three times*, etc.
- Telephone numbers, where *oh* is used instead of *zero*.
- The way we say decimal numbers. Other cultures deal with decimal places differently, so the question has to be addressed, if only in passing.

English also has about half a dozen systems which deal with time:
- The time of day.
- The days of the week.
- The months of the year.
- Dates (British and American).
- The seasons.
- Some adverbs of time such as *yesterday*, *today* and *tomorrow*, and nouns like *minute*, *hour* and *year*.

These words allow students to say sentences that are completely mastered (as good as a native speaker expressing the same idea) very early. Work on them should begin even before the work on the first Word chart has been completed.

For example, as soon as the article *the* and the verb *is* are in circulation, and once the ordinal numbers have been worked on, sentences like *Today is Monday the seventh of October* become possible. When the existential *there* is available, sentences such as *There are sixty minutes in an hour* and *There are seven days in a week* are easy. These sentences also have the advantage of being generative and easy to provoke: once students understand one such sentence, I merely write *24* or *365* on the board, and the students can do the rest. They experience a sense of power at being able to invent sentences so rapidly.

There is another advantage in working as early as possible with the various systems belonging to this third theme. Well taught, they invite the students to think and to guess intelligently and therefore indicate to them how I want them to behave throughout the course. They are fun to work on because they are so regular and yield so much for so little input. They make the students realise that the language is coherent, at least in these areas. This encourages them to look for coherence elsewhere.

At the beginning of a course, I often use elements from this theme when I need to slow the students down and give them time to assimilate what we have been doing in either of the other two themes.

WHICH THEME I'M WORKING ON

As I work through each lesson, I am always aware of which theme or themes I am working on at any one time. This means that I keep the general direction of my teaching clear in my own mind. This helps me to structure the whole course more clearly.

I know that my three themes should advance in step with each other in the early stages of the course. However, once the numbers and time systems have been put into circulation, they will be gradually acquired as they occur naturally in the class.

In a course for beginners, the Verb Tense System will not reach the same level of mastery. The class is unlikely to generate a wide enough range of situations to give students the experience they need in order to develop a strong feel for all the forms and meanings involved. I can make a good start on this, but any course is made up of only a limited number of hours.

Similarly, some of the uses of the function words will be acquired in depth, while others would need much more time than we have at our disposal.

PLACING VIRTUAL WORDS USING MENTAL IMAGERY

I always hang the charts in the same place on the wall and in the correct order. Once a chart is introduced, it will remain on the wall. This way my students and I can easily find any word we are looking for and they develop a sense of the likely paths between words.

Sometimes I want to introduce a word which is not on the present charts, but I do not want to hang a new chart on the wall yet. In this case, I introduce the word as a 'virtual word'. I do this by pointing it on the Rectangle chart so that the students know its pronunciation, then on the Fidel, so that they know its spelling; then I 'write' the word on the wall with my pointer closed (so that it looks like a pen) leaving no visible trace. I write it with drama, carefully, so that the spelling is visible as I trace the letters. Somehow that makes it really 'visible'.

When I 'write' a virtual word on the wall, I have two options. If the word is on the next chart to be hung, I write it in the exact place where it will be when I hang that chart. Or I can write it just above one of the charts that I am using at the moment. For example, say that I have the first two charts on the wall and I need the word *but* which is on the third. I simply write it exactly where it will appear when the third chart is put up. When the time comes to hang the third chart, the students will find the word in its place. Until then, whenever I touch that spot on the empty wall, the students know to say the virtual word.

Do not underestimate the power of mental imagery.

One of my colleagues, Suzette Lachaise, teaching in a primary school, took down her sixteen Word charts for learning to read in French (Lecture en Couleurs) to give a workshop elsewhere over a weekend, and arrived at work too late on the following Monday morning to put them back up before the children arrived.

She began working on the empty wall; the children recognised immediately what she was doing, and for the rest of the morning, they worked on the virtual charts, an experience they found both stimulating and joyful.

The students can usually remember a virtual word for days after I write it. They can do this because human beings have a highly developed faculty of mental imagery.

I can also 'place' the occasional luxury word invisibly anywhere on the wall near the charts if a class happens to need it.

PACING THE CLASS

All know-hows are installed slowly at first, and the know-how-to-speak-English is no exception. Developing excellence, ease and assurance in their spoken English will require a lot of work on the part of the students. It is important to be aware that the right pace at the beginning of a course might well appear to the teacher (and even more to observers) to be slow, or even very slow. We will be pick up speed later but proper foundations are essential and take time to build.

To insist that we advance in a considered way does not imply that the lessons drag. On the contrary, the students are very active at all times which makes the lessons interesting for them. But it is unhelpful for the teacher to skip quickly from one field to the next, or even from one

new word to another. A great deal of practice is necessary in each field and with each new word. Varying situations intelligently ensures that the work remains practice, and does not descend into drilling. The nature of language and the emphasis put on using function words means that once words are introduced they will constantly reappear. In this way the core of the students' language becomes more and more dense.

It is not easy to judge the right pace for a particular class. All teachers have problems in this area, even the most experienced. But a mistake in pacing that I make today will become obvious tomorrow when the students have problems with something that seemed to work well when it was done. It will need to be revisited and perhaps even reworked. I take note: next time, more work may be necessary before moving on.

A Silent Way teacher has a discipline which ensures that she will never find herself ahead of her students for long: her silence. As soon as she leaves them behind, she is met with a silence that she cannot fill. The students no longer have the ability to participate and she discovers this immediately.

TEACHING A HETEROGENEOUS CLASS

Any teacher reading this book will at some point wonder how the Silent Way approach works with a heterogeneous class. With experience she will soon realise that a mix of learners with different ages and backgrounds, aims and strengths, can actually be an asset, for several reasons.

Firstly, some differences in personality will be useful in getting people to work well. For example, the perfectionists who only speak when they are certain they are right will be drawn into the class by the chatterers who simply want to talk and don't mind how many mistakes they make. The perfectionists learn that it is by joining in and trying things out that they improve. The chatterers get pulled up short by both the teacher and the perfectionists and realise that some people care about the quality of the language. They become aware that they would be more respectful of their listeners if they were more correct in their use of English.

Secondly, the difference between the natural speeds at which the learners work allows the teacher to choose the best speed for the class at any point in time. In every class, there are the 'locomotives' who seize every opportunity to power ahead, who look for ways of making sentences more complex. And there are the 'slowcoaches' who do not understand what is happening when a locomotive starts exploring, and who have trouble saying even a few words in the right order. The locomotives see immediately how to add this or that to make the sentence longer and more interesting. The slowcoaches need to look closely at every sentence; they need to come back to a simpler form they can understand, then rebuild the sequence, perhaps several times.

The teacher uses the locomotives to move ahead, and the slowcoaches to put the brakes on, slow the class down and force everyone to deepen their understanding.

'Both in his theory and in his practice, Gattegno places much greater faith in the mental powers of even the ordinary student than does any other cognitively oriented system of which I am familiar.'

Stevick (1976)

Here is an example taken from a beginners class, but the principle remains the same irrespective of the level. The class is working on a series of sentences such as,

The rod is red. It is on the table. It is beside the green rod.

The locomotives quickly find a way to put these sentence together,

The red rod is on the table beside the green rod.

And then,

The rod which is on the table beside the green rod is red.

And also,

The rod on the table beside the green rod is red.

The slowcoaches force the watchful teacher to come back to the original sentences and reconstruct the new sentences phrase by phrase:

— The rod is red.
— The red rod is on the table.
— The red rod is beside the green one.
— The green rod is beside the red one.
— The green rod is on the table.
— The green rod which is on the table is beside the red one.
— The red rod which is on the table is beside the green one.

And finally,

The rod which is beside the green rod on the table is red.

When this work has been done, every student will understand.

Each of these sentences is said aloud by the whole class. This is when the slowcoaches have the opportunity to self-correct. Only then do I let them say some of the sentences alone. The time spent with the slowcoaches gives the rest of the class more time to develop control and fluency.

Some locomotives connect a situation and the language very quickly, and imagine that this understanding is the same as being able to perform. They may sometimes be impatient with others' problems. But when asked to actually produce a sentence they have grasped so quickly intellectually, they can be surprised at how difficult they find this. It is easy to think about what one wants to say: thoughts move freely, but the muscles of the tongue have inertia. There is a big difference between 'saying it in your head' and actually saying it aloud. The tongue is sometimes unable to produce what the mind has designed. Only through

> 'The more explicitly the teacher indicates the behaviour sought, the easier it is for the students to display that behaviour, without generating it through understanding.'
>
> *Mason (1998)*

practising speaking English will students develop the same ease of expression that they feel in their mother tongue.

Other locomotives remain on the surface of the language, without really integrating the meaning of the words with the situation in front of them. When there are only a few elements of the language in play, they can easily manipulate these mentally, from memory, quickly enough to give an impression of mastery, particularly if their pronunciation is good. But they haven't allowed the situation to educate them, with the result that at some later point they discover that what they had was a house of cards rather than an experiential foundation to build upon. Slowcoaches can render a real service to such learners.

Other locomotives are truly gifted language learners. From them, I require excellence. My secret weapon is my willingness to be exacting. I require them to produce excellent quality English every time they speak.

Between the locomotives and the slowcoaches, there are all the others, the majority, who benefit from the two speeds imposed on them by the two extremes of the class. The locomotives draw them ahead, while the slowcoaches force them to slow down and work on details.

In a different vein, I find it necessary to consider a class of one student as 'different people' in the sense that the student can be one person now and quite another in five minutes' time. In intensive courses, students tire, become saturated, need to sleep. I must remain sensitive to a student's state of being all the time.

THE TRAP

There is a trap that all Silent Way teachers will have fallen into and will have learnt to be wary of, but which is an ever-present danger. It is to believe that when a student says a sentence well, that I can infer from this that he has understood it just as well as he has said it. For a native speaker, the uttering of a sentence is the *de facto* expression of a meaning. But a learner may say a sentence beautifully while having little understanding of what he is saying, or even no understanding at all.

I fall into this trap when I don't make sure students understand what has been said. I have let the class run on, working with those who can still respond but losing the other students one by one. There soon comes a moment when I realise that I am having to feed the class with too many things to do, or I am giving them answers to my questions. When

Come back repeatedly to the weakest students in your class. You must make sure that no one is being left behind.

It's very easy to be pulled along by the locomotives and to be unaware that the slowcoaches are quietly becoming desperate.

I began using the Silent Way, individual students would just stop working, or the whole class would simply drop into silence. No one could go on. What I learned from this was that I had worked in such a way that my class had lost contact with the meaning.

At the initial stages of a beginners' class, the rods help to make sure that students understand. The teacher uses the variety of statements that rods allow—varying number, colour, length, etc., in the situations she constructs—to make sure that the students understand what they are saying, using the relationship between what they do and what they say as their feedback to her.

At later stages, when the students are freer to express themselves and the class becomes less predictable, the danger is greater. The teacher needs to remain vigilant to make sure that all the students in the class know what is being said and understand how it is being said. For this, alternative constructions, which I discuss in a later chapter, can play a similar role to rods.

Don't be disheartened when you fall into the trap. It happens to us all. On the bright side, it is one of the great strengths of the Silent Way that when you do lose your students you become aware of it quite quickly and have no choice but to remedy the situation.

FEEDBACK FROM STUDENTS

Teaching is an empirical discipline. We advance tentatively, using trial and error. When Gattegno placed *the subordination of teaching to learning* at the heart of his Science of Education, he was telling us that we should allow ourselves to be guided by our students' learning, that we should use feedback from our students as one of our principal tools for teaching. We must keep it in mind as we hang the first Word chart on the wall. Feedback is the key to all that follows.

12. Starting with Word chart 1

This chapter looks at ways of using the first Word chart. Once it is hung on the wall, it should remain in the same place for the duration of the course.

Ideally, the students are grouped in front of a central table on which the teacher can place rods. They don't take notes and don't need desks.

HOW TO BEGIN

From the beginning of a Silent Way course, the teacher works in a way which is unusual for language classes. She creates situations with Cuisenaire rods which means that the meaning of the sentence to be worked on is apprehended by the students even before the words are introduced. Thus it is not the language which communicates the meaning, but the situation. The teacher's job is to enable the students to express this meaning in English.

Cuisenaire rods and their colours

The rods allow the students to learn to use the function words of the language without the complication of having to deal with a lot of vocabulary.

I begin by showing my students what they are. I open the box, show them what it holds and take out a blue rod. I hold it up, point the two words *a rod* on the Rectangle chart and then on the first Word chart and invite the students to say them. Then I take a yellow rod and again

Scan this QR code to download the Guide to the Word charts.

A box of rods

```
a    rod  -s   -s   red   blue
green   yellow    orange
take   -n't  give   brown  's
and   me   it   to   this  's
he   two  them  here  too
the   is   her   white  the
there   an   other   these
that   one   are   us   those
put   him   black   there
```

Word Chart 1

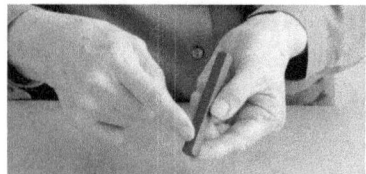

Caressing the blue rod

[1] The word pink is not on the charts. The colour of this rod varies according to the brand of rods you have, and you should choose an appropriate colour name, which might be purple or mauve.

point *a rod* on the Word chart. I do the same thing with a green rod, a red one, a black one and the other colours.

My students can deduce from this that *a rod* means the object I am showing them, whatever its colour. There is a moment when I can hear in most of their voices that this is clear; they know that whatever the colour of the rod, they say *a rod*. (Occasionally, students get upset at this point because they don't know what the word for *rod* is in their own language. Their unease disappears after a short time, when they are more confident with this way of working.)

Now I take a blue rod and run my finger along it, as if I were caressing it. If my gesture is well done, the students will guess that now we are going to talk about the colour of the rods. I point *a blue rod* and they can say it, knowing that *a rod* names the object, and *blue* therefore specifies its colour. Soon this hypothesis will be confirmed as I show them different rods and get them to use the appropriate colour each time in the whole phrase.

I use the same gesture of caressing to introduce the colour red, but this time I only point to the word *red*. Thus the students deduce the meaning of the word and they can guess where it should be placed in the phrase. After three or four different colours I introduce *orange*, which requires *an*. This provokes surprise, which I respond to with a shrug, indicating that this is just the way it is. I will deal with *a*, *an*, and the two pronunciations of *the* a little later. At the moment, this can't be done properly.

Some people will be less sure of the meaning of the colours for a few minutes, but as they see a few of them introduced—orange, blue, brown, black, green, yellow, pink,[1] red and white—they will become confident that they have understood the concept. I work on the word *orange*, which many students find difficult: that letter <a> which is pronounced with a schwi, /i/! What a strange way to pronounce the letter!

Now I put the rods on the table one by one, and the students name them as I do so. I do it again. Each time, I change the order of the rods and we gradually pick up speed. I can accelerate because the students are getting better at the job. At first they hesitate, saying *a…um…red …um…rod* but after a few minutes, the phrase becomes easier and more fluid. I adjust the speed at which I touch the rods to just a shade above the speed that the students can easily say, to maintain an element of challenge. By now the students have described the line of rods a dozen times or more.

Introducing *and* and *one*

I place two rods on the table, a yellow one and a blue one; I point to the yellow rod, prompting the students to say *a yellow rod*. Then I signal for them to stop, I touch the table between the two rods with my pointer or my finger and I point to *and* on the Word chart, so that they say *a yellow rod and …* Now I touch the blue rod, so that they say *a blue …* but I signal for them to stop again and point the word *one*. The students say *a yellow rod and a blue one*. Some students find the use of the pronoun *one* shocking. For the moment I do nothing about this but I do not accept *a yellow rod and a blue rod*. I want correct, elegant, economical, natural English. In other words, I want the students to enter into the spirit of the language from the start.[2]

Once I am sure that the students can say this sentence using many different combinations of colours—*a red rod and a green one, an orange rod and a black one*—I start increasing the number of rods: *a red rod, a green one, an orange one and a black one*. We end up with a sentence containing all the rods. To give them practice without this becoming a drill, I switch the places of the rods around.

When the students are at ease with the rods in circulation, their colours and the use of *and*, I can go on. So far the lesson has lasted between fifteen and twenty minutes, and the students have talked without stopping. I have not yet said a single word.

The plural

To launch work on the plural, I take two rods of the same colour. I usually take two blue rods and point *two blue rods*, touching the lilac <s>, pronounced /z/, beside the word *rod* on the chart.

We go through several examples: *two red rods, two green rods* before introducing chains of rods: *two red rods and two green ones*. The introduction of the word *one* in the plural often surprises students who already have a little English. No, this isn't the number *one*, but the pronoun, which can be used in the plural. (I don't say this. It remains implicit.)

If I have already introduced the number system (see Chapter 10), I can provoke an awareness of the difference between the number and the

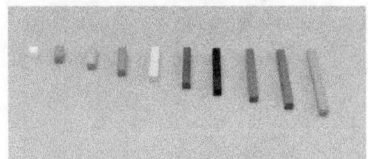

The line of rods

[2] *That said, at this point I would not accept* a yellow and a blue, *even though a native speaker might well say this in this context. Colours are exceptional among adjectives for the way they can easily be used as nouns.* A heavy and a light, *for example, would be most unusual.*

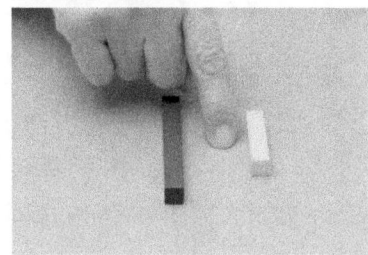

A yellow rod and a blue one

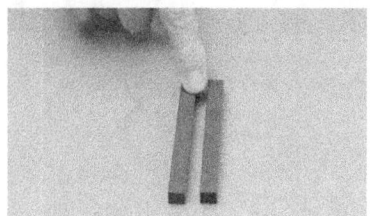
Two blue rods

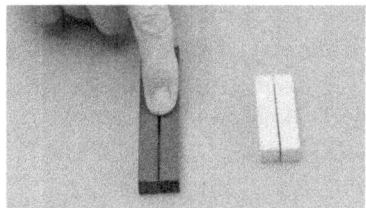
Two blue rods and two yellow ones

pronoun in the following way. While working on a phrase such as *two red rods and one blue one*, I ask a student to point the sentence on the Word charts. Almost always, he will point to the word *one* twice on the same chart. Using the aeroplane gesture, I indicate that this is not exactly incorrect, but that it is possible to do better. Who can point the phrase in a different way? (I 'say' this by holding out the pointer with the blunt end to the class.) The students begin looking for alternative ways of pointing, and someone usually realises that the word *one* should be pointed on two different charts. But he will often be unsure which of the two goes in which place in the phrase. After a few trials he realises that the first one is the number, in opposition to *two*, and the second is the pronoun. From now on, the pronoun will always be pointed on the first Word chart, and the number will be pointed on the Numbers chart. It's a useful distinction to maintain throughout the rest of the course.

If we have not covered the numbers when the plural is introduced, then this distinction cannot yet be made. It will come a little later, when it is possible.

Once the problem of *one* has been dealt with, we can launch into long chains. *One red rod, two blue ones, one yellow one, one pink one, two brown ones … and one black one*. The students need practice.

Now I create four distinct groups of rods: *a green rod and a red one; two blue rods; three pink rods and one white one; and a blue rod, a green one and a yellow one*. The nested situation requires nesting in the language.

I don't allow students to mix articles with numbers. As soon as there is even a single instance of two rods of a given colour together in a line, I insist upon the use of *one* rather than *a*. At this point, developing criteria is more important than what a native speaker might say.

The field of *Take a rod*

To begin the work on this field, I point the sequence *Take a rod* on the Rectangle chart. Once the students can say this sentence easily, I point *Give it to him*. We work on the pronunciation of the pronouns: *him, us, her, me, them* and *it*, and we practise the sequences *Give it to him, Give it to her* and then *Give them to him*, etc. The students practise these sentences as simple chains of sounds, all generated on the Rectangle chart; we are not yet working on the meaning. Only when they can say them easily are they ready to move their presence to meaning without being constantly distracted by problems of pronunciation.

I might now point *Take a blue rod* on the Word chart or I might point it on the Rectangle chart again and ask the students to find the words on the Word chart. It depends whether I feel I'm working with a slow class or a faster one. Once we have it on the Word chart, I get two students, A and B, to come out in front of the class near the table. I turn to student A and, pointing the words on the Word chart, get him to say *Take a blue rod* while looking at student B. This command only has meaning if the students face each other. I can help them to understand the meaning of *take* by taking the hand of student B, guiding it to the box of rods, and gently closing his fingers over a rod, thus indicating that he should take one. The only part of the sentence he doesn't know is *take*. He knows what *a blue rod* means, so I don't have to help with this. I make sure the whole class can see the details of what is happening. I may have to get the students to say the words and perform the action several times before I am sure everyone has seen what is going on.

Take a blue rod

When the action and the language describing it have come together (even if the performance is not entirely natural yet), I get the two students to sit down and I begin again with two others. The repeat performance usually proves that the students in the 'audience' have learned by proxy what to do. Once I can hear from their voices that they are confident, I put a single box of rods in circulation in the class. The students take the box one after the other and say the sentence to a neighbour who must act on the command. It is because everyone sees the command being carried out that I know that everyone understands what is happening.

I choose a blue rod because they are easily visible to everyone and because there are not many of them in the box. The students will soon be forced to change the colour of the rod, if no one has already done so spontaneously.

Now I wait patiently, because I know that as soon as varying the colour no longer provides a challenge, one of the students will realise that he can play a joke on his classmates with a sentence like *Take a green rod, two red ones, two yellow ones and one pink one*. Everyone can immediately see the potential of this adventure. Those who are most at ease follow suit: the sentences become longer and longer, and the students are watchful for mistakes, both in the English used and in the execution

> 'Throughout at least the initial phases, the students meet one clearly delimited new element of the language at a time. The students know that they are expected to work only on this point, using whatever resources they already have at their disposal. They feel that what they have done has moved them toward their long-term goal in an efficient way, and that they have worked both well and thoroughly. The teacher is matter-of-fact both about the students' successes and about their errors, but she always shows by her manner that she accepts the students as persons.'
>
> Stevick (1980)

of the command. The slightest error is immediately flagged up by all those who hear it.

Now I ask three male students to come out in front of the group. I give the box of rods to A, then I point *Take a blue rod and give it to him* on the Word charts. (*Give it to him* is new.) I indicate that A should say this to B who will take the rod from the box and give it to C. I turn C's hand palm upwards and indicate to B that he should put it there.

We work until the three students can say the sentence correctly (though probably very slowly) and can associate it with the actions. I make it very clear that the student who is speaking must face the student he is talking to. When I think that the whole class has understood the situation, I send the three students back to their places, and give the box of rods to a student in the class who I think will be able to re-enact what he saw and heard. Every student then has to get his neighbour to take a rod and give it to the next student.

We soon come to a female student who is to receive a rod. I stop everyone, and point the sentence *Give it to her*. The change from *him* to *her* allows the class to understand that *him* and *her* indicate that the recipient of the rod is male and female respectively.

A more adventurous student will soon try the same sentence in the plural, by saying *Take two blue rods and give it to him*. Explorers are usually aware of the risk they are taking, and often look to me to find out if the sentence is correct. I provide the explorer with *give them to him*, pointing the reduced form of *them* on the Rectangle chart. This shows him that the word *it* refers to one rod, and that *them* is needed for two rods. I ask a student to point the sentence on the Word chart, and indicate that the pale yellow dot under *them* must be pointed, to correspond to the pronunciation I gave them on the Rectangle chart.

By running into problems concerning the number of rods, and who they should be given to, we work on *Take a blue rod and give it to him. Take two red rods and give them to her. Give it to them. Give it to me. Give them to them,* etc. All these combinations will come up and be worked on. The last sentence in this list gives us the opportunity to work on how stress and reduction operate in English, since the two words *them* are not pronounced in the same way. The first is pronounced with a schwa, since the students already know about the rods it refers to, while the second is pronounced with its full vowel because it concerns significant new information.

On the Word chart, I point the reduced form of *them* by covering the ice blue <e> with the tip of my finger and pointing to the pale yellow dot. I point the full form of *them* by covering the dot and pointing the word.

In all cases, I make the student who is speaking look at the person to whom he is giving the order and point with his finger to the student who is *him* or *her*. For *Give it to them*, I make the student point to the group of males, or females, or males and females, who make up *them*.

We will come back to this field a few days later, when it will be possible to say more: *Take ten rods. Give two of them to him, another three to her. Give the others to us.* But first we need to work on other fields.

The field of *a* and *the*

To introduce a first, basic distinction between the use of *a* and *the*, I place a dozen or so rods of two or three different colours in the lid of the box, then I ask two students to come forward. I want A to make B take rods, one rod at a time. I start the ball rolling by pointing *Take a red rod*. A says this, B does it, and I motion to them to continue, making sure that they keep the lid tilted towards the class so that everyone can see its contents. While there are at least two rods of the same colour in the lid, A should say *Take a blue rod* or *Take a red rod*. As soon as there is only one rod of a particular colour left, it will be necessary for him to say *Take the blue rod*. Surprise! They swap roles several times and work until they both understand how to choose between the two words.

Now, in order to check that all is well, I put out on the table a collection such as one orange rod, three red ones, one yellow one, four white ones, one blue one, two black ones and one brown one. The task is for the students to get me to take away one rod at a time. For the line of rods described, they would have to say *Take a red rod. Take a green rod. Take the yellow rod. Take a white rod. Take the blue rod.* Etc., until no rods are left on the table. When the students are confident with this, they can begin taking multiple rods, while remaining alert to the use of *a* and *the*. For example, if there are three blue rods, two red ones and four white ones on the table, the students might say: *Take two blue rods and the two red ones*, and then *Take the blue rod and a white one*, then *Take the three white ones*.

'The work requires the learner to relate the linguistic signs to truth that he perceives with his senses.

This principle also explains why in the Silent Way there is no drilling of forms in the absence of meaning. There is systematic practice of similar sentences, but always accompanied by rod structures or some other direct "truth".'

Stevick (1980)

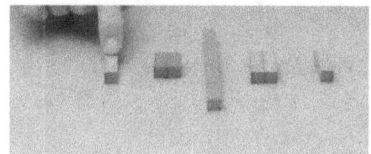

Another

'Another thing to forget is that matters called "hard," have to be postponed. The Silent Way criterion is: "if this or that is needed to make the students autonomous in the language, it must be transferred from the teacher to the student as early as possible." It is even possible to make things hard by postponing essential items of the functional language. For example en in French is essential and must be in circulation as early as it is in English, although coursebooks do leave it out for some time.'

Gattegno (1983)

The field of *another* and *the other*

An extension of this field of *a* and *the* leads to *another* and *the other*. I begin by showing the students how *another* is constructed on the Word chart, pointing to *an* and *other* then 'pinching' them together with my fingers to indicate the creation of one word.

I might put a dozen rods on the table, placing green rods in the line several times. I ask the students to name the rods: *one green rod, two red ones, one orange one, another two green ones, a blue one and another green one*. I would require them to stress the word *another* a little more each time it is said.

Now, I might put three blue rods in the lid of the box and ask a student to come out to the front of the class. I point *Take a blue rod* and gesture to the student to do it. There are now only two blue rods in the lid. I point *Take another one* ('pinching' *an* and *other* together as I point) and he takes one. The third time, there is only one rod left in the lid. I point *Take the other one*. Often it is necessary to do the whole thing a second time before the students understand which words go with each stage. When I think the students know what to say and do, I ask someone else to point the words once or twice to make sure they are aware of the spelling of *another*.

Once the students have grasped the distinction between the sentences, I might put lots of rods of the same colour in the lid of the box, and then point *Take a rod*. Someone does it. *Take another one*. He does it. *Take another two ... Take another six ...* Towards the end, when there are almost no rods left several final sentences are possible, which we work on: *Take the other ones* (if there are a few); *Take the other five* (if there are five left); *Take the other one* (if there is only one left). As they gain in confidence, I gradually complicate the situation. Then the box circulates and the students practise. In a large class I might divide students into groups of four or five for this.

I can also put various rods side by side, so that the students might say: *four yellow rods, three brown ones, six red ones, another two yellow ones, one pink one, another four red ones and one white one*.

I, or a student, can change the place and the number of rods as many times as necessary and they can describe what they see.

WORKING WITH BEGINNERS

The field of *this*, *that* and *these*

Another area waiting to be explored is the field of *this*, *that* and *these*. I have to decide whether I will introduce these words using the form *This is a blue rod* or *This rod's blue*. I choose the first if I am working with a slow class (one with no locomotives) or a class which has many unsophisticated language learners, people who have not yet realised that learning a foreign language involves changing one's vision of the world. I choose the second if I am teaching a class which is surer of its ability to learn languages or made up mainly of false beginners. *This is a blue rod* does not change the basic structure the students have been using from the beginning; it only adds two initial syllables to *a blue rod*, which they have been using for hours now, and so this form is easier to deal with. *This rod's blue* requires known words to be reordered, which can be disconcerting for slower students.

Whichever form I choose to begin with, the other will be brought in a few hours later.

I will have to put *is* and *are* into circulation since this is the first time these words have come up. They will be present in every sentence, but at this stage as vocabulary rather than as a field to work on. English uses copulas; many languages do not. Because of the nature of these words, no explanation will be given, nor is one needed. They have a function but for students whose native language does not have an equivalent they have no meaning. For them, at this point, they are simply 'there'.

Is and *are* will be used in their reduced forms in all the affirmative sentences the students meet when working with *this*, *that* and *these*. This means that the students will use *'s* for *is* and pronounce *are* as a schwa. Not only this, but I will make an effort to keep the schwa as short and indistinguishable as possible, mainly by pointing it using the schwa dot on the Rectangle chart rather than the dot under the word *are* on the Word chart for at least the first hour.

I show the contracted forms of the verb so that the students integrate the contractions from the start. When we get to the question forms, they will discover that *'s* is *is* and that the schwa is spelt <are>.

I give someone a blue rod and point the words *this*, *rod*, *'s*, and *blue* to get him to say *This rod's blue*. I take the student's free hand and stretch out his index finger so that he visibly points at the rod, indicating that

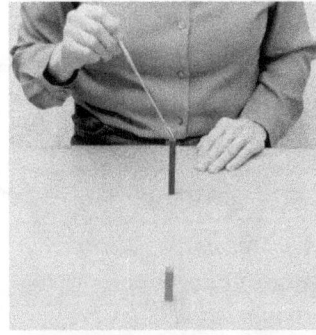

This rod's blue

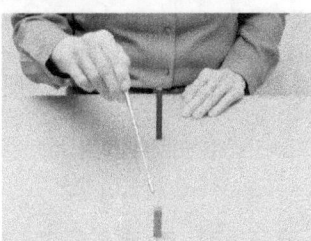

That rod's pink

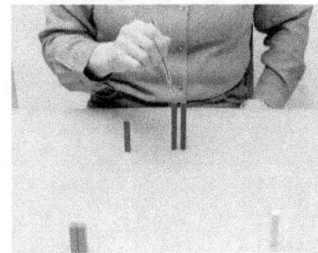

These rods are blue

he is talking about this rod and no other. These words are called 'demonstratives' for a reason! Pointing conveys their principal meaning.

I then distribute rods to all the students in the class and each says the sentence which is correct for him; I don't allow anyone to say *This rod's red* if they are holding a blue one. Every sentence must be true, as well as grammatically correct. And in this case, everyone describes, by pointing his finger, the rod in his hand.

Now I get a student to point to the rod being held by another student, and I point to the word *that*. The students can create *That rod's green* by themselves. If there are any pronunciation problems, I use gestures and the Rectangle chart to show how *this* and *that* should be pronounced.

I always take care to give students the reduced form of the forty or so words of English that have strong and weak alternatives when this would be the choice of a native speaker.

Weak forms are a distinctive feature of English pronunciation. They are difficult for students to grasp, and will need lots of practice.

Now I combine the two sentences, showing the two rods one after the other, inviting the students to say sentences such as *This rod's yellow. That rod's green* and immediately *This rod's yellow and that one's green* followed by, for example, *That rod's green and this one's red*. It can be useful, within a field, to have several similar sentences in circulation at one time, as the small differences between them allow students to pay attention to the differences in the constructions.

I listen to the students' voices and look at their faces, alert to clues about their learning. I only move on when I'm confident that the meaning of the sentences is established, and that all the students have developed a relative ease of expression and are speaking from understanding.

There is every chance that we will encounter the word *too* during this work. When a student finds someone holding the same colour rod as he is, then he will need to say *This rod's yellow. That rod's yellow, too*.

When students are at ease with *this* and *that* I can introduce the plural *these*. I do this by showing two, and then more, rods. The students work on the various combinations.

I avoid introducing all four of the demonstratives in any one session unless the students push me into it, so I would not introduce *those* yet. I find it better to work on three of them, and come back to this area of the language when Word Chart 2 is put up. Students do need to know that they are working on a system which includes singular and plural words and the concepts of *near* and *far*. However, I have found that it is not a good idea to work on all four words the same day as weaker students can get muddled. *Those*, on Word Chart 2, will give us an opportunity to use all four again in a slightly broader context.

As they speak, the students are focused on the words of the new sentences and will forget to pay attention to pronunciation and rhythm. There are too many new factors to deal with at the same time. After they have said each sentence several times, when they are certain of the words, I draw their attention to these other parameters so that they can produce the sentences in a natural way.

The contrast between *here* and *there*, and *there* /ðeə/ and *there* /ðə/

There is presented on Word Chart 1 as two separate words, with different pronunciations and different meanings.

There with a diphthong is the opposite of *here* and is only used this way. I ask the students to point to the physical location of the rods they are talking about, either *here* or *there*, when they use these words.

I start with *The green rod's here and the red one's there*. I place the two rods the students will be talking about at opposite ends of the classroom; this means that for some of the students, the red rod is *here* and the green one is *there*, while for others it's the opposite. For some students in the middle of the classroom, both rods might be *there*. The meaning is relative.

The other *there* is always used with a verb and is the beginning of the sentence *There's a green rod here* or *There are two red rods there*. It is always unstressed. Many people pronounce it with a schwa but some speakers use an unstressed /e/. I always teach the schwa form because it better distinguishes this word from the other *there*.

The plural form, pronounced /ðə rə/, has already been discussed in Chapter 7.

I introduce *There are two red rods here,* pointing to the reduced form of *there* and *are* and the liaison between them. Then we can go on to *There are two red rods there*, with the two words, two meanings and two pronunciations of *there* in one sentence.

For practice, I place rods of different colours around the room at different distances from the students. They will be able to say: *There's a blue rod there. There are two green ones here. There's a blue rod there and a red one there*, etc. I get them to point these sentences to make quite sure they know which *there* they are using on the chart.

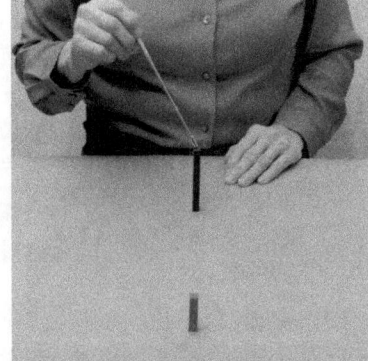

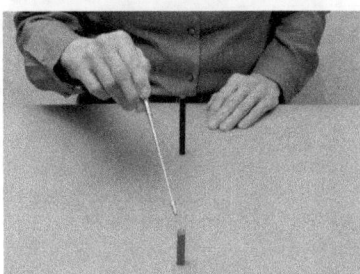

Here and there

The field of *put*

Usually, I introduce *put* with *here* and *there*: *Take a black rod and put it there. Take a blue rod and put it here.* I show *there* with the pointer to indicate that it is further away than *here* and I always make sure the students not only say the sentence but also perform the action.

It is useful, too, to vary the number of rods so as to re-introduce the plural pronoun, said using its weak form: *Take two blue rods and put them here. Take two red rods and put them there. Take two yellow rods and put one here and the other one there.* Then, when I think everything is clear, *Take two blue rods and give them to them.* With this last sentence, I can again contrast the two pronunciations of *them*. The first is said with a schwa, the second has full value. When I show the first of the two, in the phrase *and give them to them*, I cover the word with my finger and touch the yellow dot under it. For the second *them*, I cover the dot and touch the word, which is said using a blue /e/.

As with all the sentences, I work on the rhythm of the language each time. For example, the sentence *Give them to them* gives the students an insight into the way English speakers vary the pronunciation of words according to the meaning of a sentence.

Negation

The word *~n't* is easy to introduce. I hold up a red rod and point *This rod isn't blue*. Of course, as soon as I touch *this*, the students expect me to go on with *This rod's red*. After a moment, the meaning of *~n't* becomes clear. It usually take a few seconds before they understand why I'm not pointing to what they expected. They easily incorporate this word into what they can say.

I would introduce the alternative form *This rod's not green* only when *not* is introduced on Chart 3 after students have plenty of experience with variations on *This rod isn't green*.

If a student who has met the word previously asks about *not* at this stage, I can add it as a virtual word in what will become its place on the wall when Chart 3 is hung. In this case I use fingers to show that either *is* attaches to *rod* and is reduced, or *not* attaches to *is* and is reduced. There is little difference in meaning, but one reduction or the other is necessary. The absence of any reduction would make the sentence too

> 'Grammar is not visible on the functional vocabulary of the charts. It is generated by the pointer which strings words to form sequences which are sentences of that language.'
>
> Gattegno (1983)

His and *her*

I ask three students to come out to the front of the classroom. I get student A to hold a blue rod and ask student B to say *His rod's blue*, pointing to student A while he looks at student C. The word *her* can be illustrated in the same way. Then I give out a rod to everyone, and they all have the opportunity to make sentences to a third person about their neighbour's rod.

This is quickly followed by *His rods are red* and *Her rods are green*, using the weak form of the verb, of course. I pass around the box of rods and, using a gesture, invite students to take some. They can take one or more and so introduce variety. They soon make sentences like *His rods are green, red, white and pink*.

At this point, I sometimes do a 'test' with the students using sentences in this field. For this, I speak. I hold one blue rod in one hand and two blue ones in the other hand, and I stand with my hands as far apart as possible. Then I say either *My rod's blue* or *My rods are blue*, at the speed I would use with a native speaker. This means that the verb *are* is highly reduced. It is barely audible to anyone who is not primed to hear it. If the students hear *My rod's blue*, they point to the hand which is holding one rod. If they hear *My rods are blue*, they point to the hand holding two. It may take a few tries before all the students can hear the difference reliably. I would never do this until they had practised saying it first.

The point of this exercise is to make students aware of what will be to them the shocking extent to which native speakers reduce *are*. I now get them to try it for themselves.

I would usually work on *his*, *her* and *my* towards the end of work on Chart 1, since they give me a natural link to Chart 2 where the possessive pronouns are to be found.

USING THEME 3

By now, I will certainly have introduced at least some of the fields on the Time charts: the number system, time and the days of the week, probably more. See Chapter 14 for how I will have done this. I use fields from Theme 3 whenever I want to give the students a change or a break in the intensity of the work.

> 'Each time the student comes to feel that he now knows something from within himself, and not from echoing the teacher or from memorizing rules and paradigms, he has developed a new "inner criterion." The student must learn to notice these "criteria," and to trust them. It is apparently for this reason that the teacher seldom confirms a correct response on the part of the student. By not overtly approving a correct response, the teacher leaves the student alone to take note of it, and to learn to trust himself more.'
>
> Stevick (1980)

ANSWERING QUESTIONS WAITS FOR CHART 2

The reader will notice that the first chart does not allow questions to be answered because *yes* and *no* are on Chart 2. The students could construct a few questions such as *Is this rod blue?* with, as the answer, *It is*, but I would not introduce this. I prefer to wait for the second chart to be hung before we explore questions in any detail.

CLASS MANAGEMENT, BY ME AND THEN THE STUDENTS

During the work on Chart 1, and from now on, I use a little patter if I want to (with emphasis on the word 'little'). I might begin to speak in English for class management using sentences like *Say it again. Say it to him. Who would like to point? Come out and point to it again.* This gives the locomotives something else to work on. Imagine the surprise when a locomotive unexpectedly says a long sentence like this to his neighbour. That's a strong moment for the class.

Classroom patter gives me additional means to manage the class, but it also gives the students the means of working together and helping each other. For this they will need phrases like the ones above and also *Could you point to it (again), please? Could you say it louder? What does xxx mean? I don't understand what xxx means.* When I notice opportunities to introduce these sentences and others like them, I do so.

As the students learn to use more of these sentences, it becomes easier for me to subordinate my teaching to their learning because they make more of their needs known explicitly.

I remember being a student in a Japanese class taught by Fusako Allard in 1988. Out of the blue, one of the students suddenly rattled off a long sentence in Japanese! The rest of us were stunned. Slowly it dawned on us that he had been listening to the teacher's patter, and had been working on it in his spare time. (The Japanese for, Say it again please.)

I began listening quite differently.

LEARNING TO WRITE

After the first few lessons, the students can start writing phrases and sentences. Here are two possible exercises.

Firstly, I can ask my students to write a few example phrases or sentences from the work done that day. I don't present this as a test: I leave the charts on the wall, and tell them to check the spelling of words if they are in doubt. This is actually more difficult for some students than it might seem. They don't find it easy to make a mental image of the word and then carry it to their page. Students will naturally stop checking spellings when it is no longer necessary.

Then I ask them to check with their neighbour. If there is disagreement, and the Word charts cannot solve the problem, they call me.

In a school setting, there may be pressure from the parents for the children to be working with a textbook. The writing work at the end of the lesson can be adapted to meet this need. It can become the students' own personalised workbook, created as we go along. At the end of the year, the students have a faithful record of their achievement.

A second exercise is a little more challenging. I write a few words on the board and ask the students to make one sentence for each word. For example, from Chart 1: *my, this, there, 's, too.*

The students have to create a context that these words can belong to.

READING AND WRITING

For low level students, writing consists of noting what has already been learned orally. For them, writing and reading go together: students read what they can write and write what they can read. The Word charts and the Fidel help me work on both. When they are working on writing, I ask the students to actively copy words from the charts until they are sure of the spelling and no longer need to do so. This writing activity is not a test, but a chance to learn to spell.

I can help the students by hanging the Fidel on a different wall from the board. Then I can ask them to point on the Fidel the sequence being worked on, to look at it carefully and then to carry it mentally over to the board where they write it without looking back. To do this, they have to hold the spelling—and for some, even the forms of the letters—as they walk across the room from the wall to the board. This helps them to form more detailed mental images of the words they meet. If the class is not too big, I can have all the students working at this activity at once, taking the time they need to note the details and then moving to the board to write.

If writing is important, I can ask students to write sentences they have said during the class for homework and bring them in the next day. I recommend students handwrite these sentences because the act of writing by hand leaves a deeper mental trace than typing. Furthermore, I want them to puzzle out for themselves any spelling, grammatical or punctuation issues rather than having autocorrect on a word processor doing the work for them.

They can then swap these sentences with their neighbours; this gives students a chance to see various styles of handwriting which can be helpful, too.

MOVING ON

'A rule we have followed in our work is to introduce, whenever possible, one new word or expression at a time and make it become second nature before the next one is introduced. This ensures that retention takes place without drill or idle repetition, that the ground is covered systematically, that more and more of the language is integrated, and that the students use the material freely and correctly, as natives do.'

Gattegno (1976)

When I have introduced all of the words on Word Chart 1 and we have combined them in enough ways for beginners to get a sense of their meaning, I move on by hanging Chart 2. It is not necessary to exhaust all the possible uses of words on the first chart before introducing the second, but what is worked on should be done thoroughly. With complete beginners, it takes time to work through this first chart; nothing is gained by skimming over the surface and sometimes I have worked with a class for 15 or 20 hours or even longer before getting to Chart 2. If I am teaching a class of non-readers I would spend even more time.

The more in depth the work done here, the easier it will become as we move on. The students are using situations to create their own personal grammar of the language. They are integrating a new thought structure, new pronunciation habits and new intonation patterns, and these are easier to reach when the language is simple. When the students seem relatively confident, and some of what they have learned has been automatised, leaving them with functional language, I estimate that we can go on.

They have always linked what they see and do to what they say and hear. Their perceptions trigger words. Their words trigger actions. Perception, action, speaking and listening are united as a whole. Through their struggles to correct and perfect their statements, they have made progress in all areas. They know that we are working towards correct language, rather than getting by with language which is only approximately correct. Their ways of working are improving.

13. Moving on to Word Chart 2

I put the second chart up next to the first one. I leave the first chart in exactly the same place on the wall. I don't push it along to make room for the others. Once a chart has been hung, it never moves. The students will refer to the charts constantly, and I don't want to confuse them by moving things around. The second Word chart launches us into work on verb forms. On it we find *get* and *got*; *have*, *'ve*, *has* and *had*; *did*, *does* and *don't*.

All the possessive pronouns and adjectives are now visible, as are several word pairs. *Dark* and *light* allow us to talk about the two greens in the box of rods. *Same* and *different* will be used with *colour*. The word *those* completes the set of words *this*, *that* and *these* found on Word Chart 1. *Out*, *in* and *on* will allow the students to take rods out of the box, put them in or put them on the lid. *How* used with *many*, and *what* used with *colour* and *name*, and *yes* and *no*, will open the way to several types of questions and their answers. The word *of* will be used in various contexts.

Let's begin with verbs. Note that this work will be interwoven with the other themes.

THEME 2: THE VERB TENSES

I can choose to begin working on the forms of verbs in English with either *I have a rod* or *I've got a rod*. I usually choose the first of these, because the introduction of an auxiliary, *do*, to create the interrogative

Word Chart 2

and negative forms is unusual among languages and I want this unusual construction to become well established early.

I have a rod

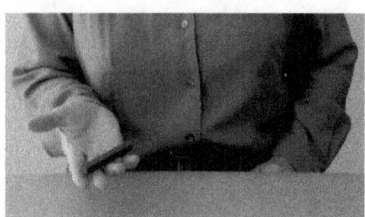
I have a rod

What I am going to describe now will take place over several lessons, interspersed with work on dates, numbers and pronouns.

To introduce *I have a rod*, I point the words on the charts and make sure that everyone can say the phrase easily. Then I hold up a rod in one hand and point the words again on the charts. Then I give a rod to each student so that everyone can say *I have a rod*. Quite quickly, a student will add the colour of his rod when he makes his sentence, and others will follow his lead. When students begin to do this, it tells me that they feel confident about the work we are doing and I know I can move on.

Next, if nothing has happened in the class to take it elsewhere, I would probably work on *He/She has ...* , varying numbers and colours of rods, and also using students' names. The students must be made aware that when they are using *he* or *she* or a person's name, they would naturally look at the person they are speaking to but might gesture towards the person they are speaking about. I make them do this; I gently turn the speaker's head if necessary and get him to make a gesture towards the third person. I want everyone to understand what the situation is, so I have to make sure it is explicit.

When this is in place, we can work on questions. To make the situation genuine, I collect all the rods, give new ones out and we go on to *Do you have a blue rod?* and from there to *Does he/she have ... ?* This requires *Yes, I do*, and *No, I don't*, and *Yes, he does*, and *No, he doesn't*.

We might then go back to *He has a rod* and *She has a rod*, to make sure everything is in order, then on to *we* and *you*. To introduce *we*, I distribute rods all around the class, making sure there is a high proportion of rods of one colour, for example, yellow; this will allow me to easily contextualise the word *we*. Each student says the sentence saying the colour of his rod, but we soon come across two people, one after the other, who say *I have a yellow rod*. I go back to the first speaker and ask him to say his sentence again, followed immediately by the second speaker who has to add *too*. This gives us *I have a yellow rod* followed by *I have a yellow rod, too*. After a few minutes practice using *too*, someone realises that *We have a yellow rod* should exist, if only he had the word *we*. He might link arms with a neighbour who is holding the same colour rod as his and indicate that he wants to know how he can express the situation he has created.

If my students know what conjugations are in their own language, they may then ask for *they* by getting other students to team up with neighbours. Then they practise all these forms until they are at ease. I periodically collect all the rods and give out others so that the colours change. This allows me to introduce *Put the rods in the box*. The word *box* is easy because the box is in front of them, and I write the word virtually on the wall underneath the first chart, a few lines down, since this is where it will appear when Chart 5 is hung.

Now we ask questions like *Do you have a red rod?* with answers like, *No, I don't, but I have three green ones*. (With a class of false beginners, I might introduce *No, I don't, but I do have three green ones*, showing how a sense of contrast can be expressed using *do*.)

This work is never formalised into a conjugation table on the board. I don't want the students to think in those terms. I want the language to live in them as words-and-actions which go together.

All these sentences can then be made negative: *I don't have a green rod, I have a red one*.

I make sure the students use the stress and reduction system as it is manifested in all these sentences. For example, in the question *Do you have a green rod?* I point to the yellow dots under the words *do* /də/ and *you* /jə/ then the full form of the word *have* /hæv/, since the verb *have* is not reduced.

I am not particularly concerned to get the quality of reduced sounds perfect. What is important at this stage is just that the students find it increasingly natural to reduce sounds in some reasonably authentic way.

The words *get* and *got*

Once the family of situations and sentences based on *I have a rod* has been fully explored and the students are starting to use the right constructions automatically, I would wait a few lessons for things to settle and then start work on *I've got a rod*. We go back over the situations used for *I have a rod* to show how they can also be expressed using this new construction. (For the moment, I am treating *I have a rod* and *I've got a rod* as synonymous.) Next, all the sentences are made into questions: *Have you got a rod? Yes I have* and made negative.

The construction *Have you got ... ?* is useful, too, because I want the students to associate *Yes, I have* with this question, and *Yes, I do* with the question *Do you have ... ?* I introduce this distinction early and make sure it is observed systematically. I require that the replies correspond exactly to the questions in order to avoid later mistakes like *May I go? Yes, you will* or *Will I? Yes, you do*. I want to make students aware that the structure of the question determines the structure of the answer. As we work on each of these sentences, I make sure that the students use the appropriate weak and strong forms of words.

I had a rod

After the work on *I have a rod* and *I've got a rod* has been completed and the students have slept on it, I can introduce the past tense with *I had* and *Did you have ... ?* To do so, I give out three or four rods to each of the students and get them to talk about them and ask each other questions: *I have ... Do you have ... ? How many red ones do you have?* I then take away the rods and using my 'Say it again' gesture, ask the students to talk about them again, which naturally introduces *I had ... he had ...* and a little later *Did you have ... ?* If people's memories of the situation differ, this can also lead directly to *No you didn't, you had ...!*

THEME 1: THE FUNCTION WORDS

Interspersed with the work on the verb forms above, I will also be working on the function words. These give opportunities for practice on the verb forms.

How many ... ?

How many ... ? naturally follows work on *Do you have ... ?* For this work, we will also need the numbers. If these have not yet been done, they should be worked on first.

With *How many*, two questions can be worked on: *How many rods do you have?* and *How many rods have you got?* It is also possible to use *How many red rods are there on the table?* working on the correct forms of the answers. I introduce the word *table* during the work on Chart 2, showing its pronunciation and spelling before 'writing' it virtually on the wall. I always do this in the same place, exactly above the word *which* at the top of Chart 2, so that I am sure myself of where it is. I write it carefully with my closed pointer simulating a pen, and it is now available there for the rest of the course.

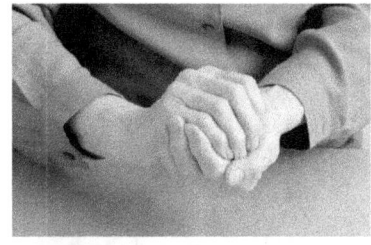

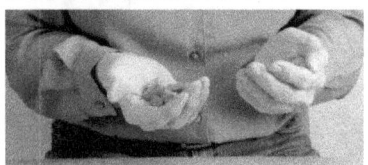

How many rods do you have?

I begin the work on *How many* by pointing to the *How many rods* on the Rectangle chart, *have you got?* on the Word charts, and asking the students to say the sentence several times, thus getting it into circulation and flowing freely. At this stage, *How many* is only a chain of sounds, having no meaning.

Now I give out a number of rods to each of the students. Often, I do this by lobbing the rods to the students as fast as I can, but making them easy to catch. I also indicate that they should close their hands around them. Thus the students have no way of choosing either the colour or the number of rods they are holding when I have finished distributing them. This means that a question about the rods someone is holding is a legitimate question.

Now I ask someone to look towards his neighbour and say the sentence *How many rods have you got?* He does so. Everyone looks back at me—what happens now? I go to the neighbour and show him that I want him to open his hand. I then count the rods *one, two …* indicating to the students that they should join in, which they do. The student is holding, say, three rods. They now understand that the question requires that they count their rods to give the answer; it must be 'the counting question'. I go back to the Word charts and point to the answer *I've got three* and ask the student to say it. Now I go back and elicit the question again, and the answer comes back more quickly. After several tries, the question and the answer sound related. Now I can get another pair of students to say them.

In a class of fifteen or twenty, almost all the students get the opportunity to say this sentence in isolation. If I have a bigger class (thirty or forty students or more), some of the students only begin speaking in the next phase I introduce, when I invite them to speak to everyone around them. This is a noisier moment.

From time to time, I collect all the rods in and lob them out again to keep the questions fresh. I encourage the students to use other pronouns.

The word *what*

This word allows us to reuse all the known question structures in new ways. For example, *Do you have a red rod?* becomes *What colour rod do you have?* Or *What colour rod do you have in your hand? I have a red one.* The question *What's your name? My name's*

'What is learned with Chart 1 will serve again when more charts are added. All that follows is expansion. Students can say more and more and express many more relationships in the new language. These relationships are concerned with people involved in space and time, in cause and effect. The people have names, sizes and positions in space and time relative to other people or places, in a culture that quantifies and qualifies. Hence the charts offer clusters of words which permit one to refer to the present, the past, and the future, to conditions, doubts, guesses; to space, orientation, location, distance, shape and position; to temporal relations, simultaneity, order, duration; to tell the time, the date, to quantify; to count, to distribute and share; to relate to words, telling, saying, showing, explaining, asking, answering; to modulate expressions via adverbs, to describe, to narrate, to question, to discuss, etc.'

Gattegno (1976)

Fred is also possible. The students almost certainly know each other's names by now, but the question can still be asked. For both questions, different pronouns can be used.

I can also set up a situation in which the sentence *What colour rod did you have?* is in context. The answer might be *I had a green one. Now I have a yellow one.* All I have to do is give out some rods, ask the students to speak about them, collect them a few minutes later, and then give out other rods. (I would 'write' *now* on the wall in its place to the left of the Rectangle chart.)

The words *same* and *different*

Opportunities to use *same* and *different* often arise in class so it is worth spending some time on them quite early.

Using the fields already worked on, I can show the appropriate rods and get the students to construct sentences such as *These two rods are of two different colours* and *These two rods are the same colour*, and a little later *This rod is the same colour as that one* and *That rod is a different colour from this one. From* appears on Word Chart 4, so I write it as a virtual word on the wall.

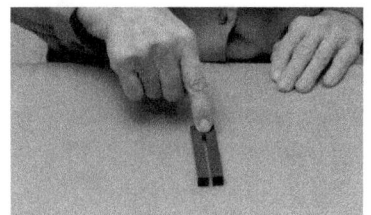
The same colour

Same and *different* are useful again when, on the third chart, work begins on *All these rods are blue. They're all (of) the same colour.* And *None of these rods is the same colour (as another). They're all (of) different colours.* Later, as we move through the charts, other opportunities come up: *Yolande and Marcel are the same age*, or *the same height*, or *the same weight. They like the same singers*, and many others.

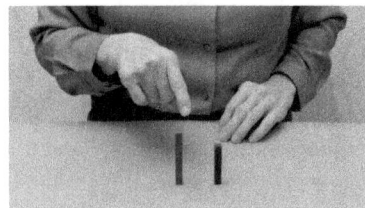
Two rods of different colours

Light and *dark*

It takes only a few seconds to show the students how to use these two words, using the green rods. I show a *light green rod* and a *dark green rod*. They are words I might have introduced while still working on Chart 1, showing them as virtual words. If so, all I have to do, as soon as the second chart is hung, is to ask the class if they recognise any of the words. Someone will almost certainly point to these two words.

The possessive adjectives

I begin with the word *my*. I give a rod to each student and take a blue one myself, then I show them my rod and hold it against my chest to indicate ownership or belonging. (I usually choose blue rods when launching a field because they are clearly visible from a distance and the colour is easy for most students to say.)

I point the sentence *My rod's blue* and invite the students to make their own sentence. To do this correctly, they have to change the colour so that it corresponds to what they are holding. Someone usually makes the proper change. Once everyone is at ease with this sentence, it is natural to move on to *His rod's green* and *Her rod's yellow*. I require each student to actually point to another student while looking at a third person. The use of *his* or *her* must be demonstrated explicitly.

For the word *your*, I give each student a rod, then ask two of them to come to the front of the class. I ask one to say, for example: *Your rod's light green and my rod's red* while using his finger to show who he is talking about. The second student must then say the same thing, using his finger: *My rod's light green and your rod's red*. The whole class then works on similar sentences.

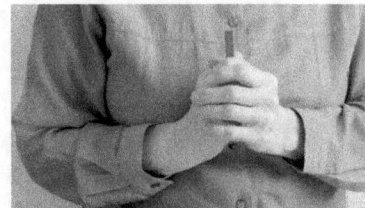

My rod's blue.

Another variant for *your* is to get students to use people's names. *My name's Anna. What's your name?* (There is no point in waiting until now to actually use the names of the students, so saying these sentences is purely formal. I never spend much time on the word *name*.)

We can also work on the apostrophe <s>. *What colour is Anna's rod?* and *What colour is her rod? Anna's rod's black* and *Her rod's black*. For these last two sentences I would use four fingers, treating the contraction of *is* as a separate word, but not the possessive apostrophe *'s*.

Introducing the plural words *our, your* and *their* requires care. It is possible to construct two different situations for each word. Either two people share two blue rods, each holding them at one end: *Our rods are blue*; or each of the two or more people involved has one or more blue rods: *Our rods are blue*. I want the students to be aware of the two possibilities. Both situations can be worked on, and then contrasted with *our* in the singular *Our rod's blue* where two people are holding the same rod.

These sentences give us another opportunity to work on the difference in pronunciation between *Our rod's blue* and *Our rods are blue*, where the verb *are* is reduced to its smallest possible form. It's the same 'test' as described in Chapter 12.

TEACHING ENGLISH THE SILENT WAY

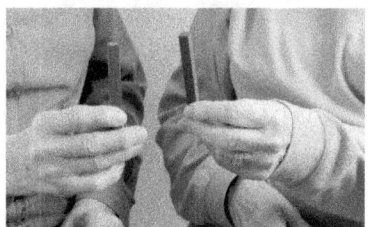

Our rod is blue.

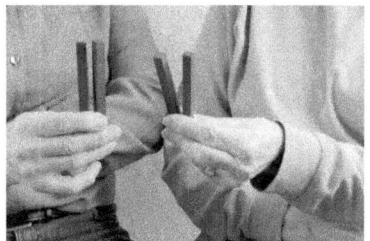

Our rods are blue.

Our rods are blue.

The possessive pronouns

To introduce the possessive pronouns, I have found that it is a good idea to create a sense of weariness from repeated use of the word *rod*. In English, it is unnatural to use the name of an object more than once when it is clear that this object is what is being talked about. The language has pronouns to avoid this. For the possessive pronouns, the forms are very easy to construct. We simply add <s> to the possessive adjective to create the pronoun. The only exceptions to this are *his* and *mine*.

Imagine a long session on the possessive adjectives which finishes with the class at ease. The next morning, I launch the same situation, and quite soon I indicate by gestures (or I say) *rod, rod, rod, rod* … I'm sick of rod!

I ask two students to come out and invite them to say *My rod's red, your rod's green*. I get one of them to place the words on my fingers, then, by lowering the finger carrying the second occurrence of *rod*, I indicate that it is possible to eliminate it from the sentence. Pointing to the relevant <s> on Chart 1, and then to the finger carrying *your*, I add a virtual <s> and so we arrive at *My rod's red, yours is green,* and the opposite, said by the second student *Your rod's green, mine's red*.

The students understand this change in the sentence very easily. It can be extended to all the other possessive pronouns by the students themselves. I simply indicate that they can guess what the word will be, and they do. They will discover that *his* is used for the pronoun as well as the adjective.

We now can go back to *Anna's rod's black,* this time reducing it to *Anna's is black* where the word *rod* is simply dropped out. We use the names of other students and then, if no one's name finishes with an <s>, I take a rod so that the students will use my name to illustrate the pronunciation *Ros's* in two syllables. We finish the session with more practice.

The words *this, that, these* and *those* (continued)

The word *those* allows us to complete the field of *this* and *that* begun on Chart 1. Whether the work was completed with Chart 1 or not, this is an excellent opportunity to go back over it. This time, the session might start with *These rods are the same colour* or *These rods are of two different colours*. This would depend on whether the students were already familiar with *same* and *different*.

I check that the class has integrated the idea that these words are relative. What might be *these rods* if they are placed close to the speaker can become *those rods* if other rods are placed closer to him.

The word *none*

To introduce the word *none*, I place just a few rods in the lid of the box.

None of these rods is white.

I get the students to take the lid and describe what they see. I vary the number and the colour of the rods so that sentences like *One of these rods is orange*, *Two of these rods are green* or *One of those rods is black* might come up, but I make sure that there are no white rods. Once the students have made some sentences, I point *None of these rods is white*. From the situation, the meaning is clear, although the sentence usually comes as a surprise. They think I have made a mistake either in the sentence I pointed or in the rods which are currently in the lid, until they realise that both were intended.

It will be necessary to work on the pronunciation of the words *none* and *no*. The vowel of *no* has two colours, and is well rounded, the vowel of *none* is yellow, and brief. The word *not* on Chart 1 adds a third pronunciation for the letter <o>, and the word *one*, in which it is pronounced /wʌ/, a fourth. The students might comment on this, either now or at some other moment. All I can do is shrug my shoulders: that's what English is like …

The word *none* can equally serve as a reply to the question *How many blue rods do you have? I have none* and then, more simply, just *None*. I will come back to this later when we work on *any* on Chart 4: *How many rods do you have? I don't have any.*

The pronunciation of *they*, *there* and *there*; *their* and *they're*

The students will need a lot of work on the pronunciation of these words. The way they are spelled is of no help in guessing how to pronounce them, so I will have to use the Rectangle chart and the Fidel as well as the Word charts to work on the problems.

Notice the position of the second *there* on Chart 1 and of *they* on Chart 2, in the bottom right-hand corners. Students need to differentiate between these words in terms of meaning and pronunciation. To the untrained ear of my students, there is very little difference between *there are* /ðərə/ and *they are* /ðeɪə/. We will need to spend some time producing both of them in authentically reduced forms so as to learn to perceive them as different, and to perceive them in native speech.

I combine all three of the words *there*, *they're* and *their* into sentences in order to highlight the fact that changes in meaning lead to changes in pronunciation. *There are three rods there. They are blue. Their rods are blue* moving on to *These are their rods, they're blue..* These sentences and other similar ones provide an opportunity to work on the vowels, diphthongs and triphthongs which sound almost identical to students' ears.

This work is not entirely new. While I was working on the Rectangle chart at the beginning of the course, I took the students through some of these differences. Now, of course, those strings of sounds have meaning.

The words *on*, *out* and *in*

In the lid of the box

On the lid of the box

Out of the lid of the box

On, out and *in* are easy since the context is clearly visible. I add the words *table, box* and *lid* to the students' vocabulary before putting them into circulation. Once they are available we can *Put the rods in the box, Take the rods out of the box, Put them on the table, Put the box on the table, Put the lid on the box*, etc. We can also *Take six green rods out of the box and put five of them on the table*.

Which

These words can then be used in sentences like *The rods which are on the table are red*, or *Which of the rods is yours, this one or that one?* and then *Which of these rods are yours, these ones or those ones?* The class can also handle *The rods which are on the table are a different colour from those which are in the box*.

Thus the sentences can become longer and more complex, more challenging.

MISTAKES TO AVOID

Don't introduce the simple present

Seeing *take* on Chart 1 and *I* on Chart 2, teachers might be tempted to work on *I take* but this would be a mistake. The meaning of the simple present form in English is best conveyed using the adverbs of frequency like *always, never* and *often* on Chart 7. So, until these adverbs are available, I would not open the field of the simple present with *I take, I put, I give, I do* and *I get*. On the other hand, *I have* can be suitably introduced in the current context.

Avoid formalising structures

Do not be tempted to formalise the structures used. I never make up a list on the board with *I, you, he, she, it, we, you, they*, for example. There are several reasons why this is counter-productive.

Firstly, I am not trying to produce an intellectual understanding of English in the students, but a living link between situations and words. We say *Give it to me* when we want a person to do something specific, and it is this desire which should trigger the language, not a thinking process which sorts through a list of words to find the right ones for the situation. That would give students knowledge about English and the satisfaction that knowledge produces. But this satisfaction is counter-productive because it leads students to stop doing the work which is necessary for them to give themselves a know-how. And knowing how to speak English—with words spontaneously presenting themselves as needed—is the aim.

If the students start making lists, I discourage them by taking them back to the sentences we have been using. If I speak their language, I ask them if they doubt whether they have understood. Of course, they have understood both the meaning of the sentence and the situation. I deliberately worked so that they would understand! I can't stop them from making lists of words or looking words up in a dictionary after class, but I can frown on the process during the lesson.

For intermediate and advanced students, when I am exploring the Verb Tense System (see Chapter 19), I do explore these conjugations systematically, because they have already met them in their previous learning and that is appropriate for their stage of learning. Even so, I still don't do this using anything like a conjugation table.

MORE ON RODS

Now that you have some experience with using rods, let me share some of Earl Stevick's (1976) observations on their use for language teaching.

> How essential are the rods, really? For years, I was skeptical on this point, preferring to use toy villages, or Tinkertoys, or real objects, and actively refusing to have anything to do with rods.
>
> My reasons for [now] preferring rods to toy houses and cars are more important. (1) The representational objects tell

> the beholder what kind of house, school, etc. to see: they preempt the functioning of imagination, which is one part of the total personality that we are trying to activate. (2) It is hard for representational objects to become what they are not. Rods, by contrast, have unbounded flexibility. The same rods may become, now a map of the Middle East, now a picture of a traffic accident, now a graphic analog of the surface structure of the Turkish noun, now a visible record of information that a student is giving about the neighborhood in which he lives. (p.145)

And,

> The presence, visibility, and manipulability of the rods mean that words are always intertwined with other kinds of interpersonal behavior. The rods are, moreover, flexible enough to parallel many different kinds of verbal behavior, whether that behavior is explaining a new point of grammar, or practicing that point in a systematic way, or telling a story, or playing a game. Students therefore remain in contact with the entire form-meaning complex at all times. Nor is this merely a theoretical feature of the Silent Way: it is, in fact, one of the features most frequently mentioned by the students with whom I have talked. (p.146)

MOVING ON

Generally speaking, I would suggest that you explore about ninety per cent of the early charts before hanging the next; unused words can be returned to later. So when we have worked on most of Chart 2, I might put up Chart 3. If I don't see what I can do with a word for the class I am working with, I feel free to decide to leave it for now. For example, if I think the class needs some time off from verbs, I might skip *have/had* or *did* and either do more work on Theme 3 or begin the work on comparatives and superlatives to be found on Chart 3.

By now, the numbers have certainly been worked on, and probably the days of the week and the months of the year, and perhaps telling the time. If not, now is a good time.

14. Expressing time

Before beginning the work proposed in this chapter, I make sure that the number system is in place, as described in Chapter 10.

I start here with the Dates chart, as the vocabulary will be useful for continuing with Charts 9 and 10. Also, it is more efficient to introduce all the days of the week and the months of the year before starting to construct sentences which will be using them.

Fri Sun Tues -day Wednes Mon Thurs Satur week autumn spring winter summer season date January March February August June April May July Septem Octo -ber Novem Decem month	past present future o'clock quarter half minute hour year first second third add once plus minus times twice divided around count point equal odd left age exact even thank century right	tomorrow yesterday now today ready time morning evening mid- day afternoon night during early late till soon until since yet before moment just last still then next ever while ago after
Dates	Chart 9: Time	Chart 10: Time triggers

THE ECONOMY OF LEARNING

We must keep in mind that learning vocabulary has a heavy cost in human energy, and that it is the students who pay. Learning the seven days of the week or the twelve months of the year is costly for those who do not speak Romance or Germanic languages. When students get to the sixth or seventh word, they are at the limit of what their memories can easily hold. These words are arbitrary for them, and so have to be remembered, stuck in place with mental glue. I am careful not to demand too much of them at any one time.

The Word charts are there to help. One of their roles is to remove the need to remember words. Instead, it is only necessary for a student who has forgotten a word to find the one he needs on a chart. During the course, a familiarity with words used in context to express what students want to say will make them as available as words in the students' native language. Memorisation should not be necessary. This is a huge economy of students' energy.

For all that follows in this chapter, I need a surface on which I can put the rods so that they are easily visible to all the students. If I am working with a class of more than twenty or twenty five students, I can fix the rods to the board in the appropriate positions with adhesive putty.

Each section below takes about an hour. However, it is easy to interrupt a session and go back to it later.

THE MONTHS

On the table I place twelve rods in four colours: three white ones, three light green ones, three yellow ones and three brown ones. I arrange them so that the students will be reading them from left to right.

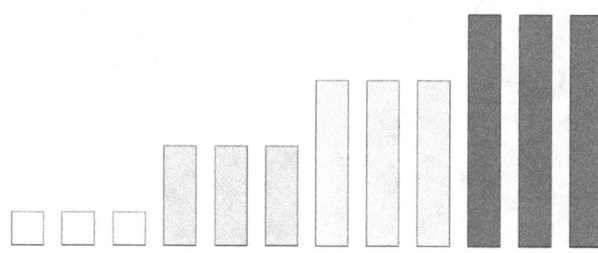

I get the students to count the rods (in English) so that everyone knows there are twelve. Then I take one of the white rods and place it on the other side of the brown ones.

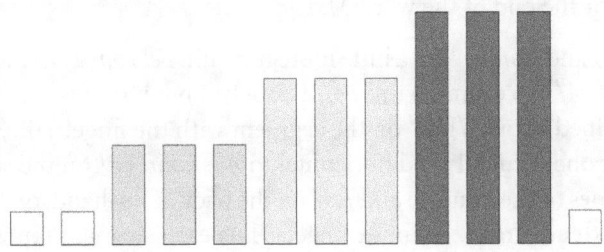

These rods represent the months of the year and the four seasons, at least in the northern hemisphere. If there is a doubt, it might be necessary to show a calendar.

I begin with the first brown rod, getting the students to say *September* by pointing the sounds on the Rectangle chart, where I can indicate the stress. Then I point the word on the Dates chart. The students say it several times, until they can confidently produce the stressed syllable surrounded by a full but unstressed vowel in the first syllable and a schwa in the final one.

Then I move to the second brown rod and, if any of the students speak a European language, I encourage them to guess, telling them that they can find the word by themselves: *October*. If not, I give it to them.

In the same way, I work on *November* and then *December*, which is represented by the white (snow-coloured) rod to the right. Depending on their linguistic background, many students will be able to guess these last two words.

If there is a mistake in the pronunciation, I have found that the problem is usually a misconception about the syllables in the word. To deal with such problems, I lift the index finger of my left hand (so that the word will unfold from left to right for the students) and curl it into a loose hook. I place a syllable virtually on each segment: *No **vem** ber*. With students who have some English, it can also be useful to simply say *Say it in English!* or *No, I'm hearing it in* (state the language)*! Make it sound English!* Often, by now, students know what to do to make it sound English.

Placing the syllables of November along my index finger..

Now, I go backwards to *August*, *July* and *June*, symbolised by the three yellow rods, then to *May*, *April* and *March*, which are the light green rods. Often both *May* and *March* can be guessed. I might pinch my thumb and my index finger together energetically to indicate the correct sound for the end of the word *March*.

February and *January* are a little more difficult. *February* has four beats /feb ru ə ri/. To examine this word closely, I put it on my index finger, as described above: /feb/ on the segment with the fingernail, /ru/ on the next one, which I hold horizontal to the floor, /ə/ on the segment which goes to the knuckle and /ri/ on the back of my hand, on the part which extends from the index finger. Thus each segment represents a syllable and, simply by indicating the segment, I can separate out each syllable of the word to make sure its pronunciation is precise. In this way, I can break the word down, get the students to establish the content of each of its syllables, and then bring these back together. I only have to touch the first segment of my finger with a little more energy to show where the stress is.

For *January*, /dʒæn ju ə ri/, I use the same technique. There are only two changes compared to *February*. *Feb* becomes *Jan* and /ru/ becomes /ju/. The ends of the words are identical. I also give the students another pronunciation which is simpler, /dʒæn jə ri/ in three syllables, which is very common and perfectly acceptable.

I can then go back to *February* and show them that it, too, can be said with three syllables, /feb ju ri/.

We spend some time saying the names of the months, in order and in any order. I touch a rod and the students name the corresponding month.

THE SEASONS

I now group the rods by colours, moving *January* and *February* to the right-hand end of the line behind *December*, and I introduce the notion of *spring, summer, autumn* and *winter,* using the colours of the rods as support.

As the students learn more English in Theme 1, we will be able to use the months and the seasons to develop sentences such as:

— There are four seasons in the year: spring, summer, autumn and winter.
— November is in autumn. July is in the middle of the summer.

I give myself the rule of thumb of trying not to introduce more than one new word in each sentence. It is always possible, and certainly beneficial, to come back to this domain later in the course when more vocabulary is available, and to extend the range of the sentences. But there is no hurry to introduce vocabulary. At this stage we are only working on the function words, leaving the luxury vocabulary for later.

THE DAYS OF THE WEEK

I place seven white rods in a line on the table, each one representing a day of the week. I stand a red rod on the white one which represents 'today'. (In this layout, the first day of the week is Sunday.)

This is what I put on the table if today is a Wednesday.

I begin by getting the students to count the rods: seven. This simple fact may give some of them an idea of what's to come, especially if we already counted to twelve for the months. I launch the work by showing the word for whatever day it is today on the Rectangle chart: let's say *Wednesday*. We then work through the other days, taking time to master the pronunciation of each. The students soon realise that it is only necessary to remember the first part of each word, since *-day* is the same for them all.

We finish with the sentence *There are seven days in a week*. Most students seem to know *week*, since they often know *weekend*. Then, if the necessary work has already been done

— Today is Wednesday, the 7th of March.
— Monday is the first day of the week.

If sentences like these can not yet be worked on, then when the work has been done on Charts 1, 2 and 3, they can be added to that.

— We go to school on Mondays, Tuesdays, Wednesdays, Thursdays and Fridays, but never on Saturdays or on Sundays.
— We have English class on Tuesdays.

Today's date

Before beginning, I might review the number system if I think it might be necessary. To prepare for this lesson, I check on the calendar for today's date, and also the day of the week that the first of this month fell on. I take a rod of the right colour for the season in which this month falls—for November I would choose a brown rod—and place it on the table. Then I put out 28, 30 or 31 white rods representing the days of the month. I put a red rod on 'today'.

In the example below, we are in the month of November which began on a Monday and today is Wednesday 17th. As always, I place the rods so that they are the right way around for the students, so the calendar will be upside down for me.

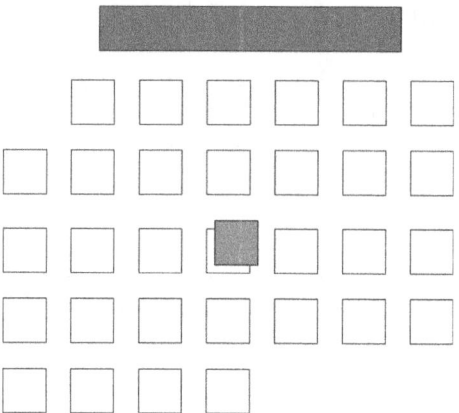

I point to the first white rod and point *The first of November* on the charts. I then point *the seventeenth of November,* to check that everyone understands the situation. I can see the certainty on their faces. We then work through the days of the month, introducing the ordinal numbers, always with the date and the month, *the sixteenth of November, the eighteenth of November*. I rapidly add the day, so that the students say *Thursday the seventeenth of November*.

The ordinal numbers are not a big leap from the cardinals. The transformation is fairly regular and predictable. The most problematic ordinals are *first, second* and *third* because they are irregular, and *fifth, sixth, eighth, twentieth* and *thirtieth* because of their pronunciation.

At the end of the work, everyone can say the day and date of all the days of the year. I don't need to check on all the days to know this, it is easy to see when the students understand the principle. I can hear the ease in their voices.

Week by week

With the same layout, I can now work on another aspect of the expression of time.

I point to the red rod and get the students to say *the 17th of November* and I indicate the current week by laying one pointer just above and another just below the line of rods.

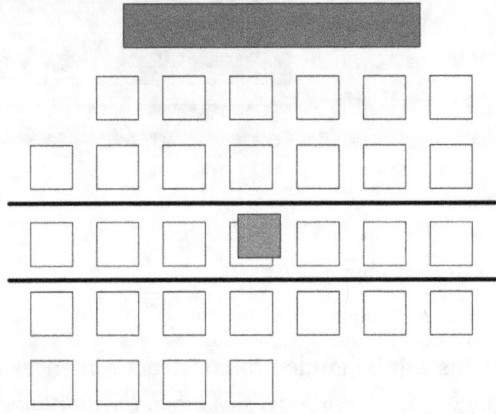

I lay two pointers across the layout

I point *this week*. I can now work on *last week*, and *the week before last*, *next week* and *the week after next*. *Before, after, next* and *last* are on Chart 10, which can be hung under the Rectangle chart for this work. If enough background work has already been done, I might try to get the students to deduce the last two of these phrases from the first two. If they know the opposite of *last*, and the opposite of *before*, they can usually manage it. It helps if I show four fingers—the answer will contain four words. Whether the students can guess these words will depend on when the work is done: if this is the first time the students have met these words, there is no point in asking them to guess. If the words have been seen elsewhere, they may be guessed.

Now we can start talking about months in the same way. Obviously, if *November* is *this month*, then *December* is *next month* and *January* is *the month after next*. Similarly, *October* and *September* can be named *last month* and *the month before last*. I elicit these phrases by putting down rods; I use the colour that I used for the season for each of the five months.

In the diagram below, I have written the words next to the rods for the benefit of the reader. However, in class I don't write these words. They are only pointed on the charts.

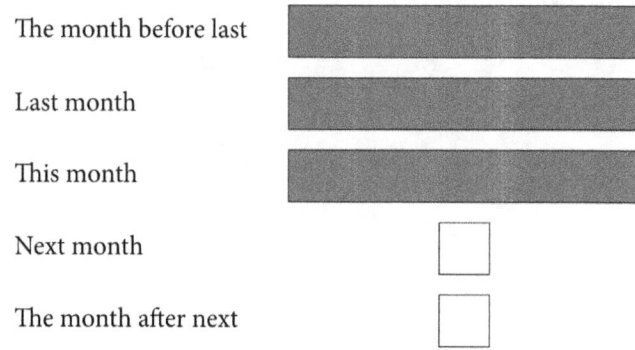

Now the students can be guided to construct sentences such as *This month is November. Last month was October, the month before last was September. Next month will be December, and the month after next will be January.* In this situation, the change of verb tense from the present to the past or to *will be* is completely logical, and never poses a problem, even if this work is done before *will* and *was* have appeared elsewhere.

If I have already taught the students how to say the year, then I write the year on the board and we go on to *next year, the year after next, last year* and *the year before last* using the same logic.

For students who are still at school, sentences like *Last year my teacher's name was Mrs. Dupont* are possible. They help to make sure that everyone (and not just nearly everyone) has understood what we are talking about. Sentences like this help to make the meaning absolutely clear.

If these ideas are launched quite late in the year, or if the work is being done as revision for the introduction of 'the past', the students will have enough English to construct sentences like

— The summer before last, we went to Toulon for three weeks.
— Last winter, we went to Chamonix for the Christmas holidays.

(If the word *Christmas* is a problem, I can show *The 25th of December is Christmas Day* and the opposite construction *Christmas Day is the 25th of December.*)

WORKING WITH BEGINNERS

All these sentences must be true. If a student did not go away last summer, the sentence will be *Last summer, we stayed at home*. The certainty that they understand is at stake. The students in a class know very well what each of them did during the summer. If they hear Marie saying *Last summer, we went to Toulon* when all her friends know she stayed at home, it might cast doubt on the meaning of the sentence in some students' minds.

As well as this, when Marie says the sentence which corresponds to her life, the words are retained much more easily by her and by her friends, since they reflect the reality of her life and touch her emotionally. So, each sentence begins as true to life, and through the teacher's correction and the class's work, it will become linguistically correct.

Yesterday, the day before yesterday …

With the rods set out in the same way, it is now easy to work from *today*, shown by a red rod on the day, to *yesterday*, *the day before yesterday*, *tomorrow* and *the day after tomorrow*. The students can now make sentences such as *Today is Wednesday the 17th of November* and add the year. *Tomorrow will be Thursday the 18th of November 20xx. The day after tomorrow will be Friday the 19th of November. Yesterday was Tuesday the 16th of November*, etc.

There is another kind of time marker in English. I get the students to count back from today: *yesterday, the day before yesterday, three days ago, four days ago, seven days ago* which we transform into *a week ago, ten days ago, a few days ago, three weeks ago, a month ago*, etc. Towards the future, *today, tomorrow, the day after tomorrow, in three days' time,*

in four days' time, *in seven days' time* which is also *in a week's time, in ten days' time, in a few days' time*, etc. Most of these phrases mark a specific day that we can show with the pointer. If I point to a rod which is quite a long way from the red rod, our anchor in the reality of time, they will have to count to know how many days they have to say.

Other relationships often become clearer too: *a week ago* and *last Wednesday* each represent a particular day, while *last week* is used for the whole seven days. These expressions are made clearer because of the way the time words are shown with the rods as well as through the sentences constructed by the class. They will be used as 'triggers' when we lay out the verb tense system in Chapter 19.

The words *month* and *year* can be substituted for *day*, which opens up still more possibilities. Students can then talk about their lives.

— The year after next, we'll be in middle school.
— Next year, Yolande is going to retire.
— Next week, we'll be on holiday for two weeks.

TELLING THE TIME

I arrange red and light green rods on the table to create a clock. The students immediately realise that we are dealing with telling the time. In the centre of the clock, I place two rods, a blue one which represents the big (minute) hand, and a pink one which represents the little (hour) hand.

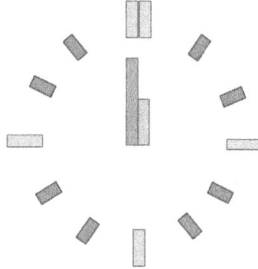

Then in order to introduce time clearly, I remove the minute hand, leaving only the hour hand.

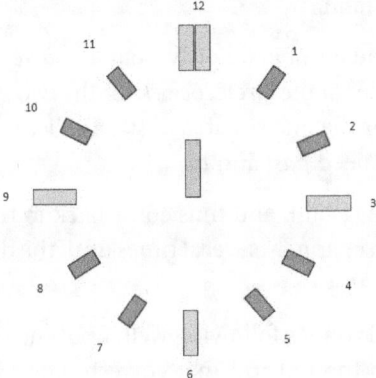

Pointing to the appropriate red rod, I show the word *one* on the Numbers chart. I invite the students to name the rods following this indication, and they can do so easily. They only have to count. In the illustration, for the benefit of the reader, the rods are numbered to show the role of the little hand. In class, the students work without the aid of written numbers, as I can rely on their powers of evocation.

When the students have named all the positions of the pink rod, I take it away and put the blue one back, pointing at twelve.

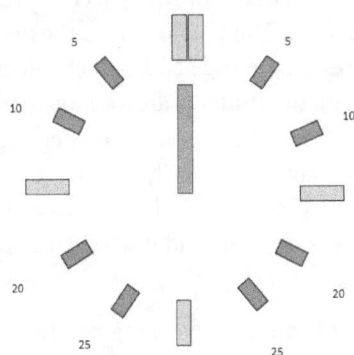

I place my two index fingers on the two red rods situated on either side of it and I say out loud *five*. The students repeat *five*. I move my fingers to the next red rods and wait a moment. If nobody says it, I say *ten*. Someone usually says *twenty* and *twenty-five* when I move my fingers to the corresponding red rods. The others see that it is possible to guess, and try to understand.

Once they have the numbers, I give them *a quarter* for the green rods situated on the sides of the circle, *o'clock* for the two green rods marking twelve and *half* for the one situated at six. To distinguish the two sides of the clock, they need *past* and *to*.

I change the hands again, and thus come back to the hours. We work on the two hands separately several times until the different use of each hand becomes clear.

When I think everyone is following well, I put the minute hand in the circle pointing to the red rod that corresponds to *ten past*, and the students say it. I add the hour hand pointing to *one*, and they say this. I run my finger along the rods to indicate the order of the words and they say *ten past … one*. I get them to put the two halves of the sentence together and they have *ten past one*.

We spend a while telling the time.

If I see that there is someone in the class who needs more practice, I have him sit in my place, facing the other students, and ask him to show combinations he finds difficult. The person sitting in my place is always silent, just like me, so sitting in my place is not a source of anxiety. The class gives the answers, the student only changes the place of the hands.

After a few minutes, I wink at him, my face expressing something like *Let's play a joke on them*. Then I take one of the two green rods marking twelve and put it beside the rod at six, which effectively turns the clock around. Suddenly, all the students are looking at the clock upside down, except the student sitting in my place. This change launches the work again, because they have to mentally turn the clock around in order to tell the time. Once they have adapted, I can place the green rod elsewhere, turning the clock as I like. Instead of changing the place of the hands, I turn the clock.

We spend the rest of the hour working on the time in this way, until everybody is at ease.

Because the students already know the numbers before working on this field, they only need to integrate six new vocabulary items to tell the time. In Gattegno's terminology, the cost of learning to tell the time is only six ogdens (or 'memory units').

Time as a game of rhythm

A few days later, I continue with the work on time, but in a different way, as a game of rhythm. I check that everyone can still tell the time, then I clap three times rather slowly (which I will indicate with the letter X, like this: X X X). I ask the students to guess the time I clapped. Usually several people guess correctly, which astonishes others. They realise that X X X can be *five past one* or *ten past two* but not *ten to one* which has to be clapped thus: X x X. In this context the word *to* is stuttered, whereas *past* contains a full vowel. We spend a few minutes with the students guessing from the rhythms and groupings I clap what time I have in my mind. If a student makes a mistake, I clap the correct rhythm for what he proposed and then my proposition. When they can guess the easy examples fairly accurately, I go on to more difficult ones.

x X x x X x can only be *a quarter to seven*. All other solutions are impossible. On the other hand, for X x X X, there are ten different combinations, all of them *twenty past... twenty past one, twenty past two, twenty past three,* etc. except *seven* and *eleven* which both have more than one syllable.

If some of the students have problems, which is often the case, I clap different combinations and ask them to decide whether I am clapping *to* or *past*. This is much easier, and almost everyone can do it.

My students thus discover that it can be possible to recognise the time in English simply from hearing it clapped, that is to say, simply from the rhythm of the sentence: the emphasis I place on the stressed syllables and the way I group the claps to reflect the grouping of words in telling the time. The words aren't necessary. This is a striking discovery for people starting to learn English, indicating the importance of rhythm in the language.

Working on time every day

After time has been introduced, I keep working on it for the rest of the course. It allows me to introduce other adverbs in real situations. There are several sentences to be said for a time that is between five to and the hour. *It's almost 4 o'clock, it's just before, just after, a little before, a little after, it's not 4 o'clock yet. Is it 4 o'clock yet?*

When I begin work on the Verb Tense System we can contrast sentences like, *It hasn't turned 4 o'clock yet. Now it has turned 4 o'clock. It turned 4 o'clock a few seconds ago.*

THE TEMPERATURE

Only a few words are necessary in order to be able to state the temperature. The word *degrees* allows students to say temperatures above zero: 6° which is said *six degrees*, 15° which is *fifteen degrees*.

For temperatures below zero, there are two possibilities: *It's minus six* or sometimes *It's six below*.

THE WEATHER

As far as the weather is concerned, the work is much less interesting, since the vocabulary 'has no future'. You cannot use the word *windy* to say anything other than *It's windy*. These words only have one usage, unlike the words on the charts, which can be used in many different ways. *It's cold* can become *It's windy* or *It's wet*, *It's cloudy* or *It's dry*. What use is that at this stage in the learning process?

The words and structures which 'have a future' are those which can be reinvested rapidly in other sentences and structures. The numbers come up all through the language. They have a future, a high yield. I never forget that my role is to make the students work on the hardest parts of the language so that these can be practised for most of the course. I prefer to introduce the vocabulary of the weather throughout the course, as the climate changes from day to day. The best day to learn to say *It's cold* and *I'm cold* is when it is actually cold.

15. Exploring Word Chart 3

When the third chart is hung, it takes its place beside the first two charts which remain on the wall in the same places. By now, Theme 3, about numbers and time, will have been worked on extensively.

THE FIELDS OF WORD CHART 3

Two areas stand out when one looks at this chart for the first time: the past forms of the verbs the students have been using, and the comparatives and superlatives. There are also a few common words such as *some*, *by*, *both*, *all*, *much* and *very*.

When I work on Word Chart 3, I run Theme 1, the function words, and Theme 2, the verb tenses, in parallel. I would never try to complete one before starting the other. The work on the verbs needs to be broken into small but coherent parts and the forms practised in a variety of contexts which the work on the function words will give me. Students need time to assimilate and practise what has been done. The new function words allow me to expand Theme 1 in many directions, working on structures which are less demanding than the verbs because the situations illustrating them are more readily understood.

Let's begin with Theme 2, the verb tenses.

at	some	longer	-est
both	go	given	much
from	as	taken	not	all
who	than	be	long	-er
but	short	by	told	's
can	if	gave	will	-ing
was	tall	tell	took	'll
come	so	like	very	'll
were	-ed	-ed	-ed	-t

Word Chart 3

THEME 2—WORK ON THE VERB TENSES

On Chart 3, we have the words *given*, *taken*, *gave* and *took*; and *put* is available from the first chart. These verb forms give me access to the Present Perfect and to the Simple Past. We also have *-ing*, *was* and *were* which allow work to begin on the two most common Progressive forms. At the end of our work on this chart, the students will have used four forms: the Present Progressive, the Present Perfect, the Simple Past and the Past Progressive. They will not yet have used the Simple Present except with *have* as a verb, and although everything necessary to begin work on the Past Perfect is available (since *had* is on the second chart), I would not launch this work either. I don't have to initiate something now just because the charts give me what is necessary for it.

What I am aiming for

When I speak, the form of the verb I use expresses my inner climate. If my inner climate involves an awareness of how I am spending my time, I use the Present Progressive: *I'm taking rods out of the box one by one* and also *I'm learning Greek at the moment* (although I am not doing it at this instant). If I locate what I am about to say at a particular moment in the past, I use a past form, and so on. For my students, I want the right form to be associated with each inner climate and the inner climate to trigger the form. The forms and a sensitivity to the climates that English allows one to express must be developed together. This is why I do not present my students with rules for each form, as a grammar book would do. This would be contrary to what I am working for. To do so would produce knowledge—an intellectual understanding of these forms—whereas I want the students to develop a know-how—a feel for what to say based in their lived experience.

Triggers

In English, most verb forms are accompanied by adverbs or other expressions of time and these can be used by students to trigger the verb forms. It is easy for students to develop an inner climate for *always* or *yesterday* which can then be associated to the forms of the Simple Present or Simple Past. Some of these expressions have been introduced by now, since the work on Theme 3 is drawing to a close, and as they become available, work can begin on the verb forms which they accompany. When students talk about their lives, if they use a trigger they can be confident of the verb form which goes with it. Triggers like *every week, once a month, always, often, never, generally,* etc. will be found in sentences like *I take the bus to work every day*. The word *yesterday* triggers the Simple Past. *Already, yet* and *not yet* are usually found with *have* as the auxiliary, etc. Instead of giving students rules to apply, I give them triggers to use. This produces a feel for the 'climate' of each verb form rather than knowledge about them.

The *-ing* form

The *-ing* form is used to describe what I am investing my time and energies in at the moment. This form describes situations I am living which extend in time: *I'm studying Greek this year* or *I'm learning to swim at the moment*. Once I can swim, I will stop learning, and swimming will become part of my repertoire of know-hows and be expressed in the form *I can swim*.

Tempting though it seems, taking a single rod out of a box is not really a satisfactory situation to illustrate the *-ing* form. By the time the student has said the sentence *I'm taking a rod out of the box*, especially at the beginning when he might be struggling with the order of the words or the pronunciation, the rod has been out of the box for some time and the sentence is no longer appropriate. So, after a few minutes spent on *one by one, two by two, three by three*, etc., I work on *I'm taking the red rods out of the box one by one* which gives them enough time to say what they are doing. Then we need to vary the pronouns and the colours in the usual way so that the students get enough varied practice. This construction is not difficult for the students since they already have most of what they need.

I might also introduce the verbs *standing* and *lying*, 'writing' them (invisibly) on the wall above the chart. This allows sentences like *The orange rod's lying on the table* or *The yellow rod's standing on the table*. Of course we work on plurals too: *The blue rods are standing on the table*.

This last sentence allows me to repeat the 'test' I gave before. I put two blue rods at one end of the table and a single one at the other end. Then I say the sentence in either the singular or plural form, using maximal reduction for the word *are*, and the students have to point to the rods that I have described. Again, the shocking extent to which *are* is reduced in English is driven home. I now give students the chance to practise saying the sentences.

The Simple Past—*I took a rod and I gave it to him*

For work on the Simple Past we will need the various time words. If these are not yet in circulation, I spend several lessons working with them. Now we are equipped to work on this form.

I get a student to take a rod out of the box and I indicate, without speaking, that he should pass it to someone of his choice. This second person then passes it to a third, who passes it on to another student. When the rod has passed through the hands of four or five people, I ask the person who is now holding the rod to put it back in the box. The situation can be described like this:

> A few moments ago, Alice took a rod out of the box and gave it to Julien. Julien gave it to Ali. Ali gave it to Philippe. Philippe gave it to Jeanne. Jeanne gave it to Fred and Fred put it back in the box.

Now that the scope of the work has been established, we begin again with a second rod of a different colour. As we go on, the trigger will change. *A few moments ago* becomes *a few minutes ago*, then *ten minutes ago*, then *a quarter of an hour ago*.

We now use pronouns rather than names. I ask the students to use a finger to point to each participant at each step:

> A moment ago he gave him a rod and he gave it to her, and she gave it to me, and I put it back in the box.

To work on the first person, I point *I took a rod and I gave it to him* to be said by the first speaker. In the end, each student will have said several sentences which correspond to different things that he did: taking a rod out of the box, giving it to someone and putting it back in the box.

In this way, each student can experience the meaning and the correctness of the sentences in a real situation. Each sentence must be established as being in the past, so the rod must be put back in the box before the description of the situation begins, and the sentence must contain an appropriate trigger.

This work takes place over several days until the students are more or less at ease with expressing these kinds of situations.

The word *who*

My next step might well be to introduce the word *who* which allows the students to say:

> Julien gave the rod to Ali who gave it to Philippe who gave it to Jeanne ... who gave it to Fred who put it back in the box.

I use my fingers to show that the pronoun *who* takes the place of *and he* or *and she*.

After the students have had at least one or two nights' sleep on this, I go on to the questions which can be asked about the situation. To do this, I take a rod out of the box and send it around the class until it has been in the hands of so many people that it becomes difficult to remember who gave it to whom. This opens the situation to questions such as:

> — Philippe, who did you give it to?
> — I gave it to Ali.
> — Ali, who did you give it to?

and then:

> — Who did Philippe give it to?
> — Who did Ali give it to?

and then:

> — Who gave it to Julien?
> — John did.
> — Who gave it to Rachid?
> — She did.
> — I gave it to Fred.
> — Fred, who did you give it to?

Fred has a problem because he put the rod away. I show *I didn't give it to anyone, I put it back in the box.* (The word *any* can easily be 'borrowed' by covering the <m> of *many* on Chart 2.)

On another day, the situation can be turned around:

> — Ali, who did you get your rod from?
> — I got it from Marcel.
> — Marcel, who did you get yours from?

The Passive voice

Since everything necessary for it is available, the Passive voice can be introduced at any time from now on. With beginners, though, I find it better to wait since they can easily get muddled by what they have learnt recently. However if a student needed the Passive and I had to illustrate it for the class, a suitable sentence might be *I was given a rod by Philippe and I gave it to Laetitia.*

HOW LONG THE WORK SHOULD TAKE

What has just been described takes place over several days in an intensive course, or over several weeks if the class meets only once or twice a week. Obviously, each step requires a lot of practice and other areas of the language provide the time for the work on the verbs to be suitably spaced over several lessons and, just as important, the time for the work to be integrated over several nights' sleep.

The Present Perfect—*I've taken a rod*

The form of the Present Perfect is not entirely new, since the students have been using *I've got a rod* for some time. So for the work we are about to do, only the words *given* and *taken* are new. The inner climate that the Present Perfect expresses, however, is entirely new.

Many European languages have a form constructed using *have* + Past Participle which is used to speak of a past event. Students whose languages have such a form for the past often equate the English Present Perfect with it and then struggle for years to distinguish this from the Simple Past. The answer they often get from their textbooks is that the Present Perfect expresses 'a past action with present relevance', but this still leaves the emphasis on the past action with the concept of present relevance rather unclear.

I regard the Present Perfect as expressing a present state by means of the way it came about. When a mother asks her child *Have you washed your hands?* she is asking if the hands are clean. For this reason, I aim for the students to develop a feel for the 'presentness' of the English Present Perfect.

At this point in a course, however, my aim is to do more than just to put the form into circulation; I want to jolt my European students out of equating what they use in their own language with the English form. I do this by presenting it in situations where they use it with the word *now*, which is an unambiguous trigger for the present.

I have already worked on some of the time triggers on Charts 9 and 10 so that students can locate themselves in time in English.

> A few minutes ago, Ali gave me some red rods, and now I've given one to Fred.

For this sentence to be correct English and true to the situation, Fred must still be holding the rod that the speaker gave him.

> A few minutes ago, Ali gave Yolande some green rods and now she has put them on the table.

Similarly, for this sentence to be true, the rods must still be on the table.

> — A few minutes ago, Marcel gave me some rods, and I gave them to Yolande. Now Yolande has put them back in the box.

In the first sentence, the trigger is *a few minutes ago* and the sentence is in the Simple Past. In the second sentence, the trigger is *now* and the rods must still be in the box.

Not yet is also a trigger for the Present Perfect.

> — Take twenty rods out of the box, one by one.

Then, while the action is being done,

> — Have you taken them all out of the box yet?
> — No, not yet. I've only taken ten out of the box.

With the language the students have at the moment, it is difficult to go further than this now. I describe more work on this verb form in Chapter 19.

Don't let yourself be tempted into giving an explanation for the Present Perfect. Explanations seem to move the class forward, but do not create a correspondence between one's inner climate and the verb form it triggers.

This treatment of the Present Perfect in the Silent Way is another example of how paradigms and constructions which have no counterpart in the students' native language are not put off until later but met head on. We do not want students to internalise an incorrect view of the language they are learning which they will find hard to modify at a later stage. Time in class is best spent on those aspects of the language which students would find difficult to master by themselves outside the classroom.

The words *go* and *come* in phrasal verbs

I present *go* and *come* as new vocabulary and soon after that I start using *go* in the construction *going to* + verb. *Go* and *come* also provide us with the opportunity to work on phrasal verbs, which behave quite differently from verbs in many other languages.

In phrasal verbs like *go in* and *come over*, both the direction of the movement and the location of the speaker are taken into account. In many other languages, a different approach is taken: only the nature of the movement is expressed. For example, in French, although *go* and *come* are translated as *aller* and *venir*, both *go in* and *come in* would be translated by *entrer* which expresses the notion of movement and its inward direction but ignores the location of the speaker.

I start the work on phrasal verbs early, using *go* and *come*. The students perform the situations when the words are said because this is the only way they will develop a feel for verbs with postpositions. I work on the pronunciation and then choose a calm student who knows he would never be sent out of the class for a misdemeanour, and point the phrase *Marcel, go out*. I get the class to say the phrase to Marcel and, using a gesture, I signal to him to go out of the room. Then we say *Come back in*.

The students practise with other members of the class, sending one or more people out and bringing them in by speaking the sentence within the room, or sending the people in and bringing them out by speaking the sentence outside the room. Once everyone is at ease with these sentences, we go on to slightly more difficult ones. They now make sentences like *Marcel, come out here. Go back into the room.* There can be a technical problem with these last sentences if I become caught up in the scenario; if I am out of the room I cannot point to words on the charts. The solution, of course, is to get students to take over, moving in and out of the classroom, giving the instructions and pointing on the charts if necessary. These sentences create a lot of movement in the class, to the delight of younger students.

I make it easier for the students to understand by using gestures and getting them to do so, too, but several examples will be needed before everyone has grasped the meaning of these words: they not only give an order, but place the speaker at the same time. Where am I when I say *Come out*? Where am I when I say *Go out*?

To enrich the situation further, we can introduce *back* and *again*, with sentences like *Marcel, go out. Come back in.* and *Go back out. Come back in again.* and other variations like *Come over here.* and *Go over there.* I use *black* from the last line of Chart 1 to produce *back* and 'write' the word on the wall just below *black*. I point *again* on the Fidel and 'write' it a few lines under *back*. When Chart 5 is hung underneath Chart 1, both *back* and *again* will appear in these places.

I'm going to take a rod

The students already know the *-ing* form. This builds on it, but with an important modification of the pronunciation compared with what they see on the charts. This signals that the speaker is using the verb *go* not to express actual motion but rather his inner feeling of involvement in an activity that has already been decided upon even though it has not yet started.

I set up the situation; as always, the meaning only becomes clear if the sentence is illustrated by actions. While the student is still seated, I would point to the following sentences and ask him to say *I'm going to go to the table, I'm going to take an orange rod* and *I'm going to put it there*. Only when he has finished speaking does he stand up and perform the three actions.

Obviously the pronouns should then be varied. Once a student has announced his intentions, but before he moves, other students can say *He's going to … She's going to …* etc. Of course, the person's destination, the place where the rod is put, the person to whom it is given, the number of rods, etc., can all be varied.

My students need to know that *going to* used for future reference is often pronounced *gonna* (/gənə/). I point the sentence *I'm going to take an orange rod* and place the words on my fingers. I close the fingers with *going* and *to* together (in the same way that my first two fingers are closed to show *I'm* rather than *I am*), and run the index finger of my other hand around them to show that they will now be said as a single unit. I now point /gənə/ on the Rectangle chart. We work on the pronunciation of the first five words until it is easy, and then vary the verb (*I'm going to give/put/take/go*) and the pronoun (*He's/she's going to …*). I write *going to* under Chart 3, about 4 lines down, where the words will appear when Chart 7 is hung.

I might also group this form with the Present Progressive and the Simple Past in a series of actions. I might get the students to say, while seated, *I'm going to take some orange rods*; then to go to the table and say *I'm taking some orange rods one by one* while performing the action; and then, after sitting down, *I took some orange rods and I put them in the box.*

At some point, the Present Progressive of the verb *go* will be needed in its literal sense, and the students will discover the pronunciation of *going to* in a sentence like *We're going to lunch*. For this, they have to construct it using *go + -ing* on Chart 3.

I was going to give it to Ali, but I didn't

A sentence like *I was going to give it to Ali, but in the end, I gave it to Fred* is not a problem for most students and I would work with it if possible, but it has to wait until a suitable situation comes up in class since I can't know what a student is thinking. The use of *was* with *going to* will come up again later in Chapter 17.

LETTING STUDENTS 'SLEEP ON IT'

I never introduce two verb forms on the same day unless I need to contrast them. I always work on each verb form until all the students are sure of its construction and have some idea of the inner climate which creates the need for this form rather than a different one. Then I stop until they have had a night's sleep. I intersperse the work on verb forms with work from other themes; this avoids students becoming muddled.

COMPARISONS

With beginners, the work on verbs described above will take many hours. It will be broken up with work based on the rest of the third chart and also the following charts.

We have three adjectives—*long*, *short* and *tall*—on Chart 3 as well as the endings *-er* and *-est* and also the word *than* (with a pale yellow schwa because it has no strong form). With these words, we can cover the field of comparison. We begin by comparing the rods using sentences like *The blue rod's longer than the yellow one*. To illustrate the meaning of this sentence, I pick up a blue rod and a yellow one and hold them together side by side, then I run my finger along the side of each rod and indicate the length with my thumb and index finger, making it clear that we are going to talk about their length. Then we work on other combinations: *The red rod's longer than the white one*, *The white one's shorter than the red one* etc., until the students have had enough practice.

The blue rod's longer than the yellow one.

When these first sentences are in place, i.e. when the students have developed a facility in comparing one rod to another, I expand the challenge. I now place three rods, then six or seven, then all ten rods, side by side on the table in any order. This produces much longer sentences: *The orange rod's longer than the blue one, which is longer than the dark green one, which is shorter than the brown one, which is longer than the red one, which is shorter than the pink one, which is longer than the white one.* It will take time before the whole class can easily produce a sentence like this, describing what they see in front of them.

I might introduce the word *centimetre* now, using the Rectangle chart rather than the Fidel so that I am giving the pronunciation without giving the spelling. The vowel in the <cen> syllable is pointed at the top of the chart and all the other vowels are pointed in the bottom section of the chart, using the dashed rectangle for the full but unstressed vowel in <me>.

Once the students can say it, I ask them to write the word on the board, which the French students I usually teach find difficult (they usually begin the word with the letter <s>, for example). It may take several guesses before they realise that it is a word they know, because the pronunciation is very different from French. They confirm the spelling by now pointing the word on the Fidel.

Words like this provide an excellent opportunity to show students from any linguistic background how English words are structured: in order to highlight the stressed syllable, the rest of the word is put into relative shadow.

The introduction of *centimetre* opens the way for sentences such as *The orange rod is ten centimetres long*, then *The yellow rod is one centimetre longer than the pink one*.

When Chart 4 is hung and the word *end* is available, we can come back and compare combined lengths, using rods placed end to end: *Three pink rods end to end are two centimetres longer than one orange one*. It is easy to move from here into a lesson on basic arithmetic if the curriculum for the learners requires this; but many people anyway enjoy doing simple arithmetical activities conducted in English. When working with literate adults these have the advantage that the content is understood by everyone.

Superlatives

To introduce the ending *-est,* I place an orange rod beside two rods of other colours—a black one and a yellow one, for example—to create a situation in which *The orange rod is the longest of the three* and *The yellow rod is the shortest of the three*. Adding the phrase *of the three* helps the students to identify what we are doing. With a similar situation, but using only two rods, sentences using *longer* and *shorter* should be made: *The red rod is the shorter of the two* compared to *The red rod is the shortest of the three*. I juxtapose examples such as these to clarify the different usages in English.

The words *tall* and *short*

The word *tall* allows us to move away from the rods to compare the relative heights of the students: *Marcel is taller than Yolande. Marie is shorter than Alice but taller than Laetitia.*

I can also introduce *very* in a sentence like *Marcel is very tall.*

From here, we might go on to *How tall are you, Marcel? I'm one metre eighty-nine.*

I take every opportunity to work on stress and reduction. When I point the word *metre*, I come back to *centimetre* to make the contrast between the two ways of pointing the <me> syllable; this will provide an example of how word stress affects the pronunciation of English. The first syllable of *metre* will be pointed red in the upper section of the Rectangle chart but the corresponding <me> syllable of *centimetre* will be pointed in the dashed rectangle at the bottom.

Then,

> Ali is ten centimetres taller than Paul who is five centimetres taller than Fred.

And

> Ali is taller than Paul by ten centimetres.

From there, we might go on to

> If Ali is ten centimetres taller than Paul and Paul is five centimetres taller than Fred, then Ali is fifteen centimetres taller than Fred

and

> If Ali is ten centimetres taller than Paul and Paul is five centimetres taller than Fred, then Ali is taller than Fred by fifteen centimetres.

Sentences that are as long as these are not necessary for mastery of comparisons. However, there is a value to their length: as is the case with saying large numbers, students have the opportunity to develop confidence and enjoy a sense of achievement in making long sentences in English which they control. These are sentences they can recreate for themselves outside the class.

To further develop comparison, I can go back to Chart 1 a few days later using *as* to create sentences such as *Yolande is not as tall as Marcel*.

OTHER WORDS ON CHART 3

The word *like*

Obviously, sentences with *like* can be constructed with what is now available, but I would not advise teachers to use this word this early because expressing similarities or one's likes and dislikes can set off a race for the vocabulary they can require.

The words *tell* and *told*

The words *tell* and *told* on this chart open up more and more complex sentences while never straying far from what is already known.

The contrast with *say* will come in soon.

    MARIE: Philippe, tell Ali to take a rod.
    PHILIPPE: Ali, take a rod!
    ALI: Philippe told me to take a rod, so I took one.

    MARCEL: Rachid, tell Julien to take a rod and give it to Elodie.
    RACHID: Julien, take a rod and give it to Elodie.
    JULIEN: Rachid told me to take a rod and give it to Elodie, so I did.

    RACHID: Julien, take a rod and give it to Elodie.
    JULIEN: Rachid told me to take a rod and give it to Elodie, but I didn't.

Starting work on the modals: *can*, *will* and *shall*

It is easy to construct classroom examples using indicative forms but more difficult to do so with modals. As I explain in Chapter 19, modals express the 'mood' of the speaker and I can't produce moods in my students at will. Instead, I need to be in a position to exploit any naturally occurring classroom situation where a student's mood is apparent or can be easily induced.

To lay the groundwork for this, I need to introduce each of the modals in a way that gives students some inkling of their meaning, but without any exploration at this point. Instead, I want the meanings to reveal themselves through natural situations that arise while the students are experiencing a 'mood' that can be expressed by a modal. For there to be plenty of examples of this, I need to be constantly alert over the rest of the course to the possibility of recasting any situation so that a modal can be used authentically.

For example, to introduce *will* and *can*, I might use the following set up:

—Will you take a green rod out of the box, please?
—I can't. There are no green rods in the box / There aren't any green rods in the box.

It is not a good idea to begin work on *will* by using the word to talk about future events. I do not want *will* to be misunderstood as a Future Tense in English when, in fact, English does not have a Future Tense in the sense that French or Latin have one. It is preferable to start the work on this word using quite different situations.

For another example of *will* and *can*, I build a tower using two or three orange or blue rods, standing one on top of the other end to end to make a tall structure. Then sentences like the following can be worked on:

—Can I put another rod here? (pointing to the top of the tower)
—No, you can't. If you put another rod there, the rods will fall.

This is a correct use of *will* and does not cause problems later on.

The words *some* and *some*—there are two of them

Some is treated as two separate words and appears twice on the charts. On Chart 3 we find *some*, the determiner, used unstressed in most contexts and found in sentences such as *Take some rods*, where it indicates a number which is appropriate for the occasion, neither too few nor too many. On Chart 5, the word is shown only in the full form, the pronoun, used in sentences such as *Some of the rods are green, others are red*.

To demonstrate the determiner, I put out the red rods in a pile and indicate to students to ask one another to either take 'some' or a specific

If you put a black rod on top of the blue one, all the rods will fall.

number: *Take some rods* or *Take four rods*. When a number is used, the rods are counted. When *some* is used, the rods are not counted, simply taken; the gesture made with the hand is quite different. Note the stress pattern: if we use a number word, we stress it because that is the number we want. If we use *some*, we don't stress it because we don't care exactly how many rods are taken.

Both rods, the two rods and all the rods

The word *both* can be surprising for those who speak a language which only possesses the opposition singular/plural.

Both can be worked on by linking it to *the two* (Chart 1) and the words *this*, *that*, *these* and *those*. The students can make sentences such as:

— The two rods on the table are green.
— Both the rods on the table are green.
— Both the rods are green.
— Both these rods are green.
— Both are green.

These sentences are contrasted with similar sentences using larger numbers:

— The three rods on the table are green.
— All the rods on the table are green.
— All the rods are green.
— All these rods are green.
— All of them are green.

These sentences can be followed by others which contrast *both* and *all* in new situations:

— These rods are both yellow.
— Both of these rods are yellow.
— Both of these rods are green, but one's light green and one's dark green.
— All these rods are green, but four are light green and three are dark green.

Starting with this last sentence, I would take away one rod at a time until the sentence requires a change from *all* to *both*.

These various constructions are best introduced one by one over several lessons, then grouped together one day to show what the various possibilities are. *Any* on Chart 4 and *some* on Chart 5 will give further opportunities to explore this system.

DON'T FORGET

All the sentences, without exception, must 'start true and finish correct'. Creating sentences which are true helps to make sure that no one gets lost (including the speaker); when students understand a correct sentence they can build reliable meanings for words and constructions. There is no place for sloppiness in language teaching.

MOVING ON TO THE NEXT CHART

I would usually introduce Chart 4 after working through the situations I have described. I leave a few of the words on Chart 3 until later. The endings for the Past Simple are available, but not yet needed. *Will* has only been used so far to create a polite request and with *If ... the rods will fall*, and I wait until I am ready to introduce the personal pronouns with *will* before using the two reduced forms of the word. See Chapter 19 for more on modals.

By now, I would have put up all the charts belonging to Theme 3 —Numbers & Time—and worked on the aspects of the language that they allow. The time triggers on these charts will be used more and more often as the class moves on.

16. Adding Word Chart 4

The fourth Word chart serves to explore spatial relations and to extend the work on verb forms and modals. If the work on the charts belonging to Theme 3 (Numbers & Time) is not yet finished, it continues while I work on this chart.

From Theme 1, the words on Chart 4 used for spatial relations include *up* and *down*; *top, middle* and *bottom*; *under;* and also *between, behind, beside* and the word *front* which allows the construction of *in front of*. A few other useful pairs and groups can be found: *more* and *less; any; for, all, with, because* and *or*, although *either* does not appear until Chart 5. The question word *where* is found here, as is the relative pronoun *that*.

The words from Theme 2 (Verb Tenses) are of two types. There are a few 'vocabulary' verbs like *end* (the verb *to end* as well as the noun), *show* and *showed*, *hold*, *live* and *let*, which expand what can be said. *Want* will open a new field of expression. We also have *goes* with its unusual spelling. We find the modal auxiliaries *must, can't* and *won't*, and *would, should* and *could*, as well as the contracted form *'d*.

As I have done up until now, I alternate work on Theme 1, the function words, with work on Theme 2, the temporal relations expressed by verb forms. By the end of the work on this chart the third theme will have been finished.

can't	up	or	top	won't
must	want	show		end
because	for	with		more
any	between		would	
hold	middle	front		'd
where	let	goes		less
showed	behind		could	
under	beside	live		that
should	down		bottom	

Word Chart 4.

TEACHING ENGLISH THE SILENT WAY

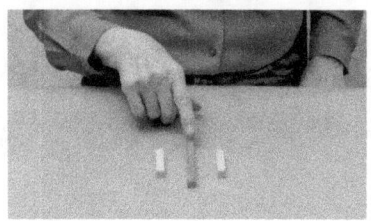
Between

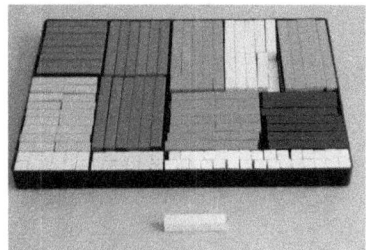
In front of the box

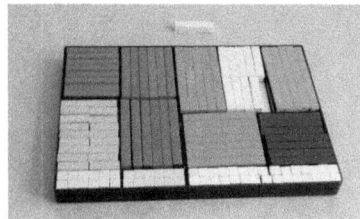
Behind the box

Beside the box

Which is on / under the...

It is quite possible to work on several spatial relation words at once, because their meanings are best made clear by contrasting them. How many I include in any one lesson depends on the aptitude of the class. I will also begin adding a little more 'luxury' vocabulary, which will allow us to talk about our immediate surroundings, always in context: *clean the board, open the window, close the door, the eraser*, etc.

SPATIAL RELATIONS AND PREPOSITIONS

When working on spatial relations, I keep in mind that not all the students are sitting in front of the table. What is *in front of* for a student sitting in the middle of the class, might well be *to the right* or *to the left* for someone sitting at either end of the front row. So this is a domain where saying sentences in chorus is not always possible, but the added variety more than makes up for this. I begin with the rods.

The orange rod is between the two yellow ones.

We spend a little time working on *between*, changing the colour of the rods.

Then I introduce *behind, in front of, on top of* and *beside*. There are no particular problems with these words because they are easy to illustrate using the rods.

— The yellow rod's in front of the box.
— The yellow rod's behind the box.
— The yellow rod's beside the box.

For these types of sentences, I also make sure to put the rods *to the left* and then *to the right* of the box. *Beside* can be on either side.

Next I might work on *on* and *under*. (*On* is revision; it first came in on Chart 2.)

The green rod is under the red one. The red rod is on the green one.

Now I can use several rods, then eight or ten, to make very long sentences like *The orange rod's lying on the green one which is lying on the pink one which is lying on … the blue one … which is lying on the table* and the opposite *The yellow rod's lying on the table under the green one which is lying under the yellow one which is … under the orange one which is lying on top.*

I soon work with the students themselves. Sentences with rods will be replaced by *Keiko is sitting behind Akiko and in front of Marie. Marie is beside Yi. Marie and Yi are sitting side by side. Pierre is between Keiko and Eliana, behind Ali and in front of Luc.* Students can then make their own sentences, and these become longer as they gain confidence.

Sometimes I ask a few students to stand in a line, and I introduce sentences like *Marie's first in the line. Akiko is in the middle. Pierre's last.* We can go on in this vein with *Marie's first in line, Keiko's second, Ali's third ... and Pierre's last in line.* By placing the students one behind the other, each one can say his or her version of *Marie is in front of me, and Ali's behind me.*

It is important for the students to grasp the general meaning of all the position words, since they are to be found everywhere in the language. In particular, they are components of some very common verbs. The meanings of combinations such as *put in, put out, put down, put up, put through* and many others will be more easily grasped if the underlying meaning of each of the elements is perfectly clear. Later on, I want my students to be able to do as I do, using their understanding of the various words as a basis for their comprehension of figurative uses of these verbs, rather than having to learn all the combinations of verbs plus postpositions as vocabulary.

Top, bottom and *middle*

The meaning of these words is easy to establish. Using a pile of three rods, the students can say *The red rod's on top of the green one. The green rod is in the middle. The orange rod's at the bottom.*

Then I might show the students the following type of sentence

— 'At' is in the top left-hand corner of the third chart.
— 'Did' is in the middle of the second chart.

Variations on this are possible: *more or less in the middle, exactly in the middle, on the second last line near the bottom* etc. When students become aware that they can use this vocabulary to speak about the position of words on the charts, it empowers them to use the language every time there is a genuine need to find a word there.

I might well use the 'Lines for Words' technique described in Chapter 18 for this kind of work. I only need to put a set of lines on the board in order to guide the students through a variety of sentences like this, until they are at ease with them. Right and left are part of Theme 3 and appear on Word Chart 9, so they will certainly have been worked on by now. The word *hand* can easily be constructed using and together with the <h> in *he* which is just below it on Word Chart 1. I show the word *corner* on the Fidel, then I might use the corner of a chart to trigger it, running my pointer vertically and horizontally a few centimetres around a corner. If I use the Lines for Words technique for the sentence above—'*At' is in the top left-hand corner of the third chart*—I might mark the word *corner* by drawing a right angle rather than a line, thus:

Because

The word *why* only becomes available on Chart 6, so I can only give a very general indication of the meaning of *because* here. During the work on the previous chart, the students learned *He asked me to put the rod here, so I did*. Now they can convey the same idea using *because*:

> I put the rod down there because he told me to.

Or, one sentence among dozens of possible examples:

> MARCEL: Put the green rods there.
> ALI: I put the green rods there because Marcel told me to.

End

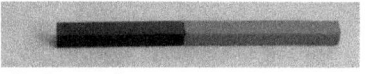

End to end

Side by side

It is easy to introduce the word *end*. I indicate by showing the ends that we will be talking about, and then place two rods end to end. I invite the students to say *The rods are end to end*.

Then, to create a contrast, I cover the *be* of *beside* with my hand and go on to sentences like *These rods are side by side*.

Any and *all*

I usually wait until we are approaching the end of the work on this chart before introducing these words, since the meaning of *any* can best be made clear when *a few, some, most, each* and *every* become available on Chart 5.

I might begin by putting out all the red rods: *All the red rods are on the table. None of the red rods are in the box.* Then: *All the rods on the table are red. None of the rods on the table are blue.*

Any can be introduced by contrasting it with numbers: *There are two green rods on the table. There are four brown rods on the table. There aren't any blue rods on the table. All the blue rods are in the box.* I vary the rods on the table and in the box until everyone has had enough practice.

We now have a second way of replying to the question *How many rods do you have? I don't have any* as well as *I have none*.

Where

Where will first be linked to *there* and *here*. Once everyone has a rod, I ask the students to put their rods on the table in front of them and then I take several rods and put them on the table at the front.

— My rod's here. Your rod's there.
— Where's mine?
— It's there, on the table.

The verbs *show* and *hold*

I ask each of the students to take a rod out of the box. We start with easy sentences and the students gradually build in more complexity. When they all have a rod, I get them to say to each other *Show me your rod*. This might lead to *I'll show you my rod if you show me yours* or *He showed me his rods because I told him to* or *I can't show you my rod because I don't have one* or *He asked me to show him my rod, but I didn't because I didn't want to* or *Show me how many rods you've got* or any of many other possibilities. This is a good example of the type of progression which develops in a Silent Way class: the sentences the students make spiral around what has been worked on previously, establishing meanings more and more firmly by their use in different contexts. While the sentences become more varied, the standards I set for pronunciation and fluency remain high.

The meaning of *hold* can be reached quite easily simply by turning over one's hand so that the fingers hang below: *I'm holding a pen*. This is quite different from *I have a pen* where the pen is simply lying in my open hand. If one of the students puts a rod in his pocket, he can say *I have a rod, but I'm not holding it*. It is not necessary for the rod to be hidden, as long as it is clear who it belongs to and that *hold* will require an energy input to maintain it where it is. (This of course is demonstrated but remains unstated.)

The practice on the verbs of the third chart continues while we explore the fourth.

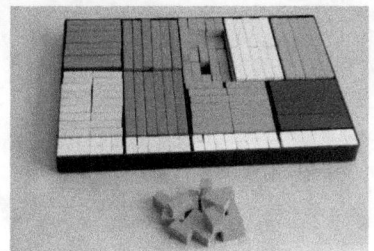

All the rods on the table are red.

The verb *live*

Obviously, the verb *live* will provide the students with the opportunity of asking each other where they live. However, more can be accomplished with this word. Some or all of the following sentences can be made about each of the students in the class.

> ALI: I live in Paris.
> CASS: How long have you been living in Paris?
> ALI: I've been living there for ten years.
> CASS: Where did you live before that?
> ALI: I lived in Bordeaux.
> CASS: What about before that?
> ALI: Before that, I lived in Lille.

Then

> CASS: Where did you live before that?
> ALI: Nowhere. I was born in Lille.

See chapter 18, for more on how *live* can be used. These sentences will have prepared the students for some of the exercises shown there. How much to undertake now and how much to keep until later is for the teacher to decide, depending on the class. A similar exercise can be undertaken later with the word *work*, which appears on Chart 6.

THE MODAL AUXILIARIES

We now have the modals *will* and *would, can* and *could,* and *must* and *should* available, and the negative forms *won't* and *can't,* and also the verb *want*.

Although it is easy to translate these words or to paraphrase them, I want them to be linked to their appropriate inner climates, not to an intellectual understanding of the meanings of each of them. However, while it is easy to use rods to create concrete situations which require the use of indicative forms, it is difficult to actively create inner climates in the classroom.

To get these words into circulation, I usually introduce them as ways of being polite. Such an opportunity might present itself if someone wants to open a door or a window.

Other opportunities will arise as part of class management. I often ask a student to point a word on the Fidel, or to write a sentence on the board. This allows me to put into context *Would you write your sentence on the board please, Marcel?* Then *Can anyone change something?* as I hold out the eraser and the marker. The contexts can be understood by the students even if the words of the sentence are not. When one student wants another to repeat his sentence more loudly, or to write it up on the board, the words *Could you* or *Would you* or *Would you mind showing it again please?* can be made explicit so that he can ask his question in English. The answers to these questions need work. *Could you/would you …* requires *Yes, of course. Would you mind …* requires *Not at all.* (*Mind* and *again* are on the next chart and can be introduced as virtual words.)

Sentences can be made which contrast levels of politeness, illustrated here with a very basic sentence, *Take a rod*, but used in the classroom many times with various situations which happen to come up. *Take a rod. Please take a rod. Would you take a rod, please?* (*Please* has certainly been pointed on the Fidel by now and 'placed' in a convenient spot on the wall.) *I'd like you to take a rod.* When Chart 5 is hung, *Would you mind taking a rod?* becomes possible.

Modals take the time they take. It is only when students have more language that they are likely to be talking about situations where their inner climates need modals to be expressed.

Using constructed situations, I have found the word *if* to be useful. It allows all sorts of clauses to be put together, most of them using one of the modals. See **Chapter 19** for examples.

THE OTHER WORDS ON CHART 4

The other words on this chart will generally be introduced in the same way as those on the following charts, and will come into conversations as required over the next lessons. More detail follows in the next chapter.

17. All the Word charts together

By now, it will have become impossible to know in advance what will be talked about. The class is working with the words on Charts 1, 2, 3, 4 and 5, as well as 9, 10 and the Dates and Numbers charts, plus some virtual words dotted here and there as the need has arisen. Each class has set off in its own direction, venturing away from the progression suggested by the order of the words on the charts, or the order of the chapters in this book.

I don't want the reader to believe that there is a fixed sequence of activities which characterises this approach. Above all else, teachers must be prepared to adapt, to change their teaching to suit the needs and perhaps also the wishes of the students they are working with. This demands constant experimentation, trial and error, success and failure. It may sometimes feel uncomfortable, but it can also be exhilarating.

Because the teacher works with complete flexibility, it is useful to have ideas for some different ways of presenting some of the key function words and structures as and when they are needed. I will now describe some of the ways I do this.

big	each	back	away
near	mind	ask	went
box	few	say	new old
when	hard	again	most
kind	done	every	says
some	little	said	-es
shown	either	together	
came	-self	young	bad
better	good	best	worse

Word Chart 5

EACH, EVERY, ALL, MOST, ALMOST ALL, SOME

This continues the work begun on Chart 4 (Chapter 16). I use several situations to show the meanings of these words and the constructions of the sentences which contain them. In what follows, the students describe the situation every time a change is made, so the pace can be quite fast since I only have to change the place of a rod to modify the situation, and hence the sentence. Thus the students pronounce dozens of sentences in one lesson.

Each of the rods ...

On the table, I place nine or ten rods, each of a different colour. I point the first sentence and then show the changes by using my fingers, or pointing if necessary. The meaning is clear from the situation.

— Each of these rods is a different colour. Each rod is a different colour.
— All the rods on the table are different colours.
— All of them are different colours.
— They are all different colours.

After the students have met words like *all* or *each* for the first time, I don't need to point to all the words in each sentence. For example, I touch *all* then sweep my hand over the pile with a wide gesture to indicate the approximate meaning, and the students launch into a guessing game with the help of my fingers. They now have enough English to construct such sentences without any more help than that. I want them to realise that *all* will need a plural verb while *each* is a singular concept.

All the red rods ...

I place all the red rods on the table, and show the students that the box no longer contains any red rods. Then I point the following sentence

All the red rods are on the table.

I turn my finger a little to indicate that the words can be rearranged, and they say, with the help of my fingers

All the rods on the table are red.

Then I show

Every one of...

and more if it is necessary

Every one of the rods on the table is red.

Almost all the red rods ...

I place one of the rods in the box and show *Almost all...* They can usually guess what should come next

Each of the rods is a different colour.

All the red rods are on the table.

Almost all the red rods are on the table, but one is in the box.
All the rods on the table are red.

I add a white rod ...

... to the pile and signal that they can say the last sentence again. They launch into the sentence, and after they say the word *red*, I signal for them to stop and show them *except*. They add it. I show them that I still have four fingers left for the end of the sentence. They hesitate for a moment, and then find the end of the sentence.

All the rods on the table are red except one, which is white.

And then

Almost all the rods on the table are red, but one is white.

Each sentence is said several times; by the end of the process each should be correct from all points of view—pronunciation, rhythm and intonation.

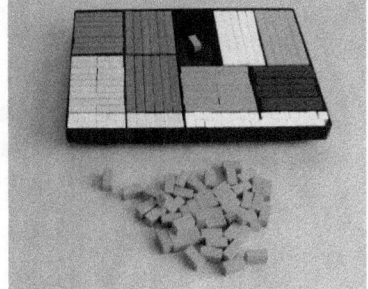

Almost all the red rods are on the table but one is in the box.

I add two other white rods ...

— Most of the rods on the table are red, but a few are white.
— All the rods on the table are red except three, which are white.

I take away a white rod...

— Most of the rods on the table are red, but two are white.
— All the rods on the table are red except two, which are white.

I add several white rods ...

Some of the rods on the table are red and some are white.

Some of the rods on the table are white.

I take away the white rods ...

... one at a time, while getting the students to say the same sentence each time. I do this until it becomes necessary to change the sentence to

Most of the rods on the table are red but a few are white.

and also

A few of the rods on the table are white, but most are red.

and then

All the rods on the table are red except one, which is white.

A few of the rods are white.

SHORTER AND LONGER ...

Using only short rods, I put about twenty rods on the table. I also put down a black rod, which is much longer.

— All the rods on the table are smaller/shorter than the black one.
— Each of the rods on the table is shorter than the black one.
— The black rod is longer than all the other rods on the table.

In this way, I show the students a variety of situations these words bring to mind. After that I launch sentences like:

— Each of the people in the class has a different last name.
— Most of the people in the class live in Paris, but Freddy lives in Lille.

and so on ...

BOTH AND *AND*, *NEITHER* AND *NOR*

Another day, I put two green rods side by side on the table. We start with:

Both these rods are green.

which has already been worked on. I separate them.

Both this rod and that one are green.

Then we can view the situation differently.

— Neither this rod nor that one is pink.
— Neither of these rods is pink.

ENOUGH

This word poses no particular problem. I sometimes introduce it with *have to have*, creating an opportunity to work on the pronunciation of *have to* and *has to*, /hæftə/ and /hæstə/ and the contrast with *have* as a verb. First I work on the pronunciation of several words from the field of geometry: *triangle, square, rectangle*, etc. Then we can begin with various sentences like

— How many rods do you have to have to make a triangle?
— You have to have three.
— I only have two.
— That's not enough to make a triangle.

or

— Freddy, take this pointer. Can you touch the ceiling?

> 'Rods let students see and handle some of the abstractions that they may find hard to follow in an explanation that consists only of words.'
>
> *Stevick (1976)*

— No I can't. I'm not tall enough. I'm not tall enough to touch the ceiling, even with a pointer. Can you?
— Yes, I'm tall enough. I'm taller than you.

BEFORE AND *AFTER*

At this point in the course, I find it useful to contextualise these two words using time.

— What's the time?
— It's a little before 3.15. It's a little after 3.10.

It is easy to come back to these sentences several times during the lesson so that the students get enough practice. Another sentence that could be used is

If it's a little before 3.15, then it's a little after 3.10.

MAKING MORE COMPARISONS

I sometimes get students to compare:

— Freddy is ten years old. Marc is nine. Freddy is older than Marc. Marc is younger than Freddy.
— Freddy is one year older than Marc. Marc is one year younger than Freddy. If Freddy is one year older than Marc, then Marc is one year younger than Freddy, of course!
— Frank is six months younger than Marc. Frank is the youngest in the class.

ONCE, TWICE, THREE TIMES …

By the time we get to these words, I know the class well, and the students know me. I can allow myself to play a joke at the expense of someone. For this exercise, I talk. I ask someone to stand up.

Stand up!	He stands.
Sit down!	He sits down.
Stand up!	He stands up again.
Sit down!	He sits down.

I do this three or four times, counting very visibly on my fingers.

He stood up three times and he sat down three times.

I show the word *times* on Chart 9, and not on Chart 10 (adding an *s*), because I want the students to distinguish between *time* going by and the word *times*, which is numerical in nature. *Time* is singular, but can

Scan to watch a video of a teacher doing a similar process with models of a sofa, a TV, a chair, a lamp etc.

While the examples are different, the process of keeping students generating language in response to a continually changing situation is the same.

be put into the plural in phrases like *the times*, whereas *times* is plural and occurs in the singular form only as a kind of strong form of *once*, for example, *I promise, it only happened one time.*

Now I ask the students to find things they can make people do several times. This might produce a series like

— Freddy, say 'hello'.
— Hello.
— Say it again.
— Hello.
— Say it again.
— Hello.
— Freddy said 'hello' three times.

I lift ten fingers and show them that I want them to say *ten times*. I lower a finger, and they say *nine times*, I lower another finger and they say *eight times*. In this way, we get to *five times, four times, three times, twice, once*. Of course, I have to give the students these last two words. They count down and up several times until everyone can do it easily.

THE SUFFIX -*LY*

This ending will be useful with many words. On Chart 6, it can be used with *slow* to make the word s-l-o-w-l-y, that the students say at the required s-p-e-e-d! This can be contrasted with *quickly* and *fast* on Chart 7.

Now we have the opportunity to go back and add the ending to words we have already seen, such as *nearly, mostly, differently,* etc. We then go to *rightly* and *wrongly, easily, shortly* (meaning *in a few minutes*), *firstly, secondly, thirdly* and *lastly*.

— Give me three good reasons to stop the lesson at four o'clock!
— Firstly, four o'clock is the time for the lesson to end; secondly, we are tired; and thirdly, we have another class at four o'clock.

Chart 7 gives us other opportunities to explore *-ly* with *loudly, softly* and *heavily*.

THE SUFFIX -*EN*

Once the students are at home in the language and have a little more vocabulary, it can be interesting to work on prefixes and suffixes. For example, the suffix *–en* is used with many adjectives to produce verbs. Words like *soften, quicken* and *heighten* can be introduced and contextualised. The colours on Chart 1 give us *blacken*, *whiten*, and *redden*, though *brown* remains unchanged.

This is the kind of field I might come back to when an opportunity comes up. We might be working with *length* on Chart 11. While we are about it, we make a sentence or two with *lengthen*. I might make a train of five red rods and measure it against an orange rod. The trains measure the same length, so the red train is ten centimetres long.

> The length of the red train is ten centimetres. If I lengthen the train by three red rods, the length of the train will be sixteen centimetres.

And of course

> If I shorten it by two red rods, the length of the train will be six centimetres.

The aim is to arrive at a point where the students are not surprised by the behaviour of a particular adjective/verb change.

SAY AND TELL

These two can be contrasted by using them in direct or indirect speech.

> — Freddy, tell Frank to stand up.
> — Frank, stand up!
> — Freddy told Frank to stand up, and he did.
> — Freddy said, 'Frank, stand up!' and he did.

Or

> — Frank, take a rod!
> — I told Frank to take a rod, and he did.
> — I said, 'Frank, take a rod!' and he did.

I think it is useful to show the contrast between the two directly, so that the students adopt the habit of using *say* for direct speech and *tell* for indirect speech. The more subtle uses are easier to introduce later on if this distinction is made early.

DISTANCES—*NEAR, FAR, CLOSE*

I stand an orange rod, a yellow one and a red one on the table. The orange one represents Paris; the yellow one, Dijon; and the red one, Besançon, the city in which the class is taking place. I try to place them at an appropriate distance apart to illustrate what will be said. Of course,

I use the English pronunciation of the names for these three cities, and any others which are introduced. This often causes laughter. Obviously, I choose towns and cities near where we live, that everyone knows.

—How far is Dijon from Paris? Dijon is 300 kilometres from Paris.
—How far is Besançon from Paris? Besançon is 400 kilometres from Paris.
—Dijon is closer to Besançon than to Paris.

I might start with a longer version of a sentence I am aiming at:

Dijon is closer to Paris than Besançon is close to Paris.

and then the actual target, with *is* stranded at the end:

Dijon is closer to Paris than Besançon is.

It is a difficult distinction to make. I often have to work on these two sentences several times until everyone is clear about their meaning. In particular, it is useful to complete the second half of the sentence, which is usually understood without being said, because it is the ellipsis which causes the confusion.

—Besançon is further from Paris than Dijon is.
—Besançon is closer to Dijon than to Paris. (Which means Besançon is closer to Dijon than Besançon is close to Paris.)

I introduce a white rod to represent Pontarlier, a small town not far from Besançon.

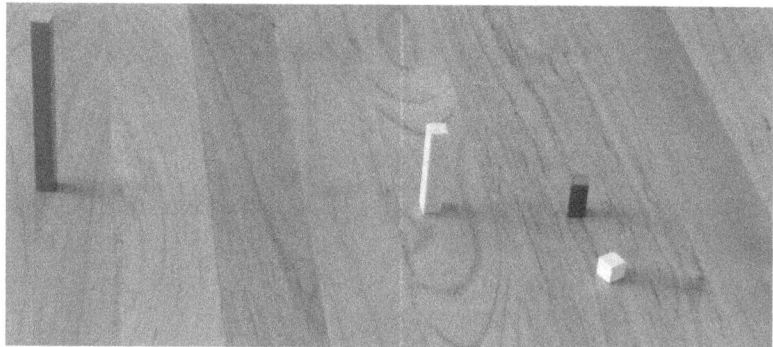

Pontarlier is close to Besançon. Pontarlier is closer to Besançon than to Dijon. Of the three cities, Pontarlier is the furthest from Paris. Pontarlier is 450 kilometres from Paris.

Now I place a black rod and a brown one to represent Lyon to the south and Strasbourg to the north.

— Besançon is half way between Strasbourg and Lyon.
— Besançon is the same distance from Strasbourg as from Lyon.

I sometimes do this exercise with a map of the world, or better still, a globe and a tape measure. I use well-known cities like Sydney, Tokyo, Moscow, London and Brussels with respect to Paris or Geneva. This gives the students a lot of practice.

— Which city is closest/nearest to Paris, Brussels or London? Which city is furthest from Paris? Sydney is. Tokyo is not as far from Paris as Sydney is.
— How far is Sydney from Paris? Sydney is 17,000 kilometres from Paris. Sydney is a very long way from Paris.
— Sydney is twenty-three hours from Paris by plane. Tokyo is twelve hours from Paris by plane, so Tokyo is closer to Paris than Sydney is. Tokyo is twelve hours from Paris and twelve hours from Sydney, so Tokyo is the same distance from Paris as from Sydney.
— Berlin is much closer to Paris than to Tokyo.

And so on...

Later we can come back to these cities and others with different sentences as the need arises. If we are working on *further* and *furthest*

— Which city in the world is furthest from Paris?
— Wellington is.
— Wellington is furthest from Paris.

Talking about distances is an opportunity for a little geography.

LOOK AND *SEE*, *LISTEN* AND *HEAR*, AND *THINK*

I try to introduce the word *see* meaning *understand* very early on, well before Chart 6. When someone becomes aware of something with an audible awareness, I use the Rectangle chart to get them to say, *Ah! I see!* The word is known well before it is associated with visual perception, which is signalled by the use of *can*.

I work on this verb by placing a box of rods on the table. I put a few rods around the box, quite close to it, so that various rods can be seen by some students but not by others.

Everyone has a sentence to make.

— From where I am, I can see four rods.
— From here, I can only see three.
— I can see three rods; that red one and those two pink ones.

And so on...

The word *look* comes in easily, when someone is looking for a word on the chart.

— If you look at the top of Chart 4, you'll see it.
— If you look at the top of Chart 4, you'll find it.

The words *listen* and *hear* often come in well before Chart 6, too. I need them when someone doesn't speak loudly enough, which happens quite often. I see that a student wants one of his fellow students to speak louder. I take the situation as an ideal opportunity to introduce,

Speak louder please. I can't hear you.

and then later

— If you listen carefully, you'll hear what he says.
— Even if I listen carefully, I can't hear what he is saying.

A quick tip: if a student is speaking too softly, I move to the other side of the classroom. This usually leads to them speaking louder.

DO YOU THINK ...? I THINK ...

I introduce *think*, from Chart 12, quite early. *What do you think?* comes in because situations naturally come up which need it.

Sometimes, for example, I construct a vertical tower made of long rods. I stand an orange rod on the table and then stand a blue rod on it, so as to make a tower that is 19 cm high. I take another long rod and start to stand it on the blue one, which of course is a challenge. Then I can show students how to make sentences such as,

— Can I put a brown rod on top of the blue one? Do you think I can put a brown rod on top of the blue one?
— I think if you put another rod on top of the blue rod, the tower will fall.
— What do you think?
— I think you can do it.
— I don't think you can.

LENGTH

The obvious way of dealing with *length* is to use rod trains. I make a train of five green rods and we measure it against an orange one.

The green train is fifteen centimetres long.

and

The length of the green train is fifteen centimetres.

Word Chart 6

When Chart 6 is hung, I might bring up the subject of triangles again, this time to deal with their length. I might use these sentences with adolescents who will know these words from their maths classes.

> The length of the three sides is different. Each of the three sides is of a different length. If a triangle has three sides of different lengths, it is called a scalene triangle.

(Obviously, it is also possible to add the word *length* as a virtual word, and work on these sentences without waiting for Chart 6.)

> — What's the difference between your three different triangles?
> — The length of the sides is different.
> — If the length of two of the sides is the same, then the triangle is called an isosceles triangle.

There is nothing to stop this work from being extended to rectangles, pentagons, etc., though it must be kept in mind that this is an English lesson, not a geometry one.

It might seem that these sentences are useless, and it is true that they would never be said in an everyday conversation! Their importance does not lie in their immediate usefulness. Rather, the language the students learnt using rods, is now being extended and consolidated in a new domain where nevertheless meaning remains crystal clear.

Furthermore, such sentences help students to discover that English is used by its speakers in exactly the same way that they use their native language. Even mathematics takes place in English! I am always astonished to see how many students are surprised by this fact.

ALTHOUGH

I'm quite tall. I stretch up and try to touch the ceiling.

> Although you're tall, you can't touch the ceiling.

I take a pointer, and try again.

> Although you're tall, you can't touch the ceiling, even with a pointer.

I ask someone fit-looking to push a cupboard standing against the wall in the classroom. He leans against it, pushing it with all his might.

> Although he's very strong, he can't move the cupboard.

Many similar sentences are possible.

DEVELOPING A FEEL FOR HOW THE LANGUAGE BEHAVES

With all these sentences, the aim is for the students to develop a feel very generally for how the language might behave.

It should be said that by now, these types of sentences take up less and less time. They are necessary only when a concept needs illustrating. Most of the time, the students discuss whatever has become the topic of the moment. I use illustrative sentences such as those given above when necessary, but as soon as the meaning has been established or the problem dissipated, we return to the original context. Consequently, I make less and less use of these kinds of sentences as the course goes on.

The more time the students spend learning functional English, as against vocabulary, the easier it becomes for them to express themselves precisely in the new language. The key word here is 'precisely'. This precision is one of the things I am aiming for: without this level of precision, quite literally, they 'cannot say what they mean'.

GOING ON FROM HERE

From Chart 4 or 5, it is possible to let adult students talk about their lives. This type of lesson is described in Chapter 20. The students themselves can perfectly well generate some of the content of the course if they are encouraged to do so. It is a pleasant and efficient way of introducing vocabulary in context, and creates an excellent atmosphere in the class. But the students may not spontaneously take hold of the reins; they have to be helped to do it.

— I don't know anything about Bernard.
— I don't know how tall he is, and I don't know how old he is either.
— I don't know what he does. I don't know if he is married.
— I don't know what his last name is.
— How old are you, Bernard?
— I'm thirty-three years old.
— I'm thirty-three.
— Where do you live?
— I live in a village a few kilometres from Besançon.
— What do you do?
— I'm a doctor at the hospital.
— Are you married?
— Yes I am. I'm married and I have two children.
— How tall are you, Bernard?

WORKING WITH BEGINNERS

Teaching a class of University students

— I'm 180 centimetres.
— I'm six foot tall.
— What's your last name, Bernard?
— My last name? Thomson.
— Is that a French name?
— Yes, it is.
— It's an English name, too.

As students speak with each other, I wait until each sentence is finished and then, if necessary, I invite the speaker to correct his sentence. If he can't do this, I invite the whole class to work on the sentence. As needed, I give clues using my fingers and the charts. I might then invite the class to provide more suitable words than those chosen. The idea always belongs to the student who is speaking, so the vocabulary is always meaningful, at least to that student and usually to all.

Since I no longer control the whole content of each lesson, I often find myself having to improvise a rod illustration or to draw on the board to make sure everyone understands the situation.

This chapter illustrates that I have prepared for my classes over many years, by making sure I have good examples to illustrate all the words on all the charts in case they are required. This preparation needed to be done only once, although I can often improve an illustration by changing my example. It is stimulating for the teacher to improvise on the fly new illustrations which relate to the current sentence rather than to a hypothetical 'standard' sentence or situation. I live on my wits, and the whole class stays wide awake because the students are doing the same thing—we are inventing the class as we go along. Often the students themselves find ways of illustrating questions and meanings for the others in the class. Very occasionally, no one,

Adrian Underhill's (2015) article 'Training for the Unpredictable' is well worth reading for advice on improvisation and other classroom issues.

including me, has a solution, and I tell them that I will think about it and try to find one for the next lesson. They are always willing to wait.

As each class progresses, there is a change in the balance between work on structures (that was predominant during the earlier part of the course) and spontaneous conversation which is now beginning to happen. The job of the teacher evolves from presenting new structures to monitoring conversations.

TOWARDS THE CLASS CONVERSATION

Learning to speak, speaking to learn

18. Verb tenses—laying the foundations

The forms of the English verb—tenses, aspects and modals—make up a coherent system and they should be presented so that the students can develop a sense of this system and build criteria for using it.

I don't do this by teaching rules. Instead, I work on verbs in a three-step process.

STEP 1 - Introduction to the forms.

These introductory steps have been described in previous chapters as one of the three themes—the function words, verb tenses, numbers and time—that I work on with beginners. During this introductory step, it is best to limit both the contexts in which the verbs are used and the vocabulary around them to what is found on the charts and can be illustrated using rods, adding little else.

For non-beginners, when a new verb form is encountered I will work on it using the teaching techniques of Step 1 before I move to Step 2. The students must find it easy to say the verb forms.

STEP 2 - Expanding the students' experience.

This second step moves work on verb tenses to situations where students can gain a wider understanding of the use of the forms. I do this by using 'triggers' in guided conversations and rod stories. Step 2 is the topic of this chapter.

STEP 3 - A comprehensive view.

The third step is the laying out of the whole system. This will be presented in the next chapter.

I keep these three steps apart in my mind for any particular class, and I make a conscious decision when I feel we have done enough work to move from Step 1 to Step 2 or to Step 3.

As ever, the sequence of exercises I present here is not strict, and should be adapted to the particular needs of your students and supplemented with other activities that you and they create.

USING TRIGGERS

From experience, I know that adverbs will help students to sense the required inner climate for a verb form, so I insist on them using adverbs with the verb forms they are learning.

For example, if I cut my finger a few minutes ago, then, depending upon my purpose, it is possible in English to say either *I have cut my finger* or *I cut my finger a few minutes ago*. The presence or absence of the words *a few minutes ago* signals my state of mind. If these words are present, the sentence will necessarily be in the Simple Past; if they are neither present nor implicit, the sentence will usually be in the Present Perfect (*Oh look! I've cut my finger. Where are the plasters?*)

Similarly, *not yet* is much more likely in *I haven't finished yet*; unlikely, at least in British English, in *I didn't finish yet*; and impossible in *I don't finish yet*. *Yet* is very common in *Have you ... yet?* and extremely uncommon in *Do you ... yet?* or *Did you ... yet?*

The adverbs of frequency are very common with the Present Simple and, except for *always*, highly unusual with the Present Progressive.

Triggers give students a simple way to think about which form to choose without anything to unlearn later. For students who have started learning English elsewhere, they are an excellent antidote to the rules-based approach they have probably encountered.

A strict use of triggers at this stage allows students to sort out the forms clearly in their minds and make a lot of correct sentences about themselves in a short period of time. They can gradually build up a feel for the correct usage.

VERBS AT STEP 1

Last week **as a trigger**

This little phrase opens the way to the Simple Past. This tense has been available since the work on the second Word chart, but it will now be possible to explore it in more detail and extend its use.

Last Monday, last month, last December, last year and many other phrases allow us to launch small conversations. According to the age of the students, the content will differ in the details, but the sentences will all describe their real life.

— Last summer, we went to the beach at Arcachon.
— Last Christmas, I got a Playstation.
— Last week I was sick.

Obviously, I encourage supplementary questions if possible. Thus

— Last week, I saw 'Titanic' again.
— Did you like it? / Was it good?
— Yes I did. / Yes it was.

Or

— Last week, I was away because I was in Belgium.
— Why did you go to Belgium?
— I went there for my work / job.
— Did you have time to visit Brussels / to see the sights?
— No I didn't. I worked fourteen hours every day / a day.

Conversations in the Present

I can ask a student to ask another one the question, *What time do you get up in the morning?* The answer might be

— I get up at 8.00 am. What about you?
— I get up at 7.15.

The exchange might develop.

— If you get up at eight o'clock, do you have time to have breakfast?
— No, I don't, I have hot chocolate. I only have hot chocolate for breakfast.

WORKING AT STEP 2—ROD STORIES

Once the structure of a verb form has become clear to the students, I can launch 'Rod Stories' which illustrate the form being used in richer situations. Initially I create a Rod Story around a single form, then I put several forms together to contrast their meanings relative to each other.

What follows in this chapter describes a series of exercises which take several weeks or months of work—depending on how many hours the class meets each week—and includes work on other aspects of English; in particular, work on Word Charts 9 and 10, the charts which show some of the main triggers in English.

Rod Stories are 'stories' which are materialised using rods to show situations and the movements of characters within them. Rod Stories have several advantages: they make it easy for the teacher to create a situation without saying very much, and then to move within the story or to come back to some point in it by simply moving a rod here or there. Here is an example.

MR. AND MRS. GREEN—THE PRESENT PROGRESSIVE

Using the longest rods, I make a simple plan of a house or an apartment on the table. In one of the rooms, I place three brown rods side by side to symbolise a bed, and put two dark green rods on the bed, Mr. and Mrs. Green. I might even fix a few tiny rolls of adhesive putty to the end of one of the green rods, to symbolise Mrs. Green's hair.

Beside the house, I create a clock with the hands on seven o'clock.

Phrase by phrase, I construct the story of Mr. and Mrs. Green's morning activities, miming and making sound effects, using the Word charts for the structure and the Fidel to provide vocabulary. I do not talk. I only make the necessary sound effects—of the alarm clock, the coffee machine,

Chart 9: Time

Chart 10: Time triggers

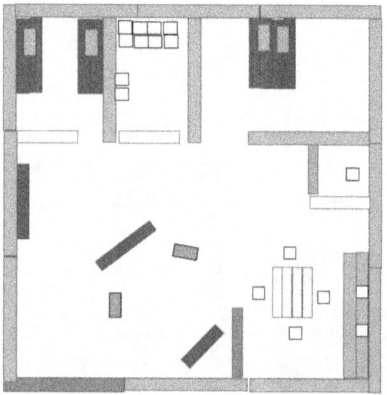

etc. The students tell the story as time moves on around the clock. Each time it is possible, I supply them with alternative constructions.

>(I make the alarm clock ring. Brrrr! Using gestures, I ask the students to read the time on the clock.)
>ALL: It's seven o'clock

>(I point on the Word charts and the Fidel: *The alarm clock's ringing*.)
>ALL: The alarm clock's ringing.

>(I theatrically open my eyes, stretch and point the words.)
>ALL: Mr. and Mrs. Green are waking up.

>(I move the minute hand on by five minutes.)
>ALL: It's five past seven.

>(I stand the green rods up to indicate that Mr. and Mrs. Green are getting up and point.)
>ALL: Now, it's five past seven. Mr. and Mrs. Green are getting up.

>(I start moving Mr. and Mrs. Green around the house, miming their actions and pointing to the sentences as we go.)
>ALL: Mr. Green is going to the bathroom. Now he's having a shower. Now he's shaving. Now he's getting dressed.

At this point, I put the clock back to seven o'clock and ask the students to begin the story again, from memory. If they have trouble doing it, I help.

Usually they manage collectively. Word by word, I select the version proposed by the student who is closest to the original words or has a good alternative.

Now we go back and look after Mrs. Green.

>ALL: It's five past seven. Mrs. Green is going to the kitchen. Now she's preparing breakfast / Now she's getting breakfast ready.

>(I move the big hand of the clock on, put Mr. & Mrs. Green to opposite sides of the kitchen table and then mime the next few words.)
>ALL: Now it's twenty past seven. They're eating breakfast / They're having breakfast. Mrs. Green's having toast with butter and jam, Mr. Green's having bacon and eggs. She's having.../ he's having... They're both drinking tea.

>(I let the students choose the menu. Often they choose the food I have suggested above. If they don't know any English words for food, I give these.)

I now get them to begin the whole story again from the beginning. They like this challenge, which remains a collective job. Then we go on …

> ALL: It's twenty to eight. They're doing the washing up / They're washing up / They're washing the dishes.
> ALL: Now, it's a quarter to eight. Mrs. Green's having her shower /Mrs. Green's having a shower. Now she's getting dressed / Now she's dressing. She's brushing her teeth / She's cleaning her teeth. Now she's doing / combing her hair. Now she's putting on her make-up.
> ALL: It's eight o'clock. Mr. & Mrs. Green are putting on their coats. They're leaving the house. They're going to work.

If the students have found this easy, we can take the Greens to the station and make the train arrive on the platform. If not, we leave this for another day …

THE STATION

I lay some long rods on the table to represent the waiting room and the tracks of a station, and use white rods to represent the people in the waiting room and on the platform. I put some others down end to end to suggest a train which is arriving at the station, and add two upright green rods, Mr. & Mrs. Green.

'Rods have no unnecessary markings or details of shape. Therefore they present an open field for the students' imagination. They are like concrete abstractions which we can put to an incredibly wide range of uses.'

Stevick (1976)

The Greens are coming towards the station, and may or may not miss their train. I can make the train pull into the station and leave while they are still some distance away, or have them run and get there in time. The students can decide whether they catch it or not.

Work on writing

Once the students have told the story orally, I ask for volunteers to write it on the board. This is also a collective job.

I write '(1)' in the top left-hand corner of the board, hold up the marker and silently propose that someone take it and write the first sentence. When the student has finished writing his sentence, he goes back to his place. I now have several ways that I can work. I might silently hold up the eraser in one hand and the marker in the other to invite the others to correct what he has written if they think it is necessary. Or, I might just hold up the marker, and invite students to underline any words they think are incorrect. Then I give the student who wrote the sentence a chance to review it.

I continue this until everyone thinks we have the correct version or until differences of opinion are well-established. If no one can correct a mistake, I do so on the Word charts or the Fidel or with my fingers. Normally, if I have worked well during the previous part of the lesson, then the story has been told enough times for the students to recreate it easily. It is retained because of the number of times they have told it—perhaps five or six times or more for the earlier parts and at least two or three for the later parts.

Introduction of the Simple Present

When Word Charts 9 and 10—which contain the major triggers for the Simple Present—have been hung on the wall, it becomes possible to tell the same story in another way, using *every* as a trigger.

> Every morning, Mr. & Mrs. Green wake up at 7 o'clock. They get up. Mr. Green goes to the bathroom and has a shower. Etc.

When we reach the point where the story has been written on the board, I rub out all the instances of *Every morning* ... and write in *It's seven o'clock* ... and invite the students to make all the necessary changes. The story moves into the Present Progressive.

Obviously, I then ask the students to talk about their own morning routines, which involve all sorts of variations on this theme. (See Chapter 20 onwards.)

THE STORY OF THE GREENS—LATER ...

It is possible to come back to the Greens many times in different ways with different verb forms according to the triggers used. So when the triggers for the Past become available a few hours or days later, the students might produce the following.

> Yesterday morning, Mr. & Mrs. Green woke up at 7 o'clock ...

In the Present Perfect

— It's twenty past seven. Mr Green has had his shower, he has dressed, he has shaved, but he hasn't yet had breakfast.
— Mrs Green has ... but hasn't yet had her shower.

'LINES FOR WORDS' FOR LONGER TEXTS

I sometimes use the Lines for Words technique when constructing paragraphs with low level students. I draw short lines of about seven or eight cm length on the whiteboard, corresponding to the words in a sentence. This helps students to hold a series of sentences in their minds for the duration of a period of work.

Suppose I want the class to work on a Rod Story, such as the ones in this chapter involving Mr. and Mrs. Green. The story contains the following details.

It's seven o'clock. The alarm clock's ringing. Mr. and Mrs. Green are waking up.

I don't want the students reading the story from the board. I want them to construct it from within themselves. But I know they need some help to do so.

As the students are saying each sentence, I draw the lines. I make the punctuation clearly visible since it guides the students as they 'read'. These sentences might look like this:

—' — — — . — — — ' — — . — — — — — — — .

I can add a few cues if necessary.

—' — 7 — . — — — ' — — . — — — G — — — .

I get the students to read the sentence from the lines several times.

Once the work has been done on the story in some form or other, we might work to develop several sentences using this technique.

Mr Green went to the bathroom to have a shower and shave. Then he got dressed. While he was having his shower, Mrs Green went to the kitchen to prepare breakfast.

— G — — — to — — — and — . Th — — — . While — — — — —, — G — to — — — — — .

With my pointer, I get the class to 'read' the sentence, pointing by sense groups as we go along. I put the pointer at the beginning of the group of words to be read, and then loop it across in a single smooth movement under the words I want the students to keep together. I hold it there until the class reaches the end of the group, then loop it on through the next group of words. *Every morning,* then *Mr. and Mrs. Green* then *get up at seven o'clock* and so on.

I can regulate the speed at which the students 'read' by changing the speed of my pointing. The whole sequence can be repeated several times until it sounds English. I build each part of each sentence carefully as we go along, so that the students are quite sure what each little line represents.

Don't forget, use your students' minds!

This technique is quite different from reading something fully written on the board. It helps students become more fluent in their speaking by helping them to create mental images.

MUCH LATER ...

Much later, after the Verb Tense System has been introduced (see Chapter 19) more complex versions of the story can be told to give students practice with sequences of tenses and forms if necessary.

Using the Present Perfect and *will*

> It's seven o'clock. Mr. & Mrs. Green are waking up. Now Mr. Green is having his shower. When he has had his shower, he will shave. When he has shaved, he will / 'll get dressed.

With some variation:

> It's seven o'clock. Mr. & Mrs. Green are waking up. Now Mr. Green is having his shower. When / After he has finished having his shower, he will shave. When / After he has finished shaving, he will get dressed. When Mrs. Green has finished eating her breakfast, she will have her shower.

USING STUDENTS' EXPERIENCE

Working on Mr. & Mrs. Green prepares students to talk about themselves. Here are examples of situations which the students might be able to explore from their own lives. (See also Chapter 20.)

My house or my flat

Who would like to show us what his house is like using the rods? The students who respond have to make a plan like the one used for the

Greens' house and explain to the rest of us who sleeps in which bedroom, for example.

Your job

A little later, if I am working with adults, I might ask someone to talk about his job, drawing the plan of the place where he works on a large sheet of paper. This can only be tried with students who are at least at the lower intermediate level.

Your car accident

Who has had a car accident? Can you show us how it happened using the rods? Traffic lights can be shown by placing red rods or green rods at appropriate corners of a crossroads.

The scar

Who has a scar? I show one or two of mine so that they understand. *Can you tell us how you got it?*

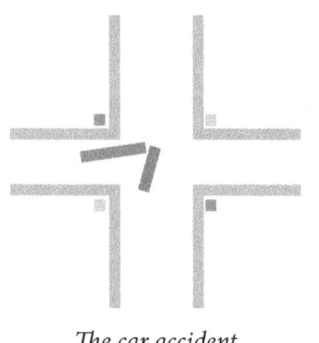

The car accident

USING WALL PICTURES

When working with pictures (discussed in Chapter 5) the teacher should be careful to introduce only a limited amount of vocabulary and only introduce it in response to students' need for it. Learning new vocabulary imposes a heavy memory burden. When introducing new words she should first point them on the Rectangle chart or Fidel, getting the class to practise saying the word so that its proper pronunciation is established from the start.

When students reach lower intermediate level and have gained a foothold in using the functional vocabulary, pictures can be useful to help students move into talking about more than situations involving rods or their everyday lives. Pictures are a bridge to the Class Conversation (see Chapter 23).

THE WORD *LIVE* AND WHERE IT CAN TAKE US

I usually bring *live* in when I have done some work on Word Chart 5, and I hang Word Chart 6 soon after. By now we are entering the stage where we can broaden the discussion to include more personal details of the learners' lives. This process is explained in more detail in coming chapters.

As a precaution, before this lesson begins, I make sure I know where a few of the students live and, for the following lesson, how old they are.

We start with the obvious question *Where do you live?* for which everyone will have an easy answer. I show the words on the Word charts, and then show the most simple answer—the place. If necessary, I might speak and say just *Paris? Besançon?* Students ask each other this question until it becomes easy. Sometimes, the answers lead us to add sentences like *He lives in the same city / suburb / street as I do* or *He lives in the same city as me*.

However, it is possible to explore far beyond this simple question with the vocabulary at hand by making concurrent time lines.

I draw a vertical line close to the right-hand side of the board and label it with the date of the current year. Then I draw a horizontal line from one side of the board to the other. I know before the lesson begins that the length of this second line will represent the age of the oldest person in the class. Thus, if the oldest person is eighteen, then each year will take more of the width of the board than if the oldest person is sixty or more. The greater the range of ages, the less length each year will occupy on the line.

Now I choose a student who is open and talkative, who has shown himself to be willing to share, and who speaks as freely as the level of the class allows. Let's call him Pierre. I ask Pierre if we can ask him questions. I have never had a student refuse.

We start again with *Where do you live?* The student gives his answer, which I note at the right hand end of the horizontal line. The next question is *How long have you been living there?* (how I introduce this is shown in Chapter 16).

I construct *been* using *be* on Chart 3 and the ending *–en,* borrowed from *taken*, which allows students to realise that *be* functions like *taken* or *given*, and is a 'regular irregular' verb. I show them the pronunciation on the Rectangle chart. A few minutes later I 'discover' *been* in Chart 6—how silly of me to have forgotten where it is!

If anyone does not understand the question, I move my hand along the line from right to left, with an inquisitive look on my face, stopping here and there to signal to Pierre the question *Here? Here?* Now, suppose the answer, when it comes, is *I've been living there for six years*. I measure off a suitable length of the horizontal line, put a small vertical line across it and to the right of it, I write *6*.

big	each	back	away
near	mind	ask	went
box	few	say	new old
when	hard	again	most
kind	done	every	says
some	little	said	-es
shown	either	together	
came	-self	young	bad
better	good	best	worse

Chart 5

look	word	lot	almost
small	well	high	thing
feel	talk	listen	wish
see	across	also	throw
why	work	whom	hear
answer	heard	sound	
speak	enough	bigger	
walk	seen	low	about
saw	wrong	been	slow

Chart 6

The next question from the students is *Where did you live before that?* I write the answer to the left of the small line. *How long did you live there?* or *How long did you live there for? For five years.* I note 5 in the appropriate place. In this way we ask the same questions until the student indicates that he can go no further back in time. I can now introduce *I was born in* (the name of the place).

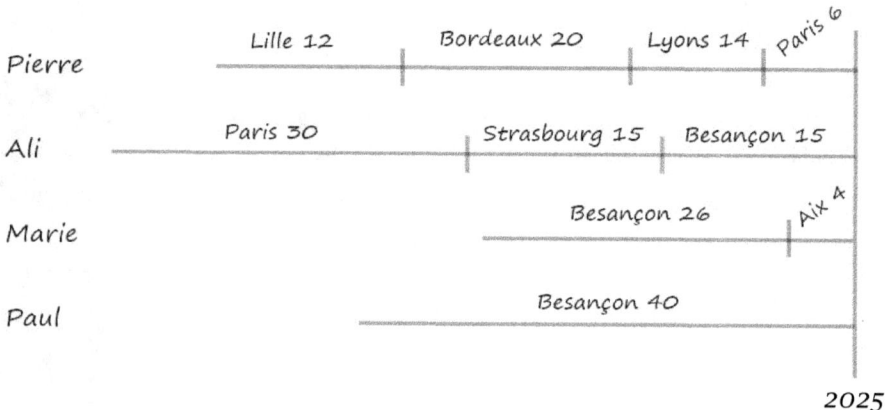

Now we can make sentences about Pierre.

> Pierre was born in Lille and lived there for twelve years. Then he moved to Bordeaux. He lived in Bordeaux for twenty years and then moved to Lyon. He moved from Lyon to Paris six years ago, and now he lives in Paris.

There can be many variants of sentences such as these, and I give the students as much freedom as they are willing to accept to make their own sentences.

I now ask for another volunteer, the students ask him the same questions, and I note the answers in the same way. We do this for several students.

Now the students make sentences about each other's lives.

> Ali was born in Paris. He lived there for thirty years and then he moved to Strasbourg. He lived in Strasbourg for fifteen years before moving to Besançon. He has been living in Besançon for fifteen years.

> Paul was born in Besançon forty years ago. He has lived in Besançon all his life. He has been living in Besançon since he was born.

Then we can easily venture into structures such as:

> When Pierre had been living in Lille for twelve years, he moved to Bordeaux where he stayed until he was thirty-two.

If we choose to talk about two students in the same sentence, then other types of complexity are introduced.

> Pierre was living in Bordeaux when Marie was born.

or

> Paul had already moved to Paris when Marie moved to Aix.

or

> Paul had been living in Paris for two years when Marie moved to Aix.

Sentences such as the following are possible, and easy, since they are contextualised.

> The year Paul was born, Marie was still living in Algiers, Pierre had already moved to Bordeaux, and Ali had not yet moved to Strasbourg.

My aim is to give the students an excellent grounding in the use of the verb forms while not overloading them with vocabulary. To reach mastery takes years and is beyond the scope of any course. But these are things that I can do to open the way to mastery.

When the students have a few hours of experience in the use of the main English verb forms—and not before—I give them a comprehensive overview of the whole verb tense system. That overview is described in the next chapter.

WRITING

With lower intermediate students, I have often asked them to write me letters. I don't want them to write about ecology or climate change; I want to read about the things they do during the week: the cinema and whether they liked the film; shopping for clothes; a concert; whatever they might have done. I never correct these letters. Instead, I write a letter back to the student, saying in the second person what they have said in the first: *You tell me that you went to the cinema and saw* The Count of Monte Cristo, *and that you enjoyed it very much. I haven't seen it yet, but I might go one evening this week.*

In class, I don't work on writing very much, unless the students either write using a different script or are illiterate. My courses are mainly about learning to speak, and the emphasis is placed on this skill.

With intermediate and advanced students I rarely work on writing because they have usually spent much of their time at school reading and writing, commenting on texts and listening to recordings. Now they need the spoken language.

19. Laying out a comprehensive view

The world's languages have many different ways of considering how human lives relate to time. Some languages have no tenses and rely on adverbs and expressions of time; some have many tenses; some add tense markers to adjectives or adverbs; the variety is considerable, and the subject is worth pursuing using the link in the QR code. However, I'm certain that almost all our students will come from a language which has a quite different way of relating its speakers' lives to time from what we find in English.

Scan for the Wikipedia entry on Grammatical tense.

Coming to grips with anything complex is easier if one can see the whole as well as its parts, and the parts in the context of the whole. One can then zoom out and look at the main patterns, and zoom in to work on details. Here, I want to show how the Verb Tense System of English functions, and how it can be built up into one coherent, organised whole, where all the different forms have been synthesised into a single schema. This schema can be taught dynamically using the spoken language almost exclusively. In what follows, I will be describing how I would work with a class of intermediate or higher level students.

Glenys Hanson working on the Verb Tense System with a class.

THE ORIGIN OF THE VERB TENSE SYSTEM

This approach to teaching verb tenses was invented by Glenys Hanson, one of the members of the Silent Way team working at the Centre de Linguistique Appliquée (CLA). She produced it in the early 1980s and it has been used extensively by the CLA team and others ever since. Several different versions exist. Glenys describes one version in the

Scan for Glenys Hanson's article on the Verb Tense System.

article linked to this QR code. She often worked with more advanced students.

I will present a slightly different version here, one which I think is more suited to lower-level groups. The Verb Tense System is not set in stone, and both the level of detail presented and the teaching should be adjusted on an ongoing basis, depending on how the class responds. However, the underlying idea remains the same. This is clear in Glenys Hanson's presentation and will, I hope, be clear in mine.

WHO MIGHT BENEFIT FROM THE WORK ON THE VERB TENSE SYSTEM?

I want to begin by emphasising that this is not a way of teaching tenses, but a way of organising them once they have been met and used extensively.

At the CLA, this system is used with:

- beginning and low-level students—only at the very end of their course, and with the forms they have worked with, to create coherence;
- intermediate students—once they have gained in fluency and can speak at least a little;
- high-level students who have five or more years of school English but who have not yet mastered the language—from the beginning of their course.

Even students who have seven years of school English, the normal secondary curriculum in schools in France, typically have no idea of the regularities of English, of its high level of coherence. They often have the impression that there are many tenses and forms, that the teacher can produce a new tense every term until they leave school, and that they can never get to know them all, much less master them. Often, they are not too sure whether forms they have in mind actually exist or not. Their English needs some serious housekeeping.

PREPARATIONS—SOME PRELIMINARY EXPLANATIONS

The day before, I prepare the students by giving them a list of irregular verbs. My list contains the most common of these verbs, about sixty altogether, presented in three columns, with all three forms, in alphabetical order. (I often get a funny reaction to this list—*now she's*

Scan to access a comprehensive online course on using the Verb Tense System.

finally revealing her true colours, now we get down to the real business of learning English ...)

I point out to the students that there are families of irregular verbs, like: *put-put-put; cut-cut-cut; hit-hit-hit* or *speak-spoke-spoken; break-broke-broken; wake-woke-woken* or *bring-brought-brought; teach-taught-taught*.

I tell them **not** to learn the verbs by heart; in fact, I expressly forbid them from doing so. Then, for homework, I ask them to reclassify all the verbs on the list into families. To do this, I know they will have to look at each verb several times to compare it with the others, and a good part of the necessary work will happen naturally as a consequence.

The following day, I check the work, discuss with them various possible right answers, then tell them I am going to give them a test. In fact, my 'test' consists of asking them to guess into which family they should put other verbs which were not on the list. They realise from this 'test' that they rarely have to learn any new verbs they meet because they can usually guess how the other forms of unknown verbs will behave. (I should admit here that I do cheat a little: my first test verb is *to cleave*, which gives either *cleave-cleft-cleft*, which they can guess from *leave-left-left* or *cleave-clove-cloven* like *speak-spoke-spoken*. The first has given us a cleft palate, the second, a cloven hoof.) Other verbs I include in my test are *bend-bent-bent* and *bind-bound-bound*, both of which can be guessed easily. This gives the students a real boost.

Scan to download the list of irregular verbs that I use.

I also ask them which verbs are the most common in English. They usually come up with *be* and *go*, or occasionally another they may have encountered. I ask them why these verbs might be irregular. They have never considered this question. I point out to them that these words are among the most common in the language; that even very small children already know them; and that this is why they don't change over time. More uncommon irregular verbs tend to become regular over time, but these ones are stuck as they were hundreds of years ago. This means that by simple contact, they will soon know them. So please, do not learn them off by heart. That would be a complete waste of time.

Before we begin, I want to emphasise that I don't have to teach my students everything about the language. I only have to set them on the right track. Their experience learning English will extend far into the future, long after they have left my class, and they will gradually be exposed to many aspects we can't cover in the time we have. It is important to keep this in mind; I have to be accurate, but not comprehensive.

STEP 1—THE WORK BEGINS

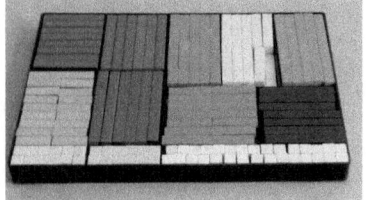

A box of Cuisenaire rods.

I would suggest that the reader take out a box of Cuisenaire rods and actually lay out the system while reading, so as to form a clear image of the whole system as it emerges.

The work will take place in four steps. First the students need to know the forms. Then we work through each form making examples which help them to sense how each is used. Thirdly, the various forms are tied together into complex sentences and lastly, the class is now in a position to engage fully in a Class Conversation, a conversation in which the students talk to each other as they would in any conversation, except that this conversation is being held in a foreign language (See later chapters on the Class Conversation).

I start by laying out a very big sheet of flip chart paper. With a thick black marker, I divide the paper into eight sections or boxes, as in Figure 1:

Figure 1. The layout at the start

I will be using a small coin for the subject of the verb, and different rods for the various parts of the system. I impose my own choice of colours and I always use the ones on the right.

If the class is not too big, I get the students to sit around my table, with a good view of the paper. They will not need paper and pencils, so these should be taken away if necessary. The aim is not to take notes, but to make sentences. The students will do this until it becomes completely natural for them. They can be seated quite close together. If I have more than about fifteen students, I draw the diagram on the board and stick, or have the students stick, the rods to the board with adhesive putty.

I tell them that we are going to work on verbs and we are going to begin with the verb *to work*. I usually choose this verb because it is well known by now, it is regular and my students often pronounce it incorrectly, so I want to give them practice using it. If some other verb has come up which has been problematic, then I would consider using it. However, I never choose an irregular verb. I also tell them that this is a guessing game; they are always willing to play the game I am about to describe if I say this.

For the whole of this lesson and the following ones, I feel free to talk more than usual, though I do keep teacher talk to a minimum. I ask questions rather than give explanations.

Off we go

I begin by placing a coin and a yellow rod in the box in the top right-hand corner, as seen from the students' side of the table. I say, *I work*. I point to the coin as I say the word *I*, and to the rod as I say *work* so as to indicate what each represents.

Using my 'your turn' gesture, I prompt the students to say this. I change the verb; pointing to the same coin and rod, I say *I take*. I ask them what else they could represent. They give a few verbs: *I play, I speak* ... I want them to understand intuitively that we are working on a symbolic level, that what is on the table represents whatever verb we want to experiment with. Then I come back to the verb *work*.

Moving on to two forms, then more

I now ask the students if they know another form of this verb. Someone usually proposes either *I worked* or *I am working*. I offer a coin, hold out the box of rods and ask the person to put down what he has just said. The student might ask what colour rods to use, but at this point, although I am going to impose colours, I tell him to choose his own. Students often ask where the new form should go, and I tell them to put it down anywhere they want to, and that we will deal with that later. I say this because I want them to think about where the various forms should go, so mistakes at this point will become useful because they will create discussion a little later. The colour of the rods is unimportant, but their number is not; it's part of the system.

The student lays down the coin and puts out one or more rods. If he lays the rods across lines, I tell him that he must keep within the boxes. I can point to what he has laid out and ask him to show us which rod corresponds to each element of the sentence by lifting my fingers. Supposing he has suggested *I'm working*, but lays out a coin and one single rod. I might ask him to say it again, and, at the same time, I hold up three fingers. He will probably realise that he has too few rods, and will add one. I might hold up the yellow rod I laid out and say *work*, then indicate his single rod and ask, *Where is work?* or I might say, for example, that I can't see *'m*, which encourages the student to add another rod. Sometimes just 'reading' the rods leads him to change the colours he has chosen, and sometimes he leaves what he has put out as it is. In this case, I lift my eyes to ask other students, to see if anyone else can suggest laying out an extra rod. However, once they realise what they need to symbolise, I start to introduce my colours.

At each step, all the students are invited to comment on what has been placed on the table. If they propose other ways of symbolising the oral form, I try to make sure, by asking leading questions, that the version closest to mine is retained.

When everyone can say both the structure that I laid out for *I work* and what the student has just put down, I ask for another form. Again I offer a coin and the box of rods, and get the student who makes the suggestion to lay it out. In this way, we build up four or five forms. As each new form is placed, I take the students around all the constructions laid out up to now, getting them to say each one with the verb *work*. I don't have to say anything. I simply point to the sets of coins and rods and say 'using *work*', and the students give the corresponding form of the verb. I do not get them to do this too much, however, as I don't want them to remember incorrect positions.

Working on getting the system correct

Once four or five forms have been set out, I ask the students if they think the present layout is coherent and, if they are not happy with it, how they would like to change it. I sometimes ask leading questions to help them see what choice of colour might be more coherent. I also point out to them that the only structure that they know for sure is correct, and is in the correct place on the table, is the one I put out, the Simple Present. (I point to it and say *'this one'*—I never use the official names of the various forms in my classes, and certainly never while doing this presentation.)

Thus, as we go along, I keep the students aware that the forms and the places may have to be changed. They discuss the layout and finally agree on which rods should be used for which element of each form, and where the various forms should be laid out. If there is disagreement, I ask someone to place the rods where he wants to, and then to tell us why he prefers this arrangement. Then I ask someone else to do the same and defend his position. Students can do this by shifting the rods to make the relationships they have noticed more obvious. In this way, the relative merits of the different arrangements become clearer. The patterns that some have now seen are made explicit by argument and counter-argument. Although the colours can be a little messy, each form is now in the correct box. The spoken forms sound logical, but the colours representing them may not yet be standardised from form to form.

Occasionally, it has happened that students have seen the correspondences but have placed the Simple Past under the Simple Present. In this case, I inform them that the double line signals the distinction between present and past. They move all the current rod-sets so as to observe this distinction.

When the Simple Past is put out, I make sure the students understand that the white rod corresponds to *-ed* for regular verbs, but that it only symbolises the past for irregular verbs. I do this by asking them to say the verbs *put* and *hit* and then *cut*, and they realise that the word *put* will sound the same in the Present as in the Past, although the rods show that one is in the past. In a similar way, *take* and *give* will involve a change of stem, rather than the addition of *-ed*. We are concerned here with the symbolic value of the rods, not the morphemes of the language.

[1] Many years ago I painted some of my white rods beige.

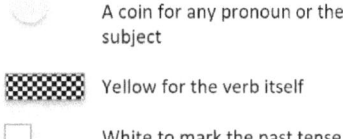

A coin for any pronoun or the subject

Yellow for the verb itself

White to mark the past tense

Beige to mark the past participle

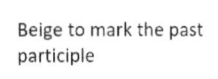

Red for all instances of the auxiliary *be*

Light green for all instances of the auxiliary *have*

Pink for the *–ing* form

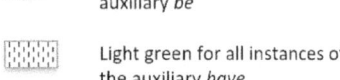

Blue for all the modals (*will, can, must, etc.*)

Black for negative forms

Brown for the auxiliary *do*

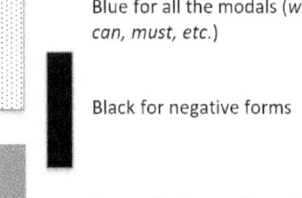

Orange for the rest of the sentence

I now make sure they see why I use a beige rod for the Past Participle ending of the Present Perfect and a white one for the Past ending.[1] The word *worked* is not the same in *I worked* and *I have worked*, even if they look the same, and this is clear in *I took* as against *I have taken* and many other verbs. I don't need to say this, only to suggest more irregular and regular verbs for them to place in the boxes.

Sometimes, especially for the Present Perfect, students place the rods across the lines between the boxes. In this case, I tell the student to keep within the boxes. With some forms, they find this very difficult; they are torn between two. All the students are invited to comment on what has been placed on the table. If they propose other ways of symbolising the oral form, I now make sure, by asking leading questions, that a version using the necessary number of rods is retained.

I ask the students if they can invent more forms. Usually a sentence with *will* is proposed and I tell the student that *will* is for later.

By now, they are moving onto shaky ground, since the easier forms have all been laid out, and those that remain to be found are not as well-known to them. As they propose new forms orally, I either agree to let them place their suggestion on the paper, or tell them that what they are proposing is 'for tomorrow', or inform them that it is not English at all. For example, *I have went* isn't English. As each new form is set out, I ask them if they are happy with where it is placed. I do this until the patterns of the forms emerge, then I stop asking that question.

Often, even with beginners, the students can lay out all eight forms. If not, and if the question has not been raised up to now, I might ask them whether they have noticed the double line in the middle of the layout, and what they think it might mean. Then I might ask how one goes from the Simple Present to the Simple Past, from the Present Progressive to the Past Progressive, from the Present Perfect to the Past Perfect, and make them aware that the presence or absence of the white rod shows this transition. Then I ask them to guess how one would go from **here** (I point) to **here** (I point to the other box). They can usually find the missing forms, deriving them from the patterns that have emerged. I use finger correction to show where to add endings if incomplete forms are suggested orally.

The only time I ever refer to more formal grammar is now. I ask them how many forms English has, and then how many tenses English has: eight forms, and two tenses, Present and Past. This is usually a great shock to them.

By now, the layout looks like Figure 2, although no words have yet been written on the paper. I have included the words below for the reader's benefit only.

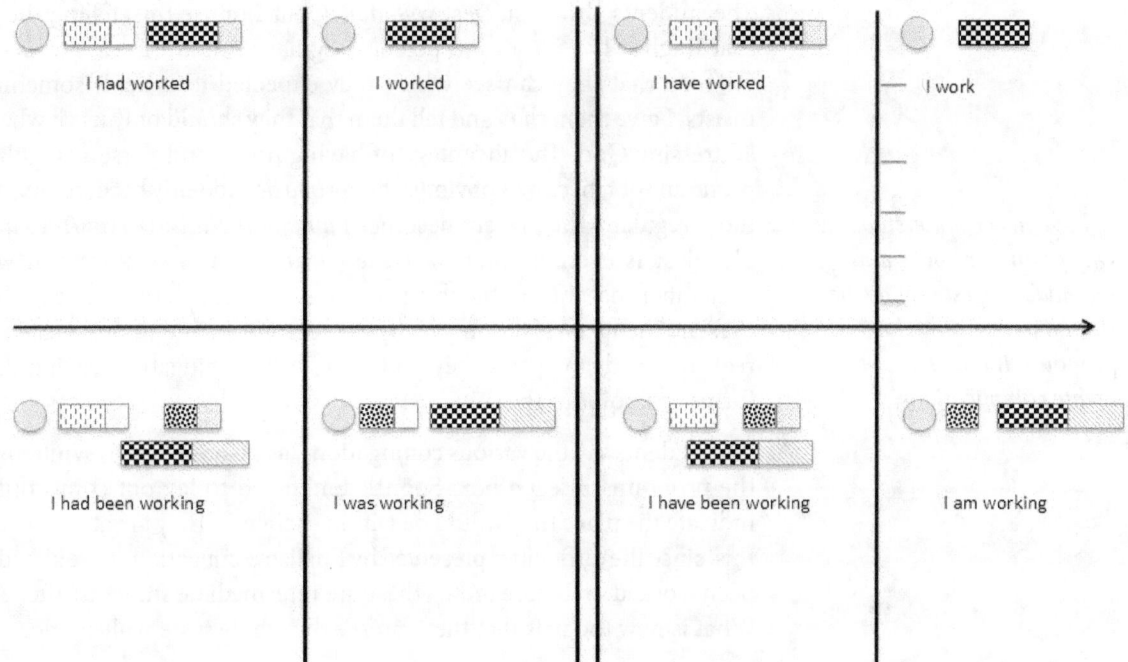

Figure 2. State of the layout at the end of the first section of the work. The length of the rods has been made regular in this representation for reasons of space. The coin representing the pronouns is the smallest possible coin in local currency. The lines for the persons are marked on the paper, as indicated in the Simple Present box. The arrowhead on the right of the centre line shows the direction of a timeline. Contractions can be indicated by overlapping coins and rods, as shown. If necessary, I might use a paperclip or something similar to represent the 3rd person singular <s>.

I now ask the students to give me all the forms of many different verbs, especially those they find difficult. We go around the layout quite a few times using these different verbs until the students realise that all verbs in English follow the same patterns, that the forms themselves are easy. They see that the same forms keep coming back in the same places.

STEP 2—CHECKING THE NEGATIVES, INTERROGATIVES, ETC.

Now I begin working on the conjugations. In the Simple Present box, I lay down coins to indicate the pronouns *I; he, she, it; we; you; they*. The students always suggest *you* after *I*, but I refuse this, telling them that English has no second person singular pronoun. I leave a space for it so that they can see where they expected it to be. If someone insists, I give them *thou* and tell them that they should only use it when addressing God. The advantage of having no second person singular pronoun soon becomes obvious; the verb *to be* suddenly becomes much more regular.[2] The Present becomes *I am; he/she/it is; we/you/they are*. The Past is even simpler: *I/he/she/it was; we/you/they were*. If we remember that the *s* of the third person runs through the whole of the Present, then *I am* is the only really irregular form. The students usually realise the advantage as they go through the conjugation, saying the forms as I point to the coins.

[2] I have never understood why grammar books and methods suggest *you* as the second person singular pronoun. It only serves to create complications.

The students say the various conjugations, as I place coins to symbolise the pronouns in each box. Soon I don't need to lay out coins, only indicate the place they would be within each box. They are at ease with this, since the difficulties presented by English conjugations have already been worked on before today; these are intermediate students, after all. What is new today is that they can see the whole system all at once.

Then we go around the whole layout, putting verbs into the negative, the interrogative, and the interro-negative. I introduce a black rod at a right angle to the others for the negative element, and a brown one, also at a right angle, for *do* and *did*, moving them around to trigger the different forms. Because I use rods, I don't have to say anything. Once the convention has been established, I simply place the black rod or get a student to place it, and they say the corresponding negative form. *Did* is obtained by taking the white rod from the stem and placing it with the brown rod. Thus they discover that in these forms, the white rod, which symbolises the Past, will move from the verb to the auxiliary. Ah!

I check with everyone that they feel fairly secure in their use of the individual forms, and that no problems remain, and then we can go on. At this stage, the students' sentences are true, but not really spontaneous. As the work progresses they become more so, until we reach the Class Conversation proper (See Chapter 21.)

STEP 3—USING THE VARIOUS FORMS

I am now going to begin the work on each of the forms separately, gradually building for each a sense of how native speakers use it to talk about their lives and circumstances. I am aiming to get the students to feel more at home with each individual form, and then with different forms grouped together using subordinate clauses. I don't really mind in what order the various forms are worked on, but what follows is probably the most common order.

The Simple Present

I tell the students we are going to explore the verb *to work*, and ask them which of the forms they find easiest. They usually propose *I work*, so we start there. I ask them what words and expressions are usually found with this form. Acceptable answers to this question include the adverbs of frequency and expressions beginning with *every*.

During the discussion of either the Simple Present or the Present Progressive, the word *now* is usually suggested. Using questions, I point out that it can be used with both of these forms equally, and I ask someone to write it at the right hand end of the horizontal line that runs across the diagram. I add an arrowhead to the right of the line, pointing to future time.

I start with the adverbs of frequency; I draw a vertical line in the box, write 100% at the top and 0% at the bottom and ask the students to suggest adverbs of frequency going from the most frequent, 100% of the time, to the least frequent, 0% of the time. They discuss where to put the various words as they make the list.

Now I give the only rule that working on the Verb Tense System requires: every sentence must be true. It will end up corrected, but it must start true to their lives. So I ask the students to make true sentences about themselves using these triggers with any verbs they need.

They produce all sorts of sentences, usually very ordinary, everyday ones: *I always drink coffee for breakfast, I never take the bus to work*. Some sentences do not need a trigger: *I live in Paris. I drive a Ford*. However, the idea of *always* or some other trigger is implicit.

As we work, other more complex forms might emerge: *every day, every second day, every other day, every so often, twice a month, etc*. Some of these are written into the box. The word *every* can be used before a

```
100% ↑  always
        almost always
        very often
        usually
        frequently
        generally
        sometimes
        occasionally
        rarely
        seldom
        almost never
 0%  ↓  never
```

```
       ⎧ morning, evening
       ⎪ day, week, month, year
       ⎪ Friday ...
every  ⎨ Easter Sunday
       ⎪ second Friday at 6pm
       ⎪ summer, winter ...
       ⎩ time, etc
```

```
tomorrow   yesterday
now   today   ready   time
morning   evening   mid-
day   afternoon   night
during   early   late   till
soon   until   since   yet
before   moment   just
last   still   then   next
ever   while   ago   after
```

Word Chart 10

```
            yesterday
            yesterday morning
            yesterday evening
         ⎧  week
         ⎪  month
         ⎪  year
last  ⎨  Friday
         ⎪  July
         ⎪  spring, summer, autumn,
         ⎪  winter
         ⎩  holidays
         •• ago
```

wide variety of nouns and we make a representative list like the one on the previous page.

I place an orange rod in the box and tell the students that it's 'the rest of the sentence'. From now on, the orange rod will stand for the rest of the sentence. It's very useful in this role.

The students also ask each other questions and get practice using the interrogative forms but, depending on the level of the students, I keep this kind of interaction fairly short, since at this point it is not the main thrust of the lesson.

The Simple Past

When everyone seems reasonably comfortable with using the Simple Present, we go on to whatever form they want to work on next. The students often select the Simple Past.

The most obvious trigger for the Simple Past is *yesterday*. *Last* requires a list like *every*, and the words which are used with it are often the same: *last summer, last Friday*, and so on. If a word like *ago* does not come up, I can suggest that they should look for a word on Word Chart 10, for example. When they have found it, I write *ago* with two big dots in front of it to indicate that there will be two other words before it: *three days ago, four weeks ago, ten years ago*, etc. We end up with a list of triggers rather like the list on the left.

Other words are also common, but they can be a little treacherous because they are not explicitly linked to the past—*on Friday, in September, at nine o'clock, during the winter,* etc. These can equally be associated with the future, so when the students use them, they need to keep in mind what they are talking about.

The students now make a number of examples drawn from their lives, pointing first to the trigger written on the paper, which, except for *ago*, I ask them to place at the beginning of the sentence, and then to the coin for the subject and to the rods when they reach the verb. I get students to point because pointing helps to cement the link between the sentence, the arrangement of rods and the reality it represents in the mind of the student who is pointing his sentence.

We work on this until the students feel at ease; only then do we go on to the next form, which is often the Present Progressive.

The Present Progressive

I start by asking the students to make a few example sentences using this form. When they have four or five, I ask them what they might use as a trigger. Someone usually finds *at the moment* or a synonym. I get them to write *at the moment* on the paper in the appropriate box.

One mistake students make with this form is to consider that *at the moment* means the same as *at this instant*. Most of their sentences will be similar to *I am listening to George at the moment*, or *I am sitting here at the moment*. I give my own example (it's not often that I give examples, but in this case, I do): *I am writing a book at the moment*, and point out to them that I started writing it many months ago. Their examples change, and become more representative of the meaning of *at the moment* which can be quite a long period of time.

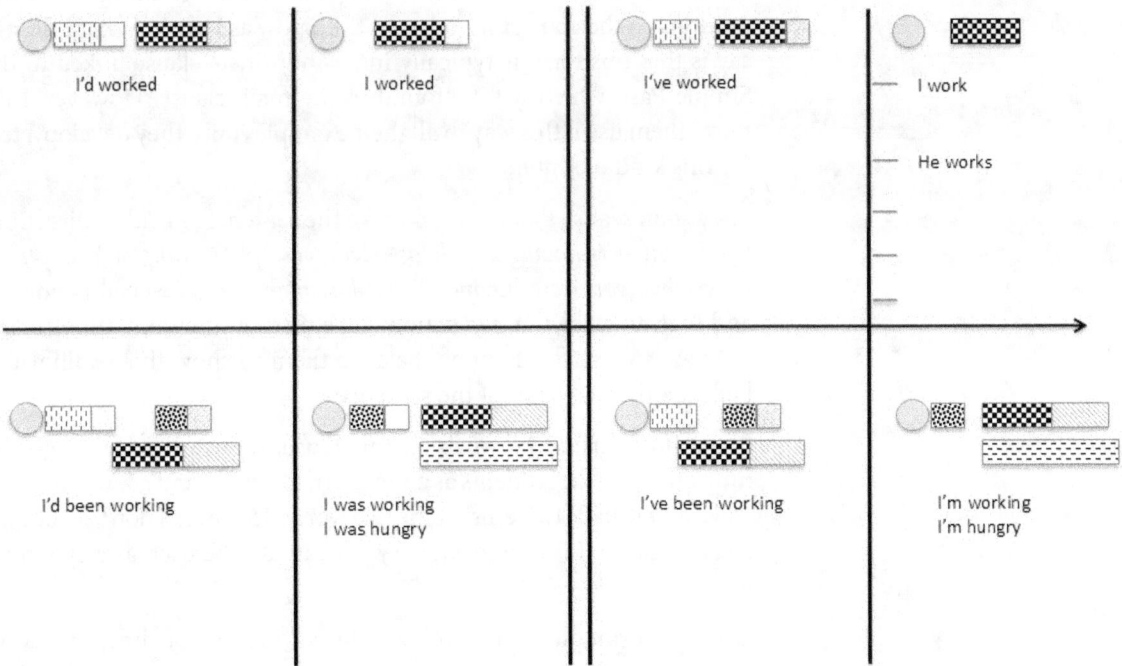

Figure 3. With the second way of using the Present and Past Progressives

At this point, I add a second, very common way this form can be used: *I'm hungry*. The word *hungry* is represented by the orange rod which I place below the *-ing* form, rather than to the right of it, as has been the case until now (See Figure 3).

In sentences like these, we are in fact using *to be* as a verb rather than as an auxiliary, but it functions in the same way however it's used, and I find it better not to make the distinction.

When everyone is more or less at ease with these examples, I ask them what they would like to look at next.

The Past Progressive

The students often suggest that we work on this form next. They are justifiably wary of the Present Perfect, and keep putting it off.

I tell them that the most common trigger for this form is *while*. I draw an arrow from the Past Progressive box to the Simple Past box and give them an example: *While I was having a bath last night, my phone rang*, pointing to the coins, the rods and the arrow as I say it. What I **do not** say is that this form is typically in a subordinate clause linked to the Simple Past, which will be found in the main clause. However, I **do** make them use it this way in all their examples until they develop a feel for this kind of sentence.

They soon realise that they can make the sentences in either direction: *While you were having a bath last night, your phone rang* or *Your phone rang while you were having a bath last night*. This reversal is normal and logical, since the two actions take place at the same time. Using my hands as scales, I simply balance them to show this equilibrium between the two parts of the sentence.

Sometime during the work on this tense, the word *when* might be introduced by the students as a synonym for *while*, and a few sentences will then be made twice, using the two words. However, I don't encourage *when* because it is a little slippery—it can also be used as a synonym for *after*.

Different examples will involve different periods of time, and soon involve the other common sequence, the same form used twice. *Last night, while I was watching television, my husband was preparing dinner* shows two similar lengths of time. We then compare this with *While I was having a bath, the phone rang* where one period is longer than the other. We can suspend the need for true sentences and play with examples like *While I was reading a book, the doorbell was ringing.* How likely is that to happen in real life? The students continue to make examples until they feel at ease with this structure. I don't explain it, I simply use examples.

The Present Perfect

They finally 'bite the bullet' and we start working on this form. The mistake students usually make with this form is to equate it with a Past. The English language uses triggers extensively, and the triggers for the Past are incompatible with this form. *I've seen it yesterday* is not English.[3]

[3] *Although I have occasionally heard native speakers say something like this, I would certainly not accept it if my students said it.*

I touch the word *Now* written on the horizontal line and ask the students, *If this is now, when is this?* pointing to the Present Perfect box. They suggest various possibilities which I deal with as appropriate: some belong in other boxes, some are not triggers, some describe the time relationship of this box. If they don't suggest what I want, I give it to them—*if this is 'now', then this is 'before now'*. I ask someone to write in *Before now*.

We finally have three or four triggers which are correct: *yet?, not yet, already, just, ever?,* etc. I ask them to write the ones which finish the sentence to the right of the box. They make many sentences using these triggers. I ask them to increase the length of their sentences to include anything which is understood but not expressed. This gives examples like *I haven't finished yet, but I hope to finish in about an hour*; or *I'm not thirsty, I've just had a drink*; or *We can't stop working yet, as it isn't four o'clock*; and *We can't stop working as it isn't four o'clock yet. Have you ever been to London? No I haven't, not yet. I've already been to Paris. I've been to Paris five times. I've already had lunch. What about you? I haven't had lunch yet.* As they speak, they point to the boxes involved.

Rather than seeing a Present Perfect form as a past event which has relevance in the present (which is what many students tell me they have been taught), it is better to think of it as a present state which is described not directly but by looking at how it has been arrived at or obtained. When someone says, 'I've eaten', they mean that they are not hungry. When a mother asks her child, 'Have you washed your hands?', she is asking whether the child's hands are clean.

As we go along, I ask them to convert some of their sentences into the Simple Past so as to establish the contrast between the two forms. They can only do this to my satisfaction if they change the trigger. *I didn't finish yesterday* is clearly different from *I haven't finished yet, but I hope to finish in a few minutes*. They make many examples, each time showing where these belong on the layout by pointing to the coins and the rods as needed.

The Past Perfect

This form is not very difficult now, since the students are starting to understand how English functions. I ask the class *If this is 'yesterday'*, (pointing to the word in the Simple Past box), *what is this?* (pointing to the Past Perfect box). They almost always find *'Before yesterday'*.

> *If this is 'three days ago', what is this? It's 'before three days ago'.*
> *If this is 'last Friday' then what is this? It's 'before last Friday'.*

I introduce the trigger *when* and give an example: *When I had eaten my dinner, I did the washing up*. The students are invited to give more examples. I don't spend too much time on this form, pointing out that the sentences can usually be made more simply by using *and then*, for example, *I finished eating my meal and then I did the washing up*. This last sentence is easy; they have been using this type of sentence for days.

The Present Perfect Progressive

This is the first form which has a double auxiliary. To draw out its underlying meaning, I point to the Present Perfect box and ask, *'What colour rods do we use for 'before now'?'* Students typically take some time before they realise that this form is represented by both the green rod and the beige one. Then I point to the Present Progressive box and ask, *'What colour is 'at the moment'?'* And they reply, *'It's red and pink'*. Then I tell them, *'Now, please be ingenious. What should we write in this box?'* pointing to the Present Perfect Progressive box. I may have to question a little more, or give another hint before they finally realise that, since the form is made up of green and beige, and then red and pink, they should write in *'before now and at the moment'*. Someone writes it in.

We then make examples. I insist that all examples begin with a sentence in either the Simple Present or the Present Progressive. This gives examples such as *I live in Paris. I have been living in Paris for five years* or *I work for Renault. I have been working for Renault for three years. I drive a Ford. I have been driving a Ford for two years*. I insist they make true sentences.

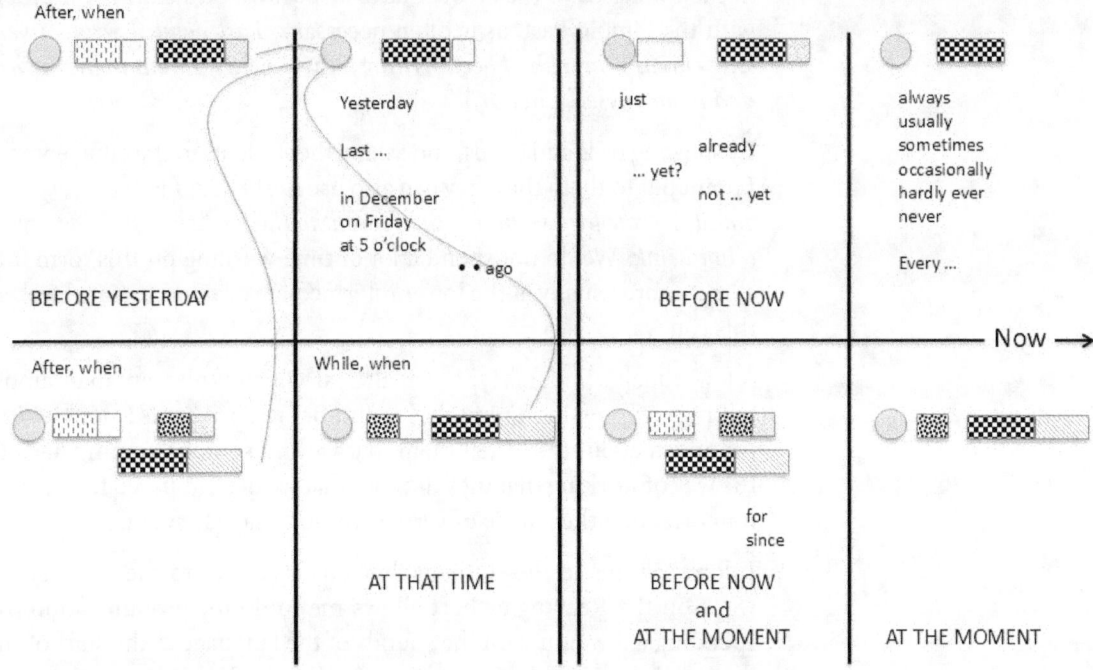

Figure 4. Some of the common 'tracks' through the system that students' examples follow.

I can also take them back to the Past for contrast: *When did you move to Paris?—I moved to Paris five years ago. I live in Paris now. I've been living in Paris for five years.* They point to the boxes as they make their examples.

From time to time, we come across a sentence which is outside my initial presentation, and which causes a problem. The system thus gradually gains in complexity. For example, *I have a new car. I have been having a new car for three weeks* is not English. I correct such sentences as they come up. One by one, verbs which behave in unexpected ways come to light. For example, *know* is typically not used in a progressive form. We make sentences with verbs like these, and the students get a feel for how they behave.

The Past Perfect Progressive

Now only this form remains to be examined. Once again, it appears in a subordinate clause. I give an example. Pointing to the coins and rods in their boxes, and the arrow I have just drawn in, I start my example with the Simple Past, as is often necessary: *Last night, I wrote a very long email. When I had been writing for two hours, I went to the kitchen and made myself a hot drink.*

By showing rods and boxes, and asking the students to start the sentence, I point out to them that they can also use *Last night, I wrote a very long email. I wrote for two hours, then I went to the kitchen and made myself a hot drink.* We do not spend a lot of time working on this form. My students are usually at the lower intermediate or intermediate level, so this can wait.

A few students find this type of analytical work less pleasant than simply talking—expressing themselves—and being corrected. I don't worry too much about this. I tell them that we will soon be coming back to the way of working that they like, but that we need a shared framework for correcting the choice of verb forms in their statements.

I don't say this to the students, but this is similar to the job that the work on the Rectangle chart allows me to do for pronunciation. By spending a few hours on the sounds of the language at the start of the course, the students' pronunciation can be worked on throughout the rest of it in micro-lessons that do not unduly impinge upon the rest of the class work. The Verb Tense System allows me to work in a similar way.

STEP 4—TAKING SOME TIME TO DIGEST

We might now spend a few minutes talking more generally about the differences between the Present and the Past. First of all, how many tenses are there in English? Only two, the Present and the Past. All the other forms derived from these. The students might come up with things like: the Present is the 'now' tense; the Past is the 'then' tense. With a class which has already studied English and knows a lot of grammar, I might point out that the forms of the Present and Past tenses are all called 'the indicative', which gives a good general idea of what they are about. They serve to indicate. We use them to give indications. A discussion like this might take five minutes at most.

Then we spend the next lesson or two simply talking, using all eight forms as needed until the students seem at ease with the system. The class needs time to digest the work that has been done to date. They need to learn to express their life experience within the constraints of the tense system of the English language. Of course, I make sure every sentence is correct before we move on to the next one.

At the same time, we meet other triggers which can be written on the paper if it seems useful.

I ask the students to lay out the system anew each day. I put out the sheet of paper on which the initial work was done once or twice. But as soon as I see that they have a clear mental picture of the layout, I change to a blank piece of paper, only marking out the boxes. The written words disappear, and now they have only the rods in the boxes as a visual support. If there is any doubt about the meaning of a sentence, I ask them to show which box they think they are in, and then check the (now invisible) triggers.

My aim is not to 'teach' the forms in the usual sense of the word. Instead I want to give the students as much experience of using the verb forms as possible in a short period of time, and to make sure that they see all the forms in juxtaposition, while using them to speak about their lives. This way, they know what they are choosing and why.

If any modals come up, I simply correct them, without explanation. They will be examined soon, but are outside the current domain.

STEP 5—THE FUTURE

By now, the students have proposed *will* on several occasions, and I have always said 'later' or 'tomorrow'. Now it is time to look at how English deals with time in the future, and there are some surprises in store.

I begin by asking in which of the boxes *next week* can be used as a trigger. After some discussion and experimentation, they finally decide that three of them can. *I'm going to Agadir next week* is of course possible, as is *I go to Agadir next week* and even *I was going to go to Agadir next week*. This last example is often a complete surprise, and sometimes provokes protest. I see if anyone can finish the sentence: *I was going to go to Agadir next week, but I had to cancel.* When I have French speaking students, I point out to them that their language behaves in the same way, which often astounds them. However they are forced to admit that it does. Time in the future does not necessarily require a Future tense.

I tell them that we will come back to this question later.

STEP 6—THE MODALS

The role of the modals is to tell us about the mood of the speaker: confidence, doubt, pressure, possibility, likelihood, certainty. For this reason, I sometimes call them the 'moodles'. In English, many moods are expressed simply using vocabulary, but the language has incorporated a few into its grammar.

In order to work on the moodles, we have to work from the moods they reveal when we use them. Thus, these words are more difficult to work with than the indicatives because moods can't be summoned on demand. I need to watch for them arising naturally in the classroom and take the opportunity to provide the language for them in the moment.

HOW I WANT STUDENTS TO UNDERSTAND THE MODALS

These words are not unknown to the students since they have usually met them previously and I have dealt with them as and when situations have come up in which they have been necessary. To my mind, students can only really understand these words if they are confronted from the beginning with the emotions the modals normally accompany and provoke.

In this section, I will describe the ideas I include in my lessons on the modals, then further down in Step 7, how I introduce them to the class.

Can and *Could*

Can is an acknowledgment of one's capabilities, and expresses a mood of certainty about one's capacity. It is used to talk about know-hows: *I can swim, I can speak French, I can drive a car*. The gesture I use to illustrate *can* is the 'all power to me' gesture often seen after a particularly good shot in a sporting event. The head is bent forward, the forearm held vertically at shoulder height and the fist turned inward toward the speaker, then the elbow is pulled down energetically a few centimetres. It means 'I did it!' and is not intended as a public display of power but rather as a sign to oneself of one's success. For me, this is its basic meaning.

Obviously, when this form is used by students, the speaker demonstrates much less merit than this gesture suggests, although the day the student first says to himself *I can swim!* he might well have felt like using this gesture. *I can come over to your place this evening* will not be written down in the record books, but it does show that the speaker is sure of his performance this evening. He knows he can come. The strength of the mood will be reflected in the level of reduction of the word *can*. *I c'n do it*, has less effort involved than *I CAN do it*, which perhaps suggests, for example, *if only I can develop a little more muscle power*.

Could is a more muted version of *can*. It introduces a certain amount of doubt. *Probably* goes well with *could*. *I could probably come over to your place this evening*. I point out that *could* is not only past, but also distant, and can have future reference. *I could come over to your place next weekend for the Bank Holiday, but I would have to organise a few things first*. There is often *but...* used with '*could*'.

May

May is fairly straightforward. The speaker is in a mood of uncertainty. The gesture I use with *may* is the aeroplane gesture: fingers outstretched, palm towards the floor, I 'rotate' the wings of my plane round the 'fuselage' of my middle finger, raising and lowering the thumb and little finger alternately.

I usually insist on much longer sentences with *may*, deliberately expressing what is omitted and must be inferred by the listener. *I may be free this evening, but on the other hand, I may not. Peter may come over tonight, but then again, he may not.*

Might

This word gives the same idea, but the uncertainty is greater. This is one of the distant forms, and distance produces uncertainty. *Fred might come over to help us, but I know Fred, and he might not. John might pay me back, but I really doubt it.*

I ask the students to be patient for *might*, it will become clearer soon after we have worked more on the sequence of tenses.

Must

The mood for *must* is an awareness of conflicting priorities, an inner pressure weighing on me to change my (or your) priorities. This mood has no particular name, but is easy to recognise. The gesture for *must* might be the one on the famous *Uncle Sam needs you* poster from the First World War—the index finger pointing at the one who is looking. I have decided what you should be doing with your time. *You must do*

your homework this evening. You must go and get a haircut. You must eat up your spinach.

Sometimes, I point the finger at myself, knowing I have other priorities, but aware that I am thinking about what my priority should be: *I really must write to mother.*

This word has no 'distant' form, although ...

Should

I usually present *should* as the distant form of *must*. I find *should* much easier to account for than *shall*. Its meaning is a weaker form of *Uncle Sam needs you*. I know better than you what you should be doing, but I'm not so assertive about saying so. Maybe I'm trying to convince you but I know that ultimately you will make the final decision. *You should be getting ready for your piano lesson, You should get dressed immediately, You should work harder at school.* Of course, I can also direct *should* towards myself: *I should save more.*

All these sentences can be made longer to illustrate what has been elided. *You should be getting ready for your piano lesson, instead of playing that (silly) game. You should get dressed immediately rather than (simply) sitting there watching television. You should work harder at school, instead of (just) sitting around talking to Kevin all day.*

And also: *I should save more instead of (stupidly) spending every last penny on junk.*

A sense of judgement is present.

Shall

Shall is now absent from some types of English, including mine, so I usually leave it to the students to work it out for themselves. If they have already studied English, they know the word, and ask for more information. If I am pressed for an explanation, I point out to the students that it is present in the Ten Commandments: *Thou shalt not kill.* Queen Elisabeth I used it, and like God, could enforce it if necessary: she had several people beheaded. Queen Elisabeth II no longer had such power. *Shall* went when the power went. I leave others to find a suitable gesture for this word. In my opinion, it is not really an important word.

Will and Would

These words are intimately related to the ideas of *willing* and of *will power*, to various degrees, often indicated by the level of reduction the speaker uses.

Will indicates that I have just thought about something, have come to a conclusion and am ready to spend energy on achieving whatever it is. The amount of energy I am ready to put into achieving it will be indicated by the 'strength' of the word *will* when I say it. For example, the doorbell rings, and I shout to the rest of the family: *Don't bother, I'll go*. I know that going to the door does not require much energy. So I use the contracted form. (The energy I have to spend is not the energy needed to walk to the door, but what is needed to pull myself away from what I am currently involved in.) At the other extreme, we have an exchange such as *Tony, eat your soup. No, I **won't**. Yes, you will. No, I will not*. Tony is indicating that he will put as much energy as he can muster into maintaining his refusal. This is implicitly recognised if the adult changes tack and says *If you eat your soup, you can have ice cream for dessert*, thus changing from the brute force approach, which she knows she will probably lose, to the carrot and stick approach, which she might think she has a chance of winning.

The gesture I would use is a decision gesture. I might hold a finger to my temple, turn it round a few times to show that I'm thinking, then I wag or flick it once firmly to indicate that I have come to a conclusion.

Would is a little more subtle. It involves distancing, which makes it more polite, since the speaker is showing he is not deeply attached to the result. *Would* is easier to deal with once we reach Step 8 below, the sequence of tenses.

STEP 7—HOW I INTRODUCE THE MODALS TO THE CLASS

Before reading this section, I again suggest that the reader lay the rods out on the table. This will help you to understand how the work develops.

Using a clean sheet of paper, I draw the usual lines and then ask the students to lay out the Verb Tense System as they have been using it for the last few lessons. The triggers are not written in. Most of the students should be able to do this very easily by now. Then I ask them to lay it out again, this time at the bottom of each box. Now I place a blue rod between the coin and the yellow rod at the bottom of the first box, at 90 degrees to these, and say *I will take* (assuming *take* is the verb we have chosen to work with). Then I hold out three more blue rods and ask the students to add them to the other boxes in the Present. This yields *I will be taking, I will have taken* and *I will have been taking*. Aaugh! This is unexpected; most of the students didn't know these forms existed. Most of them saw *will* simply as 'the Future Tense', but here it is popping up in all the forms of the present.

I now pick up four more blue rods and hold out one of them, which a student hesitantly places in the Simple Past box. If the student simply puts it there, I ask the class to read what the rods tell them—*I will took*, which they know is incorrect. They know the word they want is *would* but how should they symbolise it? Finally someone realises that the white rod should be put with the blue rod—*would* seems to function as the 'past' or 'distant form' of *will*. This gives *I would take* visually with the rods. Now they are ready to place blue rods in all four Past boxes. We examine and say all the forms that are generated, many of which are unknown to the students. These forms are easy to create, as they are completely logical and clearly symbolised by the rods. Figure 5 shows how the layout looks at this stage.

Now I take the blue rods from all the Progressive forms, i.e. the whole bottom line, and tell the students (at the level I usually work with) that they will discover these later on if they continue to learn English. I do not believe they are important for lower level students. However, I want them to know they exist, and to realise they are easy to form. Sometimes they crop up later in the conversation, and I get a student to add the rod required.

Now I come back to the blue rod in the Past box. If this is *would*, it can also represent other words. Which ones? Eventually *could* or *should* or one of the other modals appears, and we go around the layout looking at the forms generated, putting in *can* with *could*, *may* with *might*, *shall* with *should*—although *shall* will not be worked on—and *must*. Now they can place all the modals and know their forms. We can place *ought to* in the Past boxes if it comes up, but this is rare.

The next job for the students is to understand how to use the modals.

I work through what was explained in the previous section about 'moodles', getting the students to point to the rods as they produce their examples. This step of the process seems to me to be a little unsatisfactory, but I have not found a better way of doing this job. As I've said, the

TOWARDS THE CLASS CONVERSATION

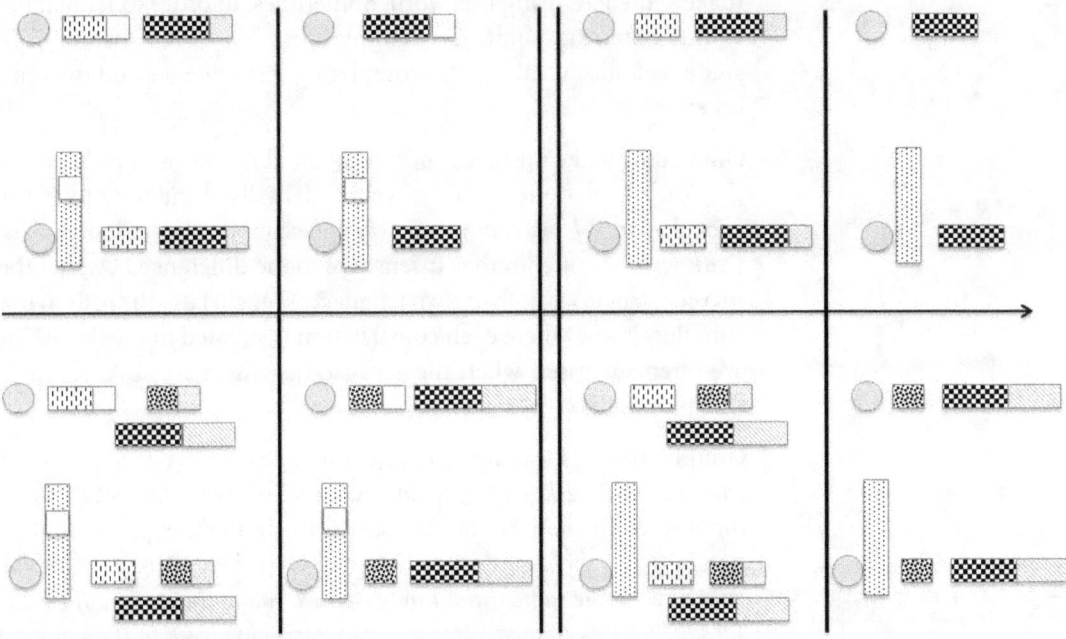

Figure 5. Blue rods are in place for all the modals.

difficulty is that one can't produce moods at will; they happen when they happen. The problem is that I can never be sure that a sentence faithfully respects the mood of the speaker. Mechanically, the sentences are correct, but there is no way of knowing if they are true.

I never spend very much time on this. The various usages of the modals will become clearer during the work described in the next section.

STEP 8—SEQUENCES OF TENSES

The meanings of the modals will become clearer because they are typically paired with the indicative forms and this grounds them. I begin with the word *if*, which gives us the opportunity of using complex language in longer and more complex sentences. At the end of the lesson, *if* will be written in at least all four non-progressive boxes, and perhaps in others too, if the need has arisen.

I begin by writing *if* in the Simple Present box. Then I ask students to make sentences using this word. Sometimes, in order to launch them, I offer a starting point, for example *If it's fine tomorrow, we …* The students find several ways of completing this sentence and then make others.

Often, they make mistakes and use a Past Tense without even noticing that they have done so. Thus we accidentally stumble onto *If I had enough money, I would buy a new car*, for example. The students I usually work with are often rather insensitive to the difference between these two constructions in their own language, French. I use the rods to make sure they know where each construction is situated in the boxes. They are often surprised when they realise that there are several types of sentences with *if*.

Grammatically speaking, the past moves left by two boxes, since *If I saw you next week, I'd say 'hello'* is compatible with *next week*. But the differences in these sentences can be made more explicit simply by finishing the sentences, often with the word *but*: *We're going to Paris next week in the same train. I may well see you at the station. If I see you, I'll say 'hello'* as against *We're going to Paris next week in the same train, but you're travelling first class and I'm in second class. If I saw you, I'd say 'hello' but I don't really expect to see you*. These are quite different from the past, *We went to Paris last week in the same train, but I didn't see you, so we didn't say 'hello'*. Or, in an example without *but*: *If it's fine tomorrow, we can have a picnic. They are predicting good weather, so we'll probably have our picnic*.

In the Past boxes, the sentences may still have future reference: *If by any chance it were fine tomorrow, we could have a picnic, but I'm expecting it to rain, so we will probably be unable to have our picnic*. But again here, there is an additional element of distance and uncertainty.

Note the presence of *were* in this example. Somewhere during the work on the *if* clauses, the form *If I were you* will certainly come up. This is the remnants of a subjunctive in English. I always teach my students to use it; it adds a certain polish to their sentences. My aim is to help them to speak excellent English, and this is part of excellence.

In the Past Perfect, we find sentences like *If I had known you were coming, I would have baked a cake* which we then continue with the information which has been elided; *but I didn't know you were coming, so I didn't bake a cake*. The students point to the boxes as they make the sentences.

TOWARDS THE CLASS CONVERSATION

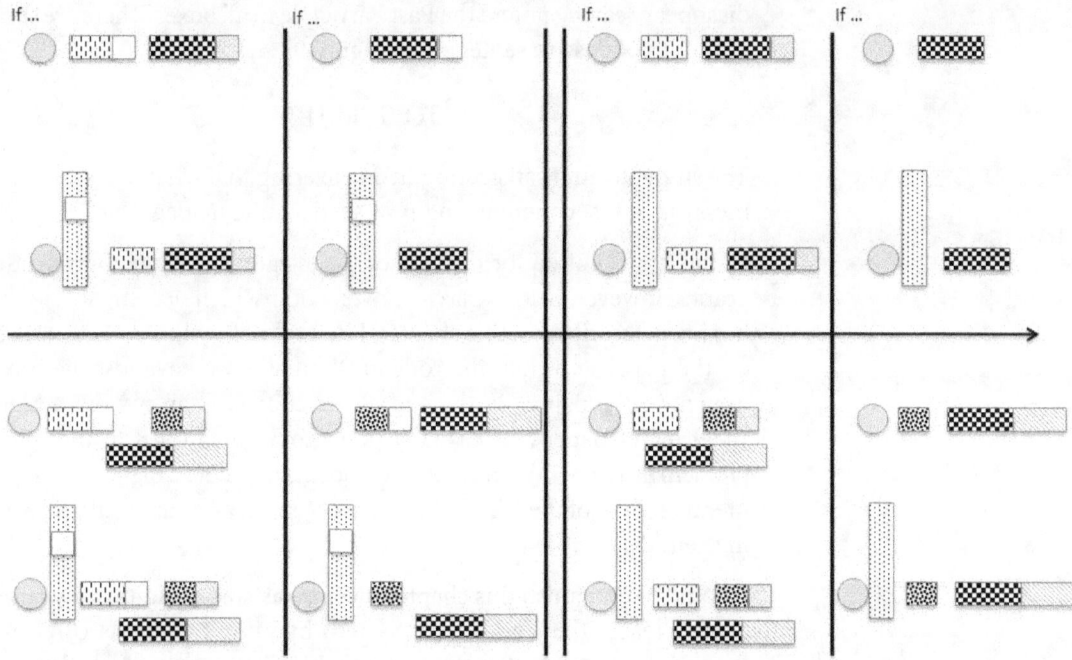

Figure 8. 'If' has been added to the layout.

They can see how English combines these forms in such a compact and logical way. The subordinate clauses are often in the same boxes, and the arrows usually go where one would expect.

Sometimes there are surprises: a sentence can jump from the Past to the Present in sentences like *If I had won the lottery, I would have bought a new car, but I didn't win the lottery, so I can't buy a new car*. Such sentences can be shortened to *If I had won the lottery, I would have bought a new car, but I didn't, so I can't*. This capacity to economise words is also a feature of English: many students are astonished by sentences like this. They love trying to use this construction.

The Passive Voice

We can also work on the Passive Voice in the same way, and I always do so when I work with students who have to write scientific articles which are often written in the Passive Voice. Placing rods makes this easy. However it is necessary to make sure that the interrogative, negative and interro-negative forms are clear in the students' minds. *Do* and *did* disappear, leaving *be* and the Past Participle in all boxes. There are some examples of passive sentences in Figure 9.

TO SUM UP

The students find satisfaction in discovering that what had seemed so messy is in fact coherent, and now seems quite manageable.

In the time allotted for my classes, I can rarely go much beyond this point. However, in the Class Conversation which accompanies what has been described in this chapter, I first take away the triggers written on the paper and then the rods until, finally, we have just the boxes drawn on the paper. By the end of the course, I can put out a blank sheet of A4 paper and casually point to an area on it to indicate a problem in a student's sentence. The students now have a highly-developed mental model of the whole Verb Tense System, and can do all the work in their heads.

I would like to finish this chapter by emphasising again that my aim is not to 'teach' the Verb Tense System by giving students rules and examples. I provide them with a suitable framework which they can use to comprehend and integrate the English they meet in the months and years to come. I want them to be able to analyse what they meet if it is unexpected, and categorise it. I hope to give them a tool for the future.

My aim is to get the students to say as many true sentences in the language as we can manage in the time allotted to the whole course so that they can learn to express their lives within this new system. The learning takes place through these examples: true things that the students want to say which we work on until they are correctly expressed. This point is fundamental. The only way students will master the spoken language is to genuinely speak it.

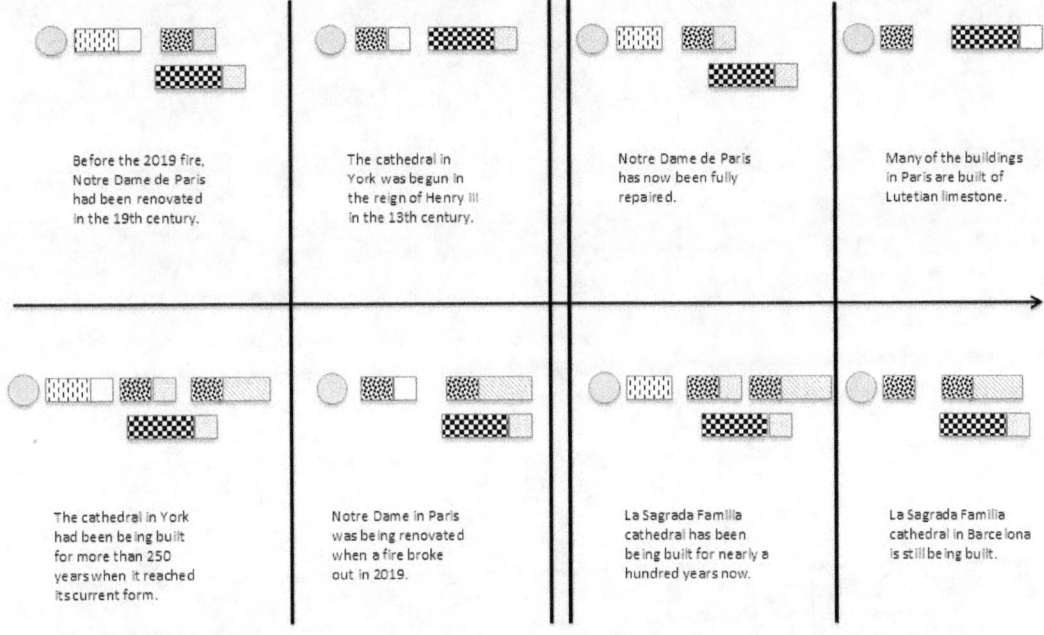

Figure 9. Some examples using the passive voice.

THE CLASS CONVERSATION

'I don't teach, I let them learn'
Caleb Gattegno

20. Low-level students

Even before the second Silent Way Word chart is introduced, I encourage the students to begin talking to each other about rods, colours and numbers. To begin with, these are mini-conversations of just a few exchanges. What makes them important is that the students decide what they want to say and who they would like to say it to. These are genuine conversations even if very short and extremely limited in scope.

— Your rod's green and my rod's red.
— Yes, my rod's red and your rod's green.
— Your rod's red and mine's green.
— Yes, my rod's green and yours is red.

— Philip, how many rods do you have?
— I have seven.
— Give me four, please.
— Here you are.
— Give me four more rods, please.
— I can't because I don't have another four, I only have three.

— I have some rods.
— I don't have any rods.
— What about you? Do you have any rods? / Do you have any?
— No, I don't.
— Do you want a rod?
— Yes please.
— How many would you like?
— As many as you can give me. I like holding rods!
— Really!?

HOW I WORK

At a slightly higher level, the students start talking more about their own lives: they ask other students about their job, their projects and their interests. They are usually interested in finding out about the other people in the class and enjoy participating in these conversations.

To give readers an idea of how I work with such a class, I will give some examples from an evening class which took place over a school year. It was for false beginners and very low intermediate students. The group consisted of twelve people, all of whom remained in the course until the end of the year. Almost all came back the following year. Twelve is on the low-ish side for a good class of this kind—I would have preferred more people in the group. Most of the participants were over fifty, and several had already retired.

THE HISTORY OF THE ENGLISH LANGUAGE

I began the class in mid-September by telling the students my version of The History of the English Language (see Appendix 2). I wanted them to know that they already possessed a lot of English simply because they were French, and that it would be useful to activate what they had in order to begin to speak the language. I then told them that from now on, they would have the responsibility for the content of what would be talked about in the lessons.

I asked everybody to find a question they would like to ask someone else in the class, and ask the question. For a few lessons, they found this difficult.

NO NOTES

I had a problem: some of them were adamant that they wanted to take notes, but I did not want them to. I knew that if they were occupied writing things down, they would not be present to the conversation and the feedback I was giving.

Finally we reached a compromise. I would record the lesson, type up the corrected versions of what they said and give it to them on paper the following week. This is what we did until the end of the year, and it is the reason that I can accurately recount what took place. While we were waiting for everyone to arrive each week, they could read the text of the lesson from the week before. If they had questions, I would answer. In general, there were no questions, since the work had been well done.

HOW I WORKED

I said very little; I left as much space as possible for the students to talk, knowing that the more active I am, the less active students are.

When a sentence was proposed for the first time, I would ask the class with a gesture and a quizzical look if everyone understood the gist of what the speaker was trying to say. If there was the slightest doubt, I would show the sentence on the Word charts and the Fidel or write a word on the board. The message almost always got across immediately.

This was important, as the students quickly realised that getting people to understand the message does not require a good level of language. They could all communicate, but this was not the problem; the problem was with the quality of what they said. Learning to express oneself requires more than just 'getting the message across'.

I would then spread out my hands in an open gesture meant to imply, *Any suggestions for improving this?* The first attempt at a sentence might be corrected by the student himself if he could; if not, by the class or, if no one could help correct it, by me. As the class tried collectively to construct the sentence in correct English, proposing this or that solution, I would accept all the suggestions which helped us. When they had arrived at their best attempt but more was needed, I would give some little indication which was likely to help them find the sentence as it should be said. During this process, I used finger correction extensively as it allowed me to specify what part of the sentence we were collectively working on.

Note that you are reading the versions of the students' sentences after the class had worked on them and they were correct.

3RD DECEMBER, JEAN LACOUTURE WAS IN TOWN

PHILIPPE: Last Thursday, I went to a conference by Jean Lacouture, and Jean-Pierre was there.

Jean-Pierre is a member of the class.

GÉRARD: Who is Jean Lacouture?
PHILIPPE: He is a journalist and a writer.
YOLANDE: What does he write about?
THIERRY: He writes biographies.
SERGE: He writes biographies about famous people.

PHILIPPE: About Michel de Montaigne, François Mitterrand, Charles de Gaulle ...
MARCEL: What does he write?
VIRGINIA: He writes books.
PHILIPPE: He writes articles.

I pointed: *What does he write about?* I introduced this distinction because I wanted to draw their attention to the role of *about* in these sentences.

ROLANDE: He writes about famous people.
PHILIPPE: He writes about politics.
VIRGINIA: From where I am sitting I can see the moon, like in a fairy story.
YOLANDE: The moon is full tonight.
GÉRARD: It's very beautiful.
ROLANDE: Is it possible to close the door?
PHILIPPE: Of course, but we are still waiting for Claudine and Serge.
ROLANDE: Perhaps there's been an accident.
MARCEL: Maybe there's been an accident along the way.
JEAN-PIERRE: There may be an accident along the way.
YOLANDE: They may be late because of an accident.

If I could, I increased their sense of the new vocabulary by using series of words. For example, in this conversation, because the word *way* came up, I introduced *railway*, *runway* and *subway* so that they could develop a sense of the notion of *way*. The students collectively produced most of the words in the following list: *way, lane, street, avenue, boulevard* and *road* with a general idea of the kind of street involved because I used well-known streets in our city to illustrate these names. I only ever gave them words no one in the class could find.

Planches Lane
Planches Way
Plançon Street
Kennedy Boulevard
Siffert Avenue
The Belfort Road

ROSLYN: There is a railway line from Besançon to Pontarlier.
THIERRY: There are some runways at Roissy.
VIRGINIA: There is a subway in New York.
THIERRY: There is a highway between Besançon and Pontarlier.
MARCEL: There is a motorway between Besançon and Paris.

Working this way often produced several possible sentences. This is visible in the text above in the little dialogue about the accident.

Each of the different alternative constructions was said several times until I was satisfied with the quality. The students all practised together during this phase of the work. I would add vocabulary if it was useful, or necessary, to produce the current sentence. These were always words that no student had been able to think of.

Knowing that vocabulary is easy to forget, I always tried to find some idea which might make it easier for them to remember. I might find the same word in a French context, for example *snow* which they didn't know, as in *snowboard* which they did. Or I might find a word in English that they had already met: *the African bush* linked to *President Bush*, or a word with a common root. I would show them changes in spelling between the two languages—*gu* or *g* becomes *w* in English; *Guillaume* becomes *William*; *garde-robe*, *wardrobe*; *guerre*, *war*; etc. I tried to give them some way of holding on to what they met.

Once the correction of the present sentence was done and all the students could say the sentence well, I would indicate that we could go back to the conversation. The person who had launched the current sentence in the first place chose which version he wanted to use, chose the person he wanted to speak to, and the conversation went on.

DISCOVER ALL YOU CAN ABOUT ONE PERSON

With other classes, I have started the process by asking the students to spend the lesson discovering all they could about one person in the group. I choose a talkative student to reply.

The students have to think of a question and ask him. My role is to maintain the quality of everything that is said. Every sentence is corrected, using the rods, the charts and finger correction.

At the beginning, the students find the process quite laborious, not believing that they have enough English to converse. But after a few hours, they begin to take things into their own hands, asking each other more original questions for which they actually do want an answer. A certain freedom begins to develop in the group. They start to relate to each other not simply as classmates, but as real people to whom one asks a question in order to obtain a personal reply.

A LITTLE LATER IN THE COURSE

By the month of March, the conversations had become more sustained. These students had realised that they could talk about anything they wanted to, and they usually arrived in class with something to say. I could start using my 'invitation to speak' gesture at the beginning of the lesson, and they would begin. Here's an example.

18TH MARCH, DANIELLE'S TRIP

DANIELLE: I won't be present next week because I'm going to Amsterdam
MARCEL: You can sing "On the port of Amsterdam" on the port of Amsterdam!
YOLANDE: How long are you going to spend in Amsterdam?
DANIELLE: I'm going to spend a week.
SERGE: Are you taking the TGV?
DANIELLE: No, I'm not. I'm taking the new train, the Thalys.
CLAUDINE: What is the Thalys? Is it a special train?
DANIELLE: Yes it is. The Thalys is a special train for Amsterdam.
JEAN-PIERRE: The Thalys goes through Brussels.
VIRGINIA: Brussel sprouts are good to eat.
DANIELLE: The Thalys is blue. It's very comfortable.
ROLANDE: How long will the train trip last?
DANIELLE: It will last about six hours.
ERIC: Where will you take the train?
DANIELLE: I'll take the train in Besançon.
PHILIPPE: In Paris, will you take a taxi or the underground to go from the Gare de Lyon to the Gare du Nord?
DANIELLE: I will take the underground.
CLAUDINE: Where are you leaving from?
DANIELLE: I'm leaving from Besançon.
THIERRY: When are you leaving?
DANIELLE: I'm leaving on Sunday at six o'clock in the morning. I'm leaving on Sunday at six a.m.
SERGE: Do you speak Dutch?
DANIELLE: No I don't. But in Amsterdam, they speak English, and so do I!
ROLANDE: Creuff was called The Flying Dutchman.
GÉRARD: Creuff's nickname was The Flying Dutchman.
PHILIPPE: Now he is a coach.
MARCEL: No, he has retired.
ROLANDE: The Flying Dutchman is the name of an opera too.
THIERRY: The Flying Dutchman is also the name of an opera—by Wagner.

This was important, as the students quickly realised that getting people to understand the message does not require a good level of language.

They could all communicate, but this was not the problem; the problem was with the quality of what they said.

Learning to express oneself requires more than 'getting the message across'.

MARCEL: You will eat chips!
DANIELLE: No. It's a pity. Amsterdam is the capital of cheese.
MARCEL: No, no!!!
YOLANDE: Of other cheeses ... Amsterdam is the capital of other cheese.
MARCEL: Mickey Mouse cheeses!!!
DANIELLE: That's right! I agree with you.
GÉRARD: Shame on you!!!
VIRGINIA: Do you like Dutch cheese?
DANIELLE: Yes I do, especially when I eat it on the spot.

I have a spot on my trousers.
A spotlight.
Eric, stand up! On the spot!!

CLAUDINE: Do you prefer Comté or Dutch cheeses?
SERGE: I like all cheeses. I love cheese.
DANIELLE: In two weeks' time, we will eat some cheese from Amsterdam.
ROLANDE: Yes, sure!
MARCEL: I will bring a bottle of wine.
VIRGINIA: Or beer from the Netherlands.
CLAUDINE: She will bring us beer from Holland.
THIERRY: She'll bring us some beer from Amsterdam to drink with the cheese.
PHILIPPE: What sort of wine will you bring, Marcel?
MARCEL: I will bring a Jura wine or a Burgundy wine or a Provence wine, whatever you like.
VIRGINIA: I'll bring the glasses!
CLAUDINE: Your glasses are not expensive glasses!
VIRGINIA: I'll bring crystal glasses!!
MARCEL: Which wine would you prefer?
DANIELLE: Which wine goes best with Dutch cheese?
MARCEL: I will bring a bottle of Bordeaux and a bottle of Jura wine.
ERIC: One bottle per person!!!
THIERRY: If we drink a bottle of wine per person, we'll all get very drunk!
PHILIPPE: Completely drunk!!
YOLANDE: The cheese is only a pretext for drinking!
SERGE: That's true!

True is the opposite of false.
A false beginner.
A true story.
I told the truth.

VIRGINIA: That's right
PHILIPPE: A right angle
SERGE: The opposite of right is wrong.

The students had arrived at a stage where they could really talk with each other about their everyday lives using simple sentences. The lessons had become a pleasure for the participants. They came to class every week with a real desire to talk to each other. We drank champagne several times to celebrate a retirement, birthdays, the trip to Amsterdam.

Among the things that we discovered about the participants and that came up quite naturally, I could cite:

- Yolande has a new grandson.
- Marcel, now retired, sings in a semi-professional choir, distills his own plums and apples and represents our city in Burkina Faso.
- Gérard runs semi-marathons.
- Thierry runs marathons too. He was absent for a week to run the Marathon des Sables in the Sahara. He explained to us how it was organised.
- Josée's father was killed over the Christmas holidays when his house burnt down. The class talked with her for the rest of the lesson about this accident, about her mother and brothers and sisters, where they came from. I kept to my role of correcting whatever was necessary.
- Danielle loves traveling, and saw Leonardo di Caprio when she was in Italy.
- Jean-Pierre was brought up in Italy and speaks Venetian and Roman; he told us about languages in Italy, and the role of the Italian language.
- Rolande loves opera music and goes to concerts now that she has retired.
- Most of the students went to Switzerland to see an art exhibition in Montreux.

SIMPLE CONVERSATIONS, BUT GENUINE

It is probably clear that no attempt is made to control or limit the grammar in the sentences the students say. They are given whatever is necessary. When they are given grammar to fill an immediate need in this way, the construction and the associated vocabulary usually stay in their minds, even if these would be considered 'hard' or advanced in other environments.

At these moments, words are not being learnt as vocabulary items, but as ways of expressing something that the student is vividly living or evoking. This brings to mind the so-called 'vocabulary spurt' in children, when words may be learnt after just a single exposure to them, or the learning of new L1 words, also after a single exposure if the word fills an expressive need at that moment.

The level of the conversations is self-regulating. Students are sensible: they only try to say things that they think will be possible for them at their current level, and for the most part, they aim well.

I recommend following the QR code in the margin. It will take you to a booklet entitled *Rods, People, More People and Stories* showing many examples of beginner and low-level students' conversations. This will give the reader a sense of how varied the grammar that is provoked by rod situations has to be if English is to be mastered. Such conversations become more complex as the students make progress. The booklet gives examples from the very simplest conversations through to ones like those in this chapter.

Scan this QR code to download Rods, People, More People and Stories, *which illustrates how students move from speaking about rods to speaking about themselves.*

21. Upper intermediate and advanced levels

Often it takes one or two weeks of intensive lessons to bring intermediate students to the point where they feel that they can express themselves in English to some extent. To achieve this, what they need is continuous practice in expressing themselves with the teacher giving continuous feedback on their attempts, as described throughout this book.

The mistakes these students make almost always involve either pronunciation or the proper use of the functional vocabulary. Often, simply signaling the existence of a problem allows the student or failing that, another member of the class, to adjust the sentence. If no one can help, then as far as this point is concerned, I have to regard them as beginners and take the time to work on the problem as described in earlier chapters.

Intermediate students often feel that there is not much hope for their English. After all, they have already studied the language for years without achieving a good result. To my mind the problem for them is exactly that: they have studied the language rather than learning it.

- **Studying** involves learning grammar rules and their exceptions, learning lists of vocabulary, engaging in role plays and doing exercises, but not actually speaking the language to talk about themselves for their own purposes.
- **Learning** means learning a skill. Think of football: most players don't study it, but they learn something every time they go out onto the field. They have coaching sessions outside of matches because

this accelerates the learning process. Learning a language means learning to speak it; we need to do it to learn how to do it, and having a teacher who understands that her role is to be a coach brings the same benefits as seen in any sport.

PRONUNCIATION

In courses for students at an intermediate or higher level, I do not work on the pronunciation of individual sounds in any detail unless it is necessary: English tolerates a variety of vowel sounds. Students do need a coherent system but it doesn't have to be mine. I work on their consonants if any are missing from the student's repertoire of sounds.

But I do work intensively on the reduction system because this is always holding them back from understanding native speakers.

THE ARTICULATORY SETTING

To help students understand how English works, I begin with the articulatory setting of the language (as presented in chapters 8 and 9). At first sight, this setting seems an unlikely way of holding one's tongue when one speaks; it is described as being spread at the back and 'tethered' to the inside surface of the upper rear molars, with the tip therefore retracted and hovering below the alveolar ridge.

In fact, I relate this setting to suckling, one of the first activities a new-born baby develops. Indeed, videos exist of babies sucking their thumb even in the womb. For sucking to be efficient, there must be an area in the mouth which is completely closed off. The closure allows pressure to be generated inside it making sucking possible. Try it with a straw.

THE REDUCTION SYSTEM

The reduction system is the second key to pronouncing the language well. For this I use our 'noughts and crosses' diagram which I draw on the board for them very early in the course. It is left in clear view on the wall or in a corner of the board until the end of the course and will be used often.

The diagram can be described to the class by saying: *In English, there are three levels of accentuation.*

	Syllable?	Full vowel?	Pitch change?
/	✓	✓	✓
~	✓	✓	✗
...	✓	✗	✗
.	✓		
,	✗		

The noughts and crosses diagram

SOME SYLLABLES ARE STRESSED. These syllables require more effort and they usually carry a pitch change. In words said on their own, this will make the stressed syllable higher than the others, but in sentences the pitch might be lower. The vowel in these syllables is always clearly identifiable.

SOME SYLLABLES ARE FULL BUT UNSTRESSED. This means that the vowel is clearly pronounced, but that the syllable has no rhythmic stress and therefore cannot have a pitch change on it. An example would be the second syllable of *window* which is stressed on the first syllable and has a full but unstressed vowel in the second. The vowel in the <ow> of *window* is clearly articulated.

SOME SYLLABLES ARE REDUCED, like the <a> in *about*, the <y> in *hilly*, or the <o> in *to Italy*. Sometimes, the vowels in these syllables can be reduced right out of existence!

Scan to watch a video of an advanced student being introduced to the noughts and crosses diagram.

Students at intermediate and advanced level have almost always heard of stress, and for many multisyllabic words, it is often relatively easy for them to identify the stressed syllable if they know the word.

When we come to a multisyllabic word, I use a standard routine. For example, *gardening*:

> *Q: How many syllables are there? A: Three.*
> *Q: Which syllable is stressed? A: The first.*
> *Q: What happens to the second and third ones? A: ?*

For this third question, most students don't have an answer the first time we analyse a word this way. The answer is, it will be reduced, and I show them how.

TWO KINDS OF SCHWA

As discussed in Chapter 8 there are two kinds of schwa, the reduced sound in English.
- The first kind of schwa is a very short neutral sound which is nevertheless pronounced. It is found at the end of words when these come before a pause, with <er> as its most common spelling.
- The second occurs between two consonants when the first consonant is completed before the second is begun. A sound appears which creates a syllable for listeners. I use stuttering to get the students used to making these very tiny sounds, as described in Chapter 9.

WORKING ON CONSONANTS

I work on the consonants that the students have problems with by making sure that they know what to do with their mouths to produce the sounds. This is much easier with consonants than with vowels because consonants require two articulators to meet (for occlusives), or almost meet (for fricatives) so they can be found by using touch. Students can feel the movements of the articulators and can sense the changes in the flow of air.

For the first few hours, I will spend some useful time working on students' pronunciation. After they have developed a sense of what to do, I can gradually decrease my input unless any of the students want to develop excellent pronunciation.

USING THE VERB TENSE SYSTEM

For classes at this level, I base my teaching around the Verb Tense System described in a previous chapter because students are often reluctant to talk. In this way I can ease the students into speaking about themselves almost without them realising that this is happening.

People come to classes expecting to be taught as they have been taught in the past, and often expecting to make little progress. As we work through setting out the forms, they can see that this way of working is different, and can also make sense of what we are doing; they become willing to join in, taking time to think about the tenses and the forms. Then when we start looking at each form one after the other, they can make small sentences about themselves. *I get up at 7 o'clock every morning* is innocuous and unthreatening.

As we move on, one form leads to another and soon they have spent a few days talking about their lives, asking other students questions and receiving answers. At the end of the course they have spent every hour speaking about themselves in English. They have lost their inhibitions and feel themselves to be on their way to a higher level. This is often all it takes to make what they have studied available to them for speech.

GETTING THE CONVERSATION STARTED

At this level, and especially if I'm working with a big class, I might point on the charts a question such as *What did you do last weekend?* This question suits me because it is very open: everyone has something to answer, and all the answers can be different, especially when we go into the details, and there can be a huge number of details. All I have to do is break the question down into *Friday evening, Saturday morning,* etc. We could spend many hours on a question like this.

Once everyone knows how to say the question well—using good quality English—I get someone to ask his neighbour.

IT WAS A QUESTION!

It sometimes happens that the question is asked, I signal to the neighbour to answer and he asks me what he should say! He doesn't understand that it is for him to reply!

— What do you want me to say?
— How would I know? I wasn't with you last weekend!
— Ah, you want me to actually reply!
— Yes. He asked you a question.
— Ah!

For some students, asking the question is the end of the process; their co-student has done what the teacher asked him to do, he said the question to his neighbour. Now the teacher will give a new instruction. When this happens, it tells me that the student who should be answering has probably never actually talked to anyone in an English class.

This is a very important moment because it sets the tone of the class for the rest of the course. They are going to have real conversations. And, as I tell them, *every sentence must be true.*

So the conversation begins. At the end of the hour, we will have discovered a few details about the lives of only one or two of the participants, since all the sentences are corrected as they are produced and at this point there can be a lot to correct. As soon as an answer is ready, that is to say, correct and well pronounced, I get the first speaker to ask his question again, because I want the question and the answer to be related. The answer is the answer to exactly this question and not to any other.

MORE ADVANCED STUDENTS

In a more advanced class, the students will use the charts less. They can more easily correct themselves, and also more easily find alternative constructions. There's no point in giving examples of their conversations in this book; they are completely natural interchanges between people, in what becomes good quality English.

THE PERFORMANCE PIECE

A performance piece is a short text, often some verse, that it will be pleasant for a student to say many times over. Students use it as a way of practising the movements of pronunciation without the distraction of having to formulate normal speech. Because they get to know their piece so well, they can come to observe every movement of their tongue and other articulators while they are performing it. They can consciously create abdominal pushes for each stressed syllable, consciously be aware of their articulatory setting, consciously articulate the sounds, and learn to coordinate the whole.

The performance piece plays an important role in learning pronunciation. Pronouncing a language is a motor skill. If speaking with another person is 'playing the language game', then acquiring the motor skills to play the game can best be done, as in any sport, in dedicated practice sessions where the game itself is not being played.

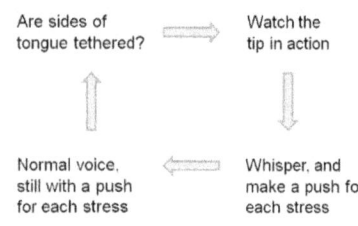

For work on a performance piece to be effective, it is important that students have already been shown how to actively practise a piece rather than simply repeating it. When practising, the student makes himself present to different aspects of his pronunciation one after the other. For example, he might start by saying the whole piece watching that the sides of his tongue are tethered against his molars, then saying it again watching the tip of his tongue in action, then a third time consciously making abdominal pushes for each stress, first in whisper then in normal speech. Finally he says it again, trying to bring all these elements together in a performance which will tell him which, if any, of them he still needs to revisit.

Cycles may consist of just a couple of aspects of pronunciation, or more.

The danger in any kind of work like this is that practice can become mere repetition. This happens when a student stops bothering: he stops being present to what he is doing and just speaks automatically. Practising in cycles where one's attention is focused on one element and then another and then another, is one way of avoiding this.

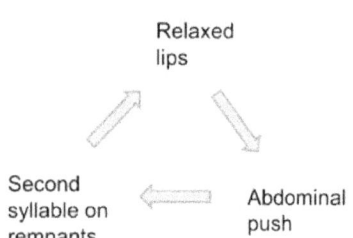

The text should not be any more than 8 to 10 lines in length. It's best if students choose their own; something that is meaningful for them.

22. The Class Conversation

By now, readers cannot fail to have noticed that from the very early stages of any Silent Way course, the students are encouraged to converse, and an increasing amount of the time in class is spent doing this.

A FREE, TO-AND-FRO CONVERSATION BETWEEN THE STUDENTS

From the beginning, then, we have been working towards a Class Conversation, a free, to-and-fro discussion involving any and all of the students. At its highest level, the content is similar to what the students might say to each other if they were enjoying some time together at the weekend, speaking in their first language.

Such conversations are spontaneous. The participants talk about their lives and interests, sharing whatever they like with the others around them. Our aim is to reach this level. They learn to do this by doing it: learning to speak, speaking to learn.

THE CONTENT

Class Conversations unfold gradually, and each sentence is worked on until it is correct. It is in this work, in the process of learning how to express each idea precisely and correctly that the learning lies. It is this that turns it into a lesson—an opportunity for the students to improve their English—rather than people using the language badly simply to chat. Students can do that themselves, outside of the classroom, if that is what they want.

Scan for an analysis of a Class Conversation between two intermediate students learning Japanese.

You may find it instructive to watch the conversation unfold, even though it may be in a language you do not know.

The video is subtitled in English.

SOME RULES

For students, Class Conversations are governed by three rules: a) be yourself, b) all sentences must be true, and c) if you don't understand, ask.

For the teacher, there is just one rule: the teacher's role is limited to coaching: correcting, encouraging, suggesting paths forward, avoiding wasted time on the part of the students. The teacher is not part of the conversation; she gives feedback for every sentence as needed, but does not participate. This is important. Imagine a football coach playing for his Under-11 side. His presence would unbalance the whole game. Clearly he already knows how to play the game that the young players are there to enjoy and learn.

EACH SENTENCE IS CORRECTED BEFORE WE MOVE ON

The first attempt made by a student might be correct. If not, it might be corrected by the student himself if he can; if he can't, by the class or, if no one can help correct it, by me.

Sometimes, I need to reflect for a few moments to decide if what has been said is actually adequate or natural. I don't rush myself. My indecision tells the students something about where the boundary between correctness and incorrectness lies.

To keep the class's command of English moving forward, I give the student an alternative or a more natural way of expressing his idea if there is one. Exploiting 'learning opportunities' in this way is quite different from having a list of 'teaching points' to be got through, because what is new is still based on the student's original motivation to speak.

At other times, I might ask the student to link the current sentence and his previous one(s) so as to make a new, more complex whole that is a more sophisticated use of the language.

There are locomotives and slowcoaches in Class Conversations, too. I need to make sure that everyone is following, and I can do this simply by regularly asking, 'Does anyone have a problem?' until each student realises that it is his responsibility to keep the class useful for him, and that he should intervene for this purpose as necessary.

As always, the aim of correction is to strengthen students' criteria for the language so that when they finally say their sentences correctly, it

'Three maxims which are at the heart of the SW:

  Watch.

  Give only what is needed.

  Wait.'

Stevick (1992)

is because they have a reliable sense of their rightness. The aim of correction is not for them to simply say the right words in the right order; little learning and no control of the language will be achieved by this.

Correcting

The student says a sentence as best he can. Correction takes place in a specific order: considering first the choice of words, then the word order, then the pronunciation, then on getting the whole sentence out smoothly, until the student reaches a point where the sentence is as satisfactory as possible given his level and ability. The order is logical: it would be counterproductive to practise pronunciation or fluency using incorrect words. The work is not repetitive or boring because the student will be changing his focus each time he speaks.

The correction process for a sentence can take seconds or it might take ten minutes or even longer in some cases, this for several reasons:

- There might be mistakes of many types to work on.
- Working on criteria, rather than on simply getting the words right, can take time; but this is time well spent.
- Some sentences will give us an entry into one of the wider systems of English, and I may open a (metaphorical) parenthesis to work on this, suspending work on the student's sentence while we explore further before returning to the student's story.

Working on criteria rather than simple correctness also gives the students' minds time to dwell on and assimilate what is new.

Once the student has said his sentence correctly, I usually invite him to say it again, more than once. This has two important functions. Firstly, it allows both of us to check his mastery of the sentence (something we all do naturally in other circumstances when we think we have mastered something, but feel the need to check). Can he say it again as well as he just did?

Secondly, it gives him space to re-evoke whatever moved him to speak in the first place and then to use the sentence to express this feeling or idea. It is this connection—between an inner state and the language needed to express it—which will enable him to express similar feelings or ideas when they occur in the future. This should be the aim of all language teaching, and it is explicitly central to the Silent Way.

THE CLASS CONVERSATION IS SELF-REGULATING

Students are good learners. They are ambitious and try to make sentences which stretch their present capacity in English but they know what they can attempt and also that they should choose what they say so that everyone else in the class can grasp their meaning. This means that each sentence is made up of things the speaker is sure of, but might also contain elements which for him are doubtful or new. The teacher, making an educated guess at exactly what he is trying to say (and checking if necessary), responds to his attempt by coaching him towards accuracy and correctness.

Usually, little new vocabulary is used in any one sentence. When anything new is introduced, it is always necessary for what is being expressed and therefore quite easy to understand and easy, too, to remember because it is in context. The teaching techniques of the approach mean that all new words are used in context several times.

USE OF ENGLISH ALONE IS INSUFFICIENT

This process is quite different from what one finds in a typical conversation class where content predominates, and feedback is intermittent. In a typical class, the aim is 'to get the message across' and as a result students are led to become speakers of 'fluent bad English'.

It is a mistake to imagine that students will reach a good level simply by saying things in the language. Some progress might be possible like this, but as soon as the student reaches a level where he can participate in the conversations taking place around him, he will be present to the content and completely ignore the language; this is normal behaviour for humans. If he is present to the conversation, then he will not be present to the way the language works, to the container.

In a Class Conversation, on the other hand, time is made for continual feedback from the coach and correction takes place, so the students are systematically kept present to the container as well as to the content.

A SPECIAL CASE: 'TELL ME' CLASSES

We can hardly call a one-to-one class a 'Class Conversation'. Instead, we call it a 'Tell me' class. The name reflects the fact that the student will be generating the content; I start by asking the student, "What are you going to tell me about today?"

The 'Tell me' class operates in much the same way as a Class Conversation. The student tries to express whatever is on his mind. I correct what is said (in the ways described earlier) and show him how to improve it when appropriate. But this is not a conversation and I'm not a partner in one. I'm an interested listener who keeps the student talking, but most of all I function as his coach.

When working in person, we sit opposite each other at a table, with a large sheet of paper between us for us to write or draw upon. Online, I use an online white board to which both the student and I must have interactive access so that both of us can point, draw and write.

At the beginning of any 'Tell me' course, most students need to build confidence, learning to feel more at ease simply speaking in English, and I need to discover what their level is. So we are likely to begin with topics like the family, the home and the workplace. Lower intermediate students might never go beyond this.

TARGETED 'TELL ME' CLASSES

In my experience, most students who enroll in a 'Tell me' course—particularly professionals—have a target, a subject they need to be able to talk about fluently and well. They invariably have problems with the use of verb tenses and with pronunciation, so we start with a few hours working on general English which serves to introduce the Verb Tense System and the noughts and crosses diagram. Then the target is addressed; the student is invited to talk until the end of the course about whatever it is that he will be using English for.

You might be reluctant to start teaching targeted 'Tell me' classes, thinking that you will need to know the specialist vocabulary of the student's subject. I have taught hundreds of 'Tell me' courses without ever having this problem. Students have almost always been exposed to the vocabulary before they come, and can supply it themselves; what they actually need is practice in speaking, leading to a better level of general spoken English and the ability to speak about their subject.

I have heard about how a liver is transplanted; how a nuclear reactor is built and insulated; how cranes are moved to a building site and how they are used to erect themselves; and hundreds of other subjects, without needing to resort to a dictionary.

'Tell me' classes are fascinating and are as deeply satisfying for both student and teacher as Class Conversations.

MOVING FORWARD

*'It is reasonable—and important—to make students
independent of their teachers and textbooks'*
Caleb Gattegno

23. Moving into the Silent Way world

To conclude this book, I want to restate the main principles from what has been said, and add some words of reassurance and advice. You can adopt and apply the principles behind the Silent Way whether or not you start using rods and charts.

SILENT WAY PRINCIPLES

CORRECTION is not just getting the student to produce the right answer. The teacher should be working so that students are developing criteria for getting it right the next time, whatever 'it' might be.

LEARNING IS CUMULATIVE. It always starts slowly, as the learner moves into an unknown field to be explored, and speeds up as he gains in experience and expertise. It never pays to speed through things at the beginning of a course. On the contrary, taking the time for students to lay strong foundations ends up producing better results.

MASTERY OF A LANGUAGE involves having an understanding of how it behaves rather than possessing a lot of vocabulary. Even the most accomplished linguist does not know the whole of a language. It follows that when teaching a language, the aim should not be for students to skim over as much as possible, but for them to gain an ever deeper understanding of the spirit of the language. Details—and in particular, vocabulary and idiomatic expressions—can always be added later, in contact with speakers, and in contexts which cannot even be imagined during the course.

ALWAYS WORK FOR EXCELLENCE. Fossilised mistakes are almost impossible to eradicate so don't let them happen in the first place. Students justifiably come to language classes with high expectations, wanting to reach as high a level as possible in exchange for the time they are going to spend. The teacher should work in such a way as to keep excellence within the reach of most students. To do otherwise is quite simply unethical. If a student decides to settle for less than this, then that is acceptable to the teacher. But it must always be the student's decision, not a limitation on him imposed by the teacher's low expectations and way of working.

How do we ensure that mistakes do not get fossilised, that reaching excellence remains possible, even if this will be at some later stage?

- By making students aware of their mistakes.
- By getting them to check constantly that what they say expresses what they want to say.
- By fostering their criteria for correctness and their sense of certainty.
- By putting into place their inner ear to monitor what they say as it does in their first language.

NO COURSE CAN TAKE ANY STUDENT TO THE END of the learning process. That is not the role of a language course. Language courses are there to help the students prepare themselves for further encounters with the language. They should come out of a course better at the language being learnt, but also better language learners than they were when they arrived.

Polyglots usually tell us that the third or fourth foreign language is much more easily learnt than the first. This is because they become better language learners as they learn more of them. They learn how to go directly to the spirit of each language. This is the kind of experience we want to give our students.

LANGUAGES ARE LEARNT. They are not acquired. As Jonathan Marks has pointed out, one can acquire a house simply by signing a cheque. But to learn a language, it will be necessary to give oneself the time and the experience that the task requires. Students can be extraordinarily unsophisticated in this respect. Some imagine that the teacher will simply 'make it happen'. They must rapidly be made to understand that there is no direct relationship between teaching and learning, and that they will have to do the job of learning the language if they want to have it.

RESIST THE TEMPTATION TO EXPLAIN. Explanations may seem to hurry the process along, but they do not produce know-hows. Speaking a language is a know-how. All the rest is superfluous. We are working to trigger awarenesses in each student which guide each of them in the use of the language, rather than giving them knowledge about it. Knowledge doesn't spontaneously become a know-how.

SLEEP is an integral part of the learning process. You will only know the next day if the work done the previous day was integrated or not. Remember what has been worked on in lessons and notice what is now appearing as automatised speech in the classroom. Notice what is not yet in place and use this to guide you in your work.

ZOOMING IN AND OUT is another general principle which is always at work in Silent Way classes: working from synthesis to analysis and back. The synthesis gives a general view of the ground being covered while the analysis allows work on the details.

Some syntheses are provided by the approach:

- The Rectangle chart shows all the sounds and relationships between them.
- The Fidel shows all the spelling-pronunciation relationships in the language, except the very rarest.
- The Word charts show the functional vocabulary.
- The Verb Tense System shows all the tenses so that students can make choices more easily.

You will create others as needed.

At any moment, the class is working in an analytic way, but the synthesis is always visible and keeps the students aware of the place of their current focus within the full context of the language.

AND NEVER FORGET, the more the teacher does, the less the students do.

YOU, THE BEGINNING SILENT WAY TEACHER

I want to make an analogy with figure skating. When I watch the figure skaters at the Olympic Games, it all seems so easy. They glide across the ice, effortlessly leap high into the air and land with poise. However,

'I had to understand that in order for the Silent Way to work I had to make it my own, for my language and for my classes. After attending a workshop in Spanish, I tended to take whatever I saw as a model for my own classes, but I soon discovered that I was betraying the whole idea of the Silent Way because I was not taking into consideration the reality of Italian in relation to my class. This is one of the reasons why I don't think it would be possible to work out a teachers' guide: the beginner teacher, overwhelmed by the novelty of the approach, would tend to rely heavily on the guide and therefore on the techniques rather than developing his or her own way to use the materials offered.

Instead, one should become aware that there is no magic in the materials per se *and that, if necessary, they could all be thrown out and replaced. Nothing is sacred in the Silent Way not even the silence, and to follow the "letter" of the approach (using the rods, the charts, being silent etc., etc.) is no guarantee of really using the Silent Way. It is the "spirit" of the Silent Way that needs to be grasped and followed—as Dr. Gattegno once pointed out—if one wants real learning to take place.*

Bartoli (1972)

occasionally I have the opportunity of watching the heats of a national or regional competition and there, the story is quite different. The effort, the lack of stability, the lack of poise is immediately obvious.

In this book, I have tried to share more than fifty years of experience which have given me a certain ease. You, the beginning Silent Way teacher, will find that a situation I describe does not work as well for you as you had hoped. What went wrong? Post-paration will help you to find out. Bear in mind that one possible reason is that I have described my classes with me as the teacher; your classes with you as the teacher will necessarily be different.

You have the right to be a beginning Silent Way teacher. Perfection is not required, nor even excellence. It will take time to feel even moderately comfortable improvising lessons with the students, and more time to feel at ease. You have the right to take this time.

Occasionally a lesson will 'fly'. You and the students live a moment of deep complicity. You all leave the classroom with a sense of exhilaration and the knowledge that this is how it is meant to be.

Most of the time, however, things go less well than this. Although you know that you are doing the right work, you may nevertheless take out of the classroom a sense of what could have been better. Don't despair! As you become a more sensitive teacher, as you learn to watch your students learning, your work will certainly improve. Being in touch with a sense of slight dissatisfaction is one of the reasons why.

Observe other teachers

Whenever possible, observe other teachers working, whether or not they describe themselves as Silent Way teachers. Ask yourself to what extent they are subordinating their teaching to the students' learning; to what extent the students' learning is visible; and how much the teacher takes it into account as she works. Ask yourself how present the students are to the work being offered to them. Does the work proposed bring them anything useful? Are they being corrected? Are mistakes being allowed to fossilise? Then go back to your own work and see whether you are inspired to change what you do in some way.

Learn a language with the Silent Way

I strongly recommend that you take at least 30 hours of a foreign language taught using the Silent Way, whether in person or online. Do it more than once. The repeated experience of being a learner in a Silent Way class inspires and informs many teachers who use the approach.

QUESTIONS, AND SOMETIMES ANSWERS

Questions and questioning are major parts of the Silent Way teacher's toolbox. So let me finish this book with some questions you can ask yourself.

- At this moment, as I walk into the classroom, is my state of mind such that I can watch my students and learn from them?
- Are my students disposed to learn? If not, what can I do about it?
- What is this student aware of, here and now? What is he not aware of? What does he need to become aware of?
- When the student has a problem, can I detect the awareness that is missing?
- Is what I'm about to do going to interfere with the students' learning?
- Can I find a way of presenting "x" without speaking?
- How much time does the student need in order to do what I've just asked for?
- Can I make the challenge visible and tangible?
- Is there a way of using mental imagery in what I'm about to present?
- Is the question only my question, or has it become the students' question? If not, what am I going to do about it?
- To what extent did I subordinate my teaching to the students' learning during the lesson I just taught? What was I doing the rest of the time?
- Can I say why I wasn't subordinating my teaching to their learning? How could I do better the next time?
- Which students do I subordinate with? Which do I not? Why? Why can I subordinate with some students and not with others?
- What does it mean to be ambitious for my students without having expectations of them?

"I don't prepare a lesson—I prepare myself."

Caleb Gattegno

Scan to see a playlist of videos linked to in this book.

- Do I have expectations?
- Do I have students I expect to fail?
- How do I apportion responsibility if a student fails?
- Was I disappointed at any time during the class? Who 'appointed' me?
- Did I think to take pointers into the classroom? Did I think to take my Blu Tack with me? Have I left the board clean for the next teacher? Did I put the cap back on the whiteboard marker? Did I switch the light off as I left the classroom?

Questions the teacher can ask the students

- Can you say what you just said again?
- Do you have a question inside you? Can you express it?
- What do you understand? (This question will provoke a more thoughtful answer than, Do you understand?)
- Can you pinpoint your problem for me?
- Are you in the right frame of mind for learning?
- Are you really looking, or simply glancing and guessing?
- Are you present to the work?

The website www.silentway.online *is a reliable source of video and other material*

24. Afterword

WHO AM I TO HAVE WRITTEN THIS BOOK?

Over the last fifty years, a number of prominent ELT authors have written chapters about the Silent Way in their books. None of these writers have been users of the approach as language teachers. They were writing more generally about approaches to teaching foreign languages. With two exceptions—Earl Stevick and Robert Blair—the practical experience of these writers seems to have been limited to demonstration classes in unfamiliar languages taught to participants who weren't real students of the language.

Videos have also appeared on YouTube purporting to be demonstrating the approach. Until recently, the only videos of classes run by a real Silent Way teacher were those of Don Cherry and his classes in Tokyo. Now fortunately, others are appearing.

The result has been that all sorts of ideas circulate today about the Silent Way which in no way reflect its true nature. I should therefore state clearly why I can legitimately write a book about the approach.

CENTRE DE LINGUISTIQUE APPLIQUÉE

I worked for over thirty years at the Centre de Linguistique Appliquée (CLA), at the University of Franche-Comté, where I had the good fortune to be part of a group of eight teachers who used the Silent Way to teach English. It consisted of Andrea Tallal Biero, Glenys Hanson, Debbi Hicks, Donna L'Hôte, John Olsen, Nancy Peuteuil, Christian Torjussen and myself. Over the years, we almost always taught in teams and we met regularly for pedagogical discussion. Everyone shared their discoveries, and we helped each other to gain confidence and experience.

We experimented with many ways of using the Silent Way. Firstly, it was used with anyone who wanted to learn to speak the language, young and old alike.

Courses for the general public were gradually reduced from 200 hours in 1968 to 120 hours when I started using the Silent Way in 1971 to 50 hours when I retired, as people became less willing to spend time on learning languages. What is the best way of using 50 hours for paying students who want to speak the language and need immediate results? How can we save time? Time ... We were always looking for ways of working more efficiently. I can say without hesitation that I did a better job in 50 hours at the end of my career than in 200 hours at the beginning, because I had learnt in the meantime how to teach the spoken language, which was what the students wanted to learn.

We increasingly worked with non-beginners, so we had a recurring question: How can we best work with people who have 5, 7 or even 10 years of school English and who still don't speak the language at all, or speak it with many fossilised mistakes, with dreadful pronunciation and without understanding native speakers?

Within the university, we were able to experiment with using the principles of the approach when teaching students who had to sit for a compulsory language examination at the end of the year. They were reluctant to spend their precious time learning a language. How can the Silent Way be used to teach English to students in their first year of pharmacy, biology or computer science, or in their final year of geology? How can the approach be used for classes of 50 or more?

We learned to use the Silent Way with university lecturers and PhD students from different disciplines needing to present their work at conferences. How much importance needed to be given to the subjects they had to present, compared with the quality of the English they used? During these courses, we quickly realised the need for excellent pronunciation and fluent delivery. These are what give authority to the speaker.

We had to decide how best to prepare soldiers about to leave on a mission as peacekeepers in Bosnia, and firefighters who had to respond to calls from motorway emergency phones. We applied the principles of the Silent Way here too.

We introduced immersion courses in the mid-1970s. These were short, intensive courses for individuals or groups of two with similar aims and usually from the same company. Some wanted to sell their products: shoes, yoghurts, cranes, planes, etc. Others needed to train their users: atomic power stations for Framatome in the 1970s, tanks for the military, etc. At first, we lived in fear of not having the necessary vocabulary. We soon realised that the students' problems were not a need for specialist vocabulary, which they already had, but the English language itself. It was these courses which gave rise very early to 'Tell me' lessons.

The teachers worked in two-hour shifts, before handing over to another; there were up to five teachers in a team with the same student(s). How do you coordinate such a team? How do you maintain a sense of continuity with so many teachers? In fact, as users of the Silent Way, we encouraged the student to talk about what was important to him. We then worked on his mistakes. No coordination was required because we were subordinating our work to his learning.

We also offered evening courses. They led to the idea of letter-writing back to students who wrote to me as described in Chapter 3.

I realised very early the advantage of a synthetic approach to teaching verb tenses and had started looking for such a system even before I came across the Silent Way. Jean-Marie Zemb had created a system for French, and this suggested that a similar one could be created for English. I shared my thoughts with the team and it was Glenys Hanson who found the answer, described in Chapter 19.

With respect to pronunciation, we found better ways of teaching the sounds of the language and we explored more fundamental aspects of pronunciation like prosody which led to a real improvement in the quality of our students' spoken language and also in their comprehension. The yellow dot, separated out from the vowels and placed at the bottom of the Rectangle chart, was introduced early in the 1990s. This was a major advance in teaching English pronunciation and led to others.

I would like to thank all the members of the CLA team for their enthusiasm, their dedication and their willingness to share all the discoveries they made with anyone willing to listen. I have been aware for years of how lucky I was to be part of such a team.

UNE EDUCATION POUR DEMAIN

From 1983 onwards, I also worked as a volunteer for Une Education Pour Demain—UEPD—the French Gattegno association that was located in Besançon. This association was officially founded in 1976 at the end of Dr Gattegno's seminar on *Time*. It formalised the existence of a group of primary school teachers who had been meeting regularly from the beginning of the 1970s on a monthly basis to learn more about how to use the principles of Gattegno's teaching in their classes. I went along to their monthly meetings because I had arrived in Besançon not long before, I didn't yet have any other activities and I knew I needed to listen to French being spoken. They were talking about teaching, and they were happy to have me among them.

It was in this group that I first heard about Caleb Gattegno and a workshop he was running in Switzerland on teaching languages. The workshop took place at Easter in 1971, and was my first contact with him. I didn't understand much of what took place—my French was not yet up to that—but I saw him teach a lesson of Chinese to a class of about 50 people out in the open air beside the lake in Geneva, and I was astonished. I had never seen such presence and concentration in any class; the participants were completely absorbed in the work he presented. That was the moment when I decided I wanted to become a Silent Way teacher. I wanted to be able to teach like that. I followed almost all the seminars and workshops Dr Gattegno led in France and Switzerland, and several in England, from then until his death in 1988.

However, that lesson of Chinese wasn't enough for me to understand the approach, and I struggled to use it during the years that followed. My real entry into the Silent Way world happened when I attended a two-week Italian course taught by Cecilia Bartoli in Paris in 1976. During this course, I finally understood how the approach could be used and felt myself to be a half-way decent Silent Way teacher by about 1978.

In the summer of that year, I conducted an English course for UEPD in which there were about thirty participants, all of them members of the association that I knew very well. About half way through the course, they started joking with each other, taking charge of the content of the lesson, and they continued to do so until the end of the course two days later. It was during that week that the Class Conversation as a teaching technique came into existence, although it wasn't named as such until many years later. I still remember hearing about Pierrot's grandmother cycling around her village in her dressing gown, and people talking about Joan's blond Afro haircut. It became clear that the class could try to use English to talk about anything for hours, enjoy themselves enormously and learn to express themselves without input from me other than feedback and correction. My teaching changed completely as a result of this course.

I attended workshops and courses run by many people for UEPD, and from 1983, ran some myself on the Silent Way.

I became president of the association in the late 1980s and held this position until the early 2000s. One of the activities during this period was the production of a magazine, *Questions*, which published articles by anyone around the world who felt spurred to write about their experience using some aspect of Gattegno's model of learning, in their classroom or in their lives. *Questions* was produced by Alain and Donna L'Hôte, and was published twice a year for seven years. During the 1980s, the Silent Way teachers from the CLA became active in UEPD, adding a new dimension to the association—foreign languages—which had been rather neglected at UEPD until then.

THE 'CLINIC'

In 1979 and 1980, I had the opportunity of working in Lyon for one week a month for an association called Rhone-Alpes-Etats-Unis which specialised in teaching English. It was there that the concept of a 'clinic' was invented; rather than adding more English to what they already had, we would transform it into something more functional using the Class Conversation technique (still unnamed as such) and do intensive work on pronunciation. The clinics took place over a thirty-hour week and demonstrated that it was possible to 'operate' on the participants' English and achieve good results in this limited time. It was during these short courses that I became aware of the importance of schwa in English. Over the years, I've come to realise that this sound alone makes the difference between heavily accented pronunciation and English that sounds just right. Not only that, but at the same time, the participants' comprehension greatly improved. The way to teach excellent pronunciation opened up.

MY THESIS

I started writing what would become my doctoral thesis on Dr Gattegno's work in about 1984. In 1986, I enrolled formally in the programme. The title was *Universals in the teaching and learning of French and English in various pedagogical situations*. I was trying to establish what united the whole of Caleb Gattegno's work, beyond the particulars of any subject or age group. How could the underlying principles be presented and described? This led me to examine Gattegno's model of energy and time; his model of man in the universe; his descriptions of human activities, and in particular, his model of learning.

Some of his workshops and seminars given in French were recorded and more than twenty were transcribed, in particular by Christiane Rozet, and published by UEPD. They were invaluable for me for my thesis. The French language lends itself to Gattegno's way of thinking. His French seminars were quite different in their content from those he conducted in English. The French love discussing theories, and so he was able to work on various aspects of his theoretical work with this group. One comment he made was revealing in this respect. He had conducted a seminar in French entitled *Towards a Theory of Human Relativity*. It was transcribed and given to him when he returned for his next European trip. He asked why we had used that title, and was told that this had been the title of the seminar. He replied that this title had been chosen before the seminar, but that during the work, a theory of relativity had indeed been constructed, so we should have called the workbook *A Theory of Human Relativity*. He was using the

French group to hammer out the details of new aspects of his wider model.

Around this time, I translated several of Gattegno's books into French, (and one from French into English). I did this not because I am a good translator but because I realised that there is no better way of making quite sure that one has read every word, and has found a meaning for each, than to attempt a translation. Most of these were published by UEPD in spite of their defects as translations.

When I told Dr Gattegno that I was working towards a doctorate and told him the title, he encouraged me to continue. He called me 'Dr Young' in a Newsletter soon after, which I took to mean that he considered me capable of doing this job competently. Of my two doctorates, the University's, finally conferred in 1990, and his, conferred in this way, I am immensely more proud of his.

TRAINING TEACHERS

For about a year after Dr Gattegno's death in 1988, there was a hiatus in the activities of UEPD. But we soon realised that teachers still needed training in his pedagogical approaches to various subjects, and that if we didn't do this, no one in France would. The first collaboration between the CLA and UEPD took place during the school year of 1989-1990. We ran a year-long course officially under the auspices of the CLA. It was attended by about 30 people from France and Switzerland, and consisted of one weekend a month for the school year plus a two-week Japanese course at Easter in 1990, given by Fusako Allard, founder of The Center for Intercultural Learning in Osaka, Japan.

This led to a fruitful collaboration. She was looking for ways of promoting Gattegno's work in Japan, and from 1989 on invited me to work there for several weeks each year, teaching English and French, and running workshops on language teaching and Gattegno's wider model. This continued until the Center closed at the beginning of the twenty-first century. Her work was taken over by a team in Tokyo and they have invited me several times since then.

TRAINING TRAINERS

In 2003, the team of teacher trainers at UEPD became aware that we needed to train people to take over from us as trainers. We were ageing and wouldn't last for ever. So we created a teacher training course which ran from 2004 to 2009. It consisted of one weekend a month for each of the school years plus one or two weeks during the summer holidays for longer courses. There were about thirty-five participants in this course. More people joined after one or two years, and they stayed on for the second edition which began in 2009 and lasted for three years. This course was structured in three parts: one third detailed work on Gattegno's model of man, one third work on general pedagogy and one third more specialised work on teaching the subject matter(s) each individual needed for their classes. It covered all primary and lower secondary subjects and language teaching to older learners.

PRONUNCIATION SCIENCE

I first met Piers Messum in 1987 at a Gattegno seminar in Bristol. He had attended a seminar run by Dr Gattegno in Japan and wanted to pursue his ideas further. Piers visited the CLA on several occasions during the 1990s and early 2000s to talk with the team about teaching pronunciation. He finished his doctoral thesis in 2007, and he and I then began collaborating more closely, discussing ideas stemming from Gattegno's model. We were aware of the difficulty of understanding the model which is undoubtedly complex. We worked on an English language version of my thesis, stripping it down to the essentials which a person would need in order to move into the world as seen by Gattegno. This was published in 2011 by Duo Flumina with the title *How we learn and how we should be taught*, and in French in 2012, published by UEPD.

Piers and I founded Pronunciation Science Ltd in 2011 with the idea of creating charts which would reflect the on-going evolution of the approach. The PronSci charts were inspired by what we knew was needed for teaching more advanced students. The Rectangle chart went through many iterations until we found the one which best takes into account the fact that pronunciation is never limited to simply making sounds. This chart reflects the underlying systems of pronunciation in English and allows pronunciation to be taught well. The Fidel was reorganised to adopt the layout of the Rectangle chart, and the Word charts were also reorganised to make it easier for more advanced students to find words easily. We did similar work for French with various collaborators.

MOVING FORWARD

Gattegno's first book about the Silent Way, *Teaching foreign languages in schools*, was published in 1963 and he last wrote about teaching foreign languages in 1987, a year before he died. Throughout this period, he was creating charts for different languages—more than 40—and revising the English and French charts he had originally produced. (Examples of such charts can be found in *The Gattegno Effect* (2011), which is a collection of 100 short essays describing the effect that Gattegno had on the authors' lives.)

There has always been some controversy as to whether other people should modify Gattegno's charts in any way. Some consider that his work should remain exactly as he created it, protesting against any changes being made for any reason. I do not agree with this point of view.

In his seminars Gattegno always insisted that he considered himself to be a scientist, and one of his major works was called, *The Science of Education*. (This first appeared in 1977 as individual chapters published as a series of booklets, and then in 1987 in three parts of an unfinished book.) He was clear in seminars, workshops and in his Newsletters that he wanted the Science of Education to evolve, as any science does, when people arrive on the scene who can carry it further within the domains he worked upon and move it into entirely new areas. This is why I have never felt I should be constrained in my work by a sense of misplaced reverence towards his.

Acknowledgements

I would like to thank the many people who helped me write this book. They were interested in using the Silent Way in their classrooms, read parts of the text and made helpful comments. John Olsen proofread the final version.

Over the years, Piers Messum gave the book several close critical readings. He has worked on most of the chapters with me, in particular the earlier ones on the model and those on pronunciation. Since the early 1990s, we have spent countless hours discussing these subjects and many of our resulting insights are included.

Special thanks go to Steven Quinn from Melbourne, who read it as a beginning Silent Way teacher and offered to edit it. In doing so, he gave me extensive feedback and asked me many pertinent questions which led me to add several chapters to the text. Readers have a more complete book thanks to Steven's contribution.

Sincere thanks to MW who asked not to be named.

Recently, Laurence Howells worked on the book which had been on 'the back burner' for a long time. In the process he helped to update it for the twenty-first century, not least by creating so many of the films that now illustrate the points I make. Thank you, Laurence. You know how much I appreciate your contribution.

And finally, thanks to Christiane Rozet who gave me her support over the years on a more material level. She helped me throughout the process with her encouragement and patience.

Roslyn Young, 2025

References

Bartoli, C. (1972). Italian. In C. Gattegno (Ed.), *Teaching Foreign Languages in Schools: The Silent Way* (2nd edition, pp. 117–121). Educational Solutions.

Bartoli, C. (1981). Teaching the Silent Way. *Practical English Teaching*, 2(1), 29–31.

Gattegno, C. (1963). *Teaching Foreign Languages in Schools: The Silent Way* (First edition). Educational Explorers.

Gattegno, C. (1974). *The Common Sense of Teaching Mathematics*. Educational Solutions.

Gattegno, C. (1976). *The Common Sense of Teaching Foreign Languages*. Educational Solutions.

Gattegno, C. (1985). *The Science of Education. Chapter 13: The Learning and Teaching of Foreign Languages*. Educational Solutions.

Mason, J. (1998). Enabling teachers to be real teachers: necessary levels of awareness and structure of attention. *Journal of Mathematics Teacher Education*, 1(3), 243–267.

Mason, J. (2008). From concept images to pedagogic structure for a mathematical topic. In C. Rasmussen (Ed.), *Making the connection: Research and teaching in undergraduate mathematics education*. Mathematical Association of America.

Stevick, E. W. (1976). *Memory, Meaning & Method*. Heinle & Heinle.

Stevick, E. W. (1980). *Teaching Languages: A Way and Ways*. Newbury House.

Stevick, E. W. (1992). *Teaching and Learning Languages*. Cambridge Univ. Press.

Further Reading

Allsopp, C., Biero, A., Hicks, D., Peuteuil, N., & Young, R. (2018). *Rods, People, More People & Stories*. Duo Flumina.

Cherry, D. (1998). The Silent Way materials and what's behind them. *Bulletin of Hokuriku University*, 22, 311–317.

Gattegno, C. (1977). Further insights into learning languages: A brief history of the Silent Way. *Educational Solutions Newsletter*, 7(2), 19–21.

Gattegno, C. (1983). The Silent Way. In J. Oller & P. Richard-Amato (Eds.), *Methods that Work* (pp. 72–88). Newbury House.

Gattegno, C. (1986). A working model for health. *Educational Solutions Newsletter*, 16(2).

Hewitt, D. (2022). Calling upon human powers to work mathematically. *Mathematics Teaching*, 283, 32–35.

Hirschhorn, S. (2023). *The Cuisenaire Rods: Of Crocodiles, Castles and Clocks*.

Howells, L. (2024). A Class Conversation: Working with what students say. *Voices* (Whitstable, Kent: IATEFL), 301, 12–13.

Logan, A. (Ed.). (2011). *The Gattegno Effect*. Educational Solutions Worldwide Inc..

Messum, P. R. (2018). Why we should use a chart and a pointer for teaching pronunciation. *Speak Out!* (Whitstable, IATEFL), 58, 53–60.

Messum, P. R., & Young, R. (2017). Bringing the English articulatory setting into the classroom: (1) the tongue. *Speak Out!* (Whitstable, IATEFL), 57, 29–39.

Messum, P. R., & Young, R. (2019). Teaching the underlying systems of English pronunciation. *Speak Out!* (Whitstable, IATEFL), 61, 18–31.

Messum, P., & Young, R. (2021a). Teaching students to pronounce English: a motor skill approach in the classroom. *RELC Journal*, 52(1), 169–178.

Messum, P., & Young, R. (2021b). Uncommitted materials: support for spontaneous interaction in class. *Voices* (Whitstable, Kent: IATEFL), 280, 14–16.

Mullen, J. (1996). Cuisenaire rods in the language classroom. *Les Cahiers de l'APLIUT*, XVI(2).

Stevick, E. W. (1990). *Humanism in Language Teaching*. OUP.

The Silent Way. (2017). [Video recording]. https://www.youtube.com/watch?v=JlL_rcRY5cQ&t=46s

Underhill, A. (2014). Training for the unpredictable. *EJALTEFL*, 3(2), 59–69.

Young, R. (2018). How to use a chart and a pointer for teaching pronunciation. *Speak Out!* (Whitstable, IATEFL), 59, 20–26.

Young, R. (2024). Learning to speak, speaking to learn. *Voices* (Whitstable, Kent: IATEFL), 301, 10–11.

Young, R., & Messum, P. (2018). Other aspects of using a chart and a pointer for teaching pronunciation. https://www.pronunciationscience.com/app/download/

Young, R., & Messum, P. (2023). Pointing on charts is a third way of working in the pronunciation classroom. *Proceedings of the 7th International Conference on English Pronunciation: Issues and Practices*. Grenoble.

Young, R., & Messum, P. R. (2011). *How We Learn and How We Should be Taught: An Introduction to the Work of Caleb Gattegno*. Duo Flumina.

Young, R., & Messum, P. R. (2013). Gattegno's legacy. *Voices* (Whitstable, Kent: IATEFL), 232, 8–9.

Young, R., & Messum, P. R. (2015). Teaching English pronunciation in an intensive Silent Way course. https://www.pronunciationscience.com/downloads/

Young, R., & Messum, P. R. (2022). Teaching schwa: Using intentional "stuttering" on consonants to improve English pronunciation. In J. Levis & A. Guskarova (Eds.), *Proceedings of the 12th Pronunciation in Second Language Learning and Teaching Conference*.

Guides

At www.pronsci.com/guides you will find a comprehensive set of guides to the Silent Way and PronSci Rectangle, Word and Fidel charts.

APPENDICES

Appendix 1: A brief history of the English language

I tell the following story when I work with classes of adults who speak French. (It's not entirely accurate, but it is close enough to the truth to be helpful.) I use it for all levels including low intermediate students. I don't use it with children, because it supposes a level of general cultural knowledge that children do not yet have.

I draw on the board a very stylised map of Europe. It takes me less than a minute to do it, perhaps only thirty seconds. Often it only becomes clear that it is a map of Europe when I draw the boot of Italy. Norway and the Baltic Sea are the shape of an egg, a bit dented here and there, almost closed, with a little passage going off towards the Atlantic. I need Denmark to be reasonably well drawn with Jutland pointing up towards Norway. Then my line goes down on a slope. The west of France has to bulge out quite clearly. Spain and Portugal are almost square-shaped, the Mediterranean Sea is like another very big egg, without forgetting the boot. I finish with two triangles, one the right way up for Britain, and a smaller one, upside down, for Ireland. These have to be situated properly, just above Normandy on the map. It takes me less time to do it than to tell the story of how I do it. I can tell from the sounds made by the class that they have understood what it is.

*

I put a dot right in the middle of Italy: Rome. Then, speaking very slowly in English, repeating a sentence here and there when I have the impression that some people have not understood, I begin my story. As I tell it, I write the important words on the board so that what I say is at least vaguely comprehensible for all. I am not aiming for everyone to understand everything, and the details are unimportant.

Julius Caesar (I write his name) arrived in Britain in 55 BC (I draw an arrow from Rome to Britain and write '55 BC–before Christ'). The Romans pushed the Celts (I write the word) west to Cornwall, to Scotland and to Ireland (three arrows). For three hundred years (I write 300) the Romans spoke Latin (I articulate this word carefully) in England (I point to the appropriate triangle). In about four hundred AD, (I write the number) the Anglo-Saxons started to arrive (I write their name). Then I ask, Where did the Anglo-Saxons come from? (Often someone can reply in their language or in English, the North, Scandinavia, Germany….)

What languages did they speak? (Someone can sometimes give an answer: German. Different dialects of German.) You call people from Great Britain Anglo-Saxons. Where did the Saxons come from? (Saxony.) Where is Saxony? Here. (I show Saxony on my map.) Where did the Angles come from? A region called Angeln which is just here, just behind Jutland. (Gestures to localise it. It is in that part of Germany now called Schleswig-Holstein, just behind Jutland.) So from the 5th century to 1066 (I write the dates), people in England spoke Anglo-Saxon. Anglo-Saxon is the same as Old English (I write the words).

The next important date is 1066 (I point to the date). In France you have 1515 (I write the date, one which is known to all French people). In England, we have 1066, the date every English person knows. What happened in 1066? (Occasionally someone can say.) William the Conqueror (I write his name) won the Battle of Hastings. What is the name of William the Conqueror in French? (If I have French speakers, we spend a few moments in French so that they recognise him as being Guillaume le Conquérant.)

347

Where did William come from? (Often no one knows…) He came from Normandy. He came from Caen. (I add a dot on the map in Normandy for Caen.)

In 1066, he won the Battle of Hastings (I add a dot on the south coast of England for the town of Hastings.) He moved to England and installed his barons all around the country (I add dots here and there around the south of the triangle representing England, but nothing precise. I am not aiming at particular cities.)

What language did William speak?—French. The Anglo-Saxons spoke Anglo-Saxon, and William and the barons spoke French. So England was divided into two levels (I use gestures to indicate the two social layers, the French speakers on top, the Anglo-Saxons below.) The Anglo-Saxons were serfs. (I write the word, then pause for a few seconds…) The nobles spoke French and the Anglo-Saxons spoke Anglo-Saxon, a Germanic language (I move my hands as I speak.) And they didn't understand each other. The nobles didn't understand the serfs and the serfs didn't understand the nobles.

As you know, in German and in French you use endings—in French you have -ons, -ez, -ions, -iez, -erait (I write up one or two) and in German there are words like *gebringen*, *gesprochen* (I write up two or three). Because they didn't understand each other, they all started to speak in a simplified way. *Me Tarzan, you Jane*. (Two gestures to indicate the message 'I am Tarzan, the students are all Jane'.) They dropped off all the endings, all the complications and just kept the meaning. And everybody developed a taste for simplicity: subject, verb, complement. England was bilingual for 350 years (I write the number.) The two languages merged (gesture of my hands interlocking) by about 1400 (I write the date). This was the beginning of Modern English.

Why is this important for you? Because fifty percent (I write 50%) of English comes from French. English is a simplified version of German, with a lot of French vocabulary. There are thousands of French words in English, so you have a very big advantage. You already have lots of vocabulary in English. You just have to learn how to use it.

(My story goes on … I clean a little space on the board.) Let's look at how English functions. The barons lived in the castles (I show the word 'barons' again). The Anglo-Saxons worked for them in the fields. They were serfs. (I find the word or write it again.) In the fields, what are the names of the animals?

Cow (*cowboy*, yes!) and what is it called in modern German? *Kuh*. Cow is an Anglo-Saxon word. (I begin a table with the word *cow*.) And other animals? (Sometimes they can give me the names of other animals.)

kuh	cow
schaf(e)	sheep
kalb	calf
schwein	pig

One day, the baron says *Dimanche, nous allons manger une vache*. So the animal is killed and comes into the kitchen. But what is the cow called when it is sereved to the baron and his family? *Bœuf*.

Beef. (I build up the following table):

kuh	cow	*bœuf*	beef
schaf(e)	sheep	*mouton*	mutton
kalb	calf	*veau* → un veau, une velle	veal
schwein	pig	*porc*	pork

And now, 950 years later (I write 950), in English we have two words for animals from the farm, a Germanic word for the animals outside in the fields and a French word for when they are in the shop.

So you can see here the influence of French. French is also used, for similar reasons, for legal, military and administrative parts of English.

French is used in formal contexts, Anglo-Saxon is used in conversations between simple people like you and me. So if you want to say something, try and say it using French words. If you say them in the way an English speaker would, there is a good chance that you will be understood.

*

This is the end of my Brief History. However, during the year, I often ask if a word is of French or Germanic origin, and if it is of Germanic origin, what is the French equivalent. For example, when the word *kind* (*what kind of…*) comes into circulation, while we are looking at it, I introduce the words *sort* and *type* (*what sort of… what type of…*), both of which are of French origin. So we have three for the price of one … All that has to be done then is to learn to pronounce them correctly.

A little later in the course, I will spend another session to begin a collection of words which exist in the two languages. These are the only times in the course that I speak. And in this second lesson, once my students are launched, I limit my participation to a few remarks. I might say,

Let's spend a few minutes looking for words that are in French and in English.

I write *nation* on the board. Someone proposes another, for example *addition*. I add it. A considerable number of words ending in *-tion* exist in both languages. While we are working, we happen upon words like *parking, jogging,* and *footing* which have made the trip in the opposite direction.

Sports give us a good collection. Words of Anglo-Saxon or French origin like *basket, ball, hand, goal, corner, penalty* and dozens of others are seams to be followed and capitalised on. We finish up with a board filled with words which exist in both languages.

It is not important to give lists of words here. There are thousands. When the board is full, the work of the day is finished. The lesson is not about learning vocabulary but about the huge number of examples. My French-speaking students have a hidden treasure that they are unaware of. I want to draw their attention to it. Sometimes students ask me if there are books on the subject. When this happens, I know my lesson has been profitable. Their attitude towards English and their level of English will both be enhanced.

Appendix 2: The Silent Way Word charts

The Silent Way Word charts are used with beginners. They are introduced one by one. Once each chart has been hung its position isn't changed, so students can always find the words they need in the same place.

The final layout, once all the charts have been hung is shown at the bottom of the next page. The Rectangle chart is in the middle, Charts 1-8 are hung on the right and Charts 9-12 on the left.

The special charts for dates, family relations and numbers are shown on the extreme left, but each of these can be placed under the Rectangle chart when it is the focus of the class's work.

Charts 1-8

a rod -s -s red blue	which your my get of	at some longer -est	can't up or top won't
green yellow orange	have out has mine 've	both go given much	must want show end
take -n't give brown 's	our light I their how	from as taken not all	because for with more
and me it to this 's	many colour dark you	who than be long -er	any between would
he two them here too	yes in did what she	but short by told 's	hold middle front 'd
the is her white the	do different 'm we no	can if gave will -ing	where let goes less
there an other these	none off got same	was tall tell took 'll	showed behind could
that one are us those	on 're had am his	come so like very 'll	under beside live that
put him black there	name does don't they	were -ed -ed -ed -t	should down bottom

big each back away	look word lot almost	further above often	gone shall know mean
near mind ask went	small well high thing	may quick stand only	neither rather own sat
box few say new old	feel talk listen wish	already size loud fall	spoke least use knew
when hard again most	see across also throw	going to held fast soft	need else caught able
kind done every says	why work whom hear	make quiet made -en	chose brought whole
some little said -es	answer heard sound	never below quite far	life move choose bring
shown either together	speak enough bigger	fell begin forward -ly	nor threw sure known
came -self young bad	walk seen low about	towards begun -ness	try meant might pass
better good best worse	saw wrong been slow	sit always stood began	easy except although

351

The special charts for family relations, dates and numbers, and Charts 9-12

| aunt born boy brother |
| child children cousin |
| daughter die divorce |
| family father girl |
| grand- husband -in-law |
| love marry mother |
| nephew niece parent |
| relative single sister |
| son step- uncle wife |

| Fri Sun Tues -day |
| Wednes Mon Thurs |
| Satur week autumn |
| spring winter summer |
| season date January |
| March February August |
| June April May July |
| Septem Octo -ber |
| Novem Decem month |

| past present future |
| o'clock quarter half |
| minute hour year |
| first second third add |
| once plus minus times |
| twice divided around |
| count point equal odd |
| left age exact even |
| thank century right |

| tomorrow yesterday |
| now today ready time |
| morning evening mid- |
| day afternoon night |
| during early late till |
| soon until since yet |
| before moment just |
| last still then next |
| ever while ago after |

| eight five two four |
| nine one six seven |
| three fif nin ten -ty |
| thirteen twelve -teen |
| eigh eleven nought |
| twelf twenty forty |
| and zero thirty -th |
| a hundred oh -ieth |
| thousand million -h |

| keep through teach |
| open man drop write |
| spell women kept -ful |
| buy read close read |
| stay pretty men seem |
| -wards opposite learn |
| meet shut woman turn |
| sell pick easily -less |
| wonder length close |

| people over -body job |
| unless such question |
| matter whether among |
| usual happen true way |
| prefer think call hope |
| leave care against wait |
| apart impossible whose |
| person heavier used to |
| heavy have has had |

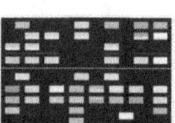

The final layout, once all the charts have been introduced

Appendix 3: The PronSci Word charts

The Pronunciation Science Word charts are designed for Silent Way work with intermediate and advanced students. All the charts are hung on the wall from the beginning of a course.

The words are grouped by function, giving students a synthetic view of the functional vocabulary—the words through which Gattegno's 'spirit of the language' is expressed. Within each group, the words are arranged alphabetically, enabling students to find them easily.

Students who already have some English will have met these words before and therefore the progression designed into the Silent Way charts is not appropriate.

The PronSci Word charts from the personal study set for American English

I me my mine it he him his she her we us our you your they them their -es no 's 's -self -s -s yes 's -selves -es this that these those any every -body one some no- thing there	and the a an the what when whom how which where whose why many much who about above across again -st ahead along all almost also among anyway apart around as at away back bit	because behind below between both but by down each n- either else end enough even except fairly for from front here if in -deed kind left like -stead lot none of off on only opposite n- or	other out over own perhaps plenty pretty quite rather right side so some sort such that there al- though through to together too top toward under unless up very -ward whether whole with
am 'm is are been was were 's 's 're have 've has had 'd do does don't did -n't not -n't will 'll won't would 'll can can't could may might must ought shall should	agree ask be been begin began begun -s bring brought buy -s call come came care choose chose close -es do does did done -es feel felt give gave get got go went gone -en -ten -n -n -ing	happen have has had hear heard hold held hope keep kept know knew let learn leave left like listen live look make made mean meant mind move need point pop put run ran -i- -ed -ed -ed -t	see saw seen seem send sent show sound speak spoke suppose take took talk think thought try turn use walk want wish wonder work supposed going to able used to want have has had

American English - Word Charts 1 to 8

TEACHING ENGLISH THE SILENT WAY

aunt born boy brother child children cousin daughter die divorce family father girl grand- husband -in-law love marry mother nephew niece parent relative single sister son step- uncle wife	Sun Mon Tues -day Wednes Thurs Fri Satur week season spring summer winter fall date January February March April May June July August Septem Octo -ber Novem Decem month	past present future morning noon evening o'clock quarter half time minute hour year first second third last once twice times man -man men -men people person woman women home job use	after ago already always before day during early ever just late mid- moment never next night now often recently seldom since soon still then today tomorrow until while yesterday yet
black blue brown rod green gray orange pink red white yellow color dark light pale add area degree divide equal fraction minus multiply percent plus point square subtract question wrong answer	eight five two four nine one six seven three fif nin ten thirteen twelve -teen eigh eleven -ty -ty twelf twenty forty and zero thirty -th a hundred oh -ieth thousand million -h	bad better best big certain close different easy exact far further few good great hard high ideal impossible large least less little long loud low more most near new nice -i- -er -est -ly than	old open probable quick quiet ready real same short small soft sudden sure tall usual well worse worst young -able -ful -less un- read read say says said spell tell told write wrote written

American English - Word Charts F, D, C & N (left) and 9 to 12 (right)

Scan to download a guide to these Word charts.

www.ingramcontent.com/pod-product-compliance
Lightning Source LLC
Chambersburg PA
CBHW081328230426
43667CB00018B/2861